SIMPLE

CLASSICS

COOKBOOK

WILLIAMS-SONOMA

SIMPLE
CLASSICS
COOKBOOK

RECIPES

Chuck Williams

PHOTOGRAPHY

Allan Rosenberg
and Allen V. Lott

First published in the USA, 1994, by Weldon Owen Inc.,
814 Montgomery Street, San Francisco, CA 94133

Originally published as:
Chuck Williams Simple American Cooking (© 1994 Weldon Owen Inc.)
Chuck Williams Simple Italian Cooking (© 1995 Weldon Owen Inc.)
Chuck Williams Simple French Cooking (© 1996 Weldon Owen Inc.)

OXMOOR HOUSE INC.

Oxmoor House books are distributed by
Sunset Books, 80 Willow Road, Menlo Park, CA 94025
Phone: 650·321·3600 Fax: 650·324·1532

Vice-President/General Manager: Rich Smeby
Director of Special Sales: Gary Wright

Oxmoor House and Sunset Books are divisions of
Southern Progress Corporation

In collaboration with Williams-Sonoma Inc.
3250 Van Ness Avenue, San Francisco, CA 94109

WILLIAMS-SONOMA
Founder & Vice-Chairman: Chuck Williams
Book Buyer: Cecilia Michaelis

PRODUCED BY WELDON OWEN INC.
Chief Executive Officer: John Owen
President: Terry Newell
Chief Operating Officer: Larry Partington
Creative Director: Gaye Allen
Vice President International Sales: Stuart Laurence
Sales Manager: Emily Jahn
Managing Editor: Margaret Garrou
Consulting Editor: Norman Kolpas
Copy Editor: Sharon Silva
Editorial Assistant: Dana Goldberg
Art Director: Jamie Leighton
Original Design: John Bull, The Book Design Company
Design Director: Paul Morales, Onyx Design Inc.
Production: Chris Hemesath, Stephanie Sherman, Linda Bouchard
Proofreader: Desne Border
Photographers: Allan Rosenberg, Allen V. Lott, Noel Barnhurst,
    Philip Salaverry
Food Stylists: Heidi Gintner, George Dolese, Sue White
Prop Stylists: Sandra Griswald, George Dolese, Carol Hacker
Illustrations: Alice Harth
Front Cover Photographer: Daniel Clark
Front Cover Food Stylist: George Dolese
Front Cover Prop Stylist: Amy Denebeim
Back Cover Photographer: Allan Rosenberg
Additional credits on page 304

The Williams-Sonoma Complete Cookbook series
conceived and produced by Weldon Owen Inc.

A WELDON OWEN PRODUCTION
Copyright © 2000 Weldon Owen Inc. and Williams-Sonoma Inc.
All rights reserved, including the right of reproduction in
whole or in part in any form.

First printed in 2000
10 9 8 7 6 5 4

Library of Congress Cataloging-in-Publication Data is available.
ISBN 0-8487-2595-6
Separations by Colourscan Co. Pte. Ltd.
Printed in China by Leefung-Asco Printers Ltd.

A Note on Weights and Measures
*All recipes include customary U.S., U.K. and metric measurements.
Conversions are based on a standard developed for these books
and have been rounded off. Actual weights may vary.*

Contents

SIDE DISHES

DESSERTS

NTRODUCTION

I have always preferred simple cooking, whether I was eating in a restaurant
or cooking for friends or just for myself at home. To me, simple cooking is the sort of
unpretentious, classic food you might have in a small country restaurant, whether you
were in Italy or France or even in America — comforting food that is enjoyed
with a bottle of wine and lively conversation.

This is a book dedicated to the simple cooking of France, Italy, and America. It compiles
in one convenient volume three separate books I wrote that first appeared several years ago:
Simple Italian Cooking, Simple French Cooking, and *Simple American Cooking.*

After I opened the first Williams-Sonoma store in 1956, I traveled yearly
to France and Italy in search of cookware, tools, and foods for our customers. On those
trips, I always enjoyed visits to city and country restaurants and cafes where classic
and regional dishes were served. That kind of honest, simple cooking wasn't really
much different from the things I had learned to cook at an early age
in my grandmother's kitchen in Florida.

Throughout the following fully illustrated pages, you will find a wide array
of such simple, classic recipes, each identified by its country of origin and organized
by the role it plays in a meal and by its featured ingredient. To help make the most
of these recipes, you will also find ample guidance on menu planning,
basic preparation, cooking techniques, key ingredients, and equipment.

Join me in enjoying the simple pleasures of classic cooking.

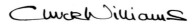

SUGGESTED MENUS

Dozens of simple meals can be composed from the recipes in this book. These suggested Italian, French, and American menus provide easy examples for putting together a meal for any time of the day. Use them as guidelines for planning typical regional meals, but please do not stop there. Let your own tastes lead you to personalized menus with Italian, French, or American themes, choosing from among the many courses represented by the chapters in this book. And feel free to cross boundaries, building harmonious meals with dishes from each of the countries. Whatever the season or the occasion, use these classic recipes to create menus as casual or formal, and as light or hearty, as you wish.

ITALIAN

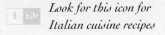 *Look for this icon for Italian cuisine recipes*

WEEKEND BRUNCHES OR LIGHT SUPPERS

(FEATURED MENU)

Assorted Antipasti 18

Farfalle with Tuna and Black Olives   176

Mixed Berries with Zabaglione 274

———

Baked Semolina Gnocchi   179

Escarole Salad with Pear and Prosciutto   78

Lemon Rice Pudding with Hazelnut Meringues   269

Shrimp and Scallops with Mixed Herbs and Baby Greens   30

Swiss Chard and Poached Eggs with Polenta   191

Grape Focaccia   236

———

Shrimp-Filled Artichokes with Mustard Dressing   26

Lentil, Tomato, and Mint Soup   52

Arugula Salad with Black Olive Crostini   77

Apple Walnut Cake   259

CASUAL DINNERS

Blood Orange, Fennel, and Olive Salad   81

Baked Salmon on Chard   90

Italian Green Beans with Mint   222

Lemon Rice Pudding with Hazelnut Meringues   269

———

Green Beans and Tuna with Basil   25

Braised Pork Loin with Sage   154

Mashed Potatoes with Rosemary and Lemon   214

Glazed Carrots with Marsala and Hazelnuts   194

Oranges with Mint and Toasted Almonds   279

Asparagus with Capers and Pine Nuts   23

Sautéed Chicken Breasts with Parmesan Cheese   121

Roasted Red Peppers with Oregano   201

Pink Grapefruit Granita   278

Almond Biscotti   254

———

Cheese and Basil Ravioli   185

Fresh Tuna with Mint and Coriander   96

Braised Fennel in Milk   202

Mixed Berries with Zabaglione   274

FRENCH

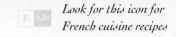 Look for this icon for French cuisine recipes

LIGHT LUNCHES OR BRUNCHES

Mediterranean Tuna Salad   71

Onion Soup   40

Cherry Clafouti   267

————

Vegetables with Three Sauces   32

Country Veal Stew   170

Couscous   283

Orange Floating Islands   268

Leeks à la Grecque   22

Artichoke Flat Omelet   190

Mango and Melon Salad   83

Walnut Wafers   248

————

Cheese Soufflé with Tomato-Basil Sauce   188

Green Beans with Shallots   203

Pear Tart with Walnuts   246

DINNERS OR LIGHT SUPPERS

(FEATURED MENU)

Asparagus with Orange Hollandaise Sauce   29

Rack of Lamb with Flageolet Beans   151

Fresh Fruit Compote with Cassis   280

————

Green Lentil Salad   224

Pork Loin with Orange   167

Broccoli Gratin   217

Endive and Mushroom Salad with Mustard Dressing   80

Sautéed Apples with Whipped Cream   277

Celery Root with Mustard Mayonnaise   28

Roast Tarragon Chicken   131

Potato and Onion Gratin   220

Chicory and Goat Cheese Salad   67

Bittersweet Chocolate Cake   256

————

Carrot Soup with Coriander   50

Halibut with Hollandaise   86

Green Beans with Shallots   203

Escarole Salad with Bacon   64

Chocolate Mousse   271

$\mathcal{A}$MERICAN

A ⊘ Look for this icon for American cuisine recipes

LUNCHES

White Bean Soup   43
Broiled Shrimp and Spinach Salad   62
Parmesan Cheese Bread   239
Lime-Pecan Butter Cookies   248
served with a fruit sorbet

————

Caesar Salad   74
Crab Cakes   114
Corn and Red Pepper Salad   65
Poached Pears and Blueberries   272

Tropical Salad with Lime Dressing   68
Corned Beef Hash with Poached Eggs   163
Cranberry-Orange Muffins   243
Apricot Bread-and-Butter Custard   264

————

Zucchini Soup   41
Chicken Salad with Apple and Walnuts   72
Ginger Biscuits   240
Lemon-Almond Butter Cake   258

DINNERS

(FEATURED MENU)
Roasted Red Pepper Soup   61
Broiled Swordfish Steaks with Basil, Olive Oil, and Capers   111
Cauliflower with Cherry Tomatoes   204
Golden Apple Cobbler   251

————

Tropical Salad with Lime Dressing   68
Braised Brisket of Beef with Port Wine   164
served with mashed potatoes and a green vegetable
Chocolate-Orange Cheesecake   261

Garden Greens and Citrus Salad   69
Roast Chicken with Apple and Sage   125
Corn and Green Beans, Circa 1935   218
Poached Pears and Blueberries   272

————

Asparagus Mimosa Salad   207
Sautéed Pork Tenderloin with Gingered Apples   161
Jasmine Rice with Shredded Zucchini   228
Toasted Walnut Quick Bread   237
Mixed Berry Shortcake   262

First Courses

GRILLED VEGETABLES WITH HERBED DRESSING

SERVES 4

Almost all vegetables cook well and easily on the grill. They require only a light brushing of oil to lubricate them for browning, and a sprinkling of fresh herbs for extra flavor and aroma.

You can grill vegetables in one of several ways. A broiler (griller) or a charcoal grill will work beautifully. Italians most often use a stove-top grill—a cast-iron or aluminum, ridged pan that provides intense, searing heat and makes the characteristic grill marks; they are available in specialty cookware stores (see page 293). If you use a stove-top grill, avoid overly juicy vegetables or too much oil, either of which can smoke up your kitchen. Slices of eggplant, zucchini, radicchio, and fennel bulb cook well on a stove-top grill.

focaccia (optional; recipe on page 283)
1 tablespoon fresh lemon juice
⅛ teaspoon salt
⅓ cup (3 fl oz/80 ml) extra-virgin olive
    oil, plus extra for brushing
1 or 2 green (spring) onions, including
    some tender green tops, minced
1 tablespoon chopped fresh mint,
    oregano, basil, flat-leaf (Italian) parsley
    or other herb
freshly ground pepper
2 or 3 small Asian (slender) eggplants
    (aubergines), or 1 small globe eggplant
2 or 3 small zucchini (courgettes)
1 head radicchio
2 small fennel bulbs

If using the focaccia, bake the bread as directed.

In a small bowl, make a dressing by combining the lemon juice and salt, stirring until the salt dissolves. Add the ⅓ cup (3 fl oz/80 ml) olive oil, the green onions, mint or other herb, and pepper to taste. Whisk until blended; set aside.

If using Asian eggplants, trim and cut lengthwise into slices ¼ inch (6 mm) thick. If using a globe eggplant, trim, cut in half lengthwise and cut each half crosswise into slices ¼ inch (6 mm) thick; then sprinkle both sides of the slices with salt, place in a single layer in a colander and let stand over a bowl or in the sink for 45 minutes to drain the bitter juices. Rinse the slices and pat dry with paper towels, pressing down to absorb all the moisture. Set aside.

Preheat a broiler (griller), or prepare a fire in a charcoal grill. If using a cast-iron or cast-aluminum stove-top grill, preheat for a minute or two over medium-high heat just before putting the vegetables on.

Trim the zucchini and cut lengthwise into slices ¼ inch (6 mm) thick. Discard any old leaves from the radicchio. Cut into 8 wedges. Trim the stems from the fennel bulbs; cut the bulbs lengthwise into slices ⅛ inch (3 mm) thick.

Brush the vegetables lightly on both sides with olive oil. Place on the stove-top grill pan, on a broiler pan, or on the rack of a charcoal grill. Grill or broil, turning once, until lightly browned and tender when pierced with the point of a knife, 4–5 minutes on each side.

Whisk the dressing again and spoon a little on the bottom of a serving platter. Arrange the vegetables on the platter and spoon a little dressing over the top. Serve warm or at room temperature with the focaccia, if using. Pass any remaining dressing at the table.

LEEKS À LA GRECQUE

SERVES 4

This splendid first course is loved the world over—and no more so than in France. An excellent cold dish, it is easily prepared and adds a touch of casual elegance to any warm-weather meal.

◑ *The dish will be at its best when made with small, tender leeks. If tiny pearl onions are out of season, use the smallest boiling onions you can find—no more than 1 inch (2.5 cm) in diameter—and cut them in half vertically, through their stem and root ends, so the halves hold together.*

2 lb (1 kg) young, slender leeks
salt
8–10 small pearl onions
¾ cup (6 fl oz/180 ml) chicken
   stock or water, or as needed
⅓ cup (3 fl oz/80 ml) dry white wine
3 tablespoons olive oil
1 tablespoon tomato paste
4 bay leaves
1 teaspoon peppercorns
paprika

Following the directions on page 291, trim the leeks, leaving about 1 inch (2.5 cm) of the tender green tops, then rinse them. If the leeks are small, leave them whole; if they are medium-sized, cut them in half lengthwise.

◑ Gather the leeks together in a bundle and tie in 2 or 3 places with kitchen string to secure the bundle. Fill a large, wide pot half full with water and bring to a boil. Add 1 tablespoon salt and the bundle of leeks and boil, uncovered, for 5 minutes. Drain the leeks and let cool for a few minutes. When cool enough to handle, snip the strings and separate the leeks. Set aside.

◑ Fill a small saucepan three-fourths full with water and bring to a boil. Add the pearl onions and boil, uncovered, for 3 minutes. Drain the onions and immerse them in cold water. Using a small, sharp knife, trim the root ends and cut a shallow X in the root ends. Using your fingers, slip off the skins. Set aside.

◑ In a large sauté pan or frying pan that will hold the leeks in a single layer, arrange the leeks in a row. In a small bowl, combine the ¾ cup (6 fl oz/ 180 ml) stock or water, the wine, olive oil, and tomato paste. Stir until well blended and then pour the stock mixture over the leeks. Tuck the bay leaves under the leeks and scatter the peppercorns over the top. Arrange the onions

around and among the leeks so that they sit in the liquid. The liquid should reach just to the top of the leeks; add more stock if necessary.

◑ Place the pan over medium heat and bring to a simmer. Reduce the heat to low and allow the liquid to barely simmer, uncovered, until the leeks are tender when pierced with a knife and the liquid is reduced to a few spoonfuls, about 45 minutes. Remove from the heat and set aside to cool completely.

◑ To serve, arrange the leeks in a row in a serving dish. Arrange the onions and bay leaves over the leeks and spoon the reduced sauce, including the peppercorns, over the leeks and onions. Sprinkle with paprika and serve at room temperature. ⬛◑

ASPARAGUS WITH CAPERS AND PINE NUTS

SERVES 4

This first course or side dish is best served immediately after cooking, when the heat of the vegetable combines with the other ingredients to produce a lovely fragrance. Small to medium-sized asparagus spears will have the finest flavor and texture. If you purchase medium-sized or larger stalks, use a vegetable peeler or an asparagus peeler (see page 294) to strip away any thick, coarse skin.

Some capers can be exceptionally salty, so drain off the brine and taste one. If they are too salty, rinse well in cold water and drain again.

If you'd prefer the asparagus spears cold, try serving them with an oil and lemon juice dressing in place of the lemon-caper sauce: Immediately after draining the asparagus stalks, plunge them into cold water to stop the cooking, then drain again. Stir together 2 tablespoons fresh lemon juice and salt and pepper to taste; then stir in ¼ cup (2 fl oz/60 ml) extra-virgin olive oil and 1 teaspoon chopped fresh tarragon. Drizzle over the asparagus and serve at room temperature.

¼ cup (1½ oz/45 g) pine nuts

1½ lb (750 g) asparagus, preferably
   small to medium-sized spears,
   6–7 inches (15–18 cm) long

salt

6 tablespoons (3 oz/90 g)
   unsalted butter

1 tablespoon fresh lemon juice

¼ cup (2 oz/60 g) drained capers

freshly ground pepper

¼-lb (125-g) piece Italian
   Parmesan cheese, preferably
   Parmigiano-Reggiano

In a heavy frying pan over medium heat, toast the pine nuts, stirring, until lightly colored and fragrant, 1–2 minutes. Transfer to a bowl; set aside.

Break or cut off any tough white ends of the asparagus spears and discard. Cut all the spears the same length. If medium-sized or larger, peel the asparagus spears as well: using a vegetable peeler or an asparagus peeler and starting about 2 inches (5 cm) below the tip, peel off the outer skin from each spear.

In a large sauté pan or deep frying pan that will accommodate the asparagus comfortably lying flat, add water to a depth of 2–3 inches (5–7.5 cm). Bring to a rapid boil over high heat. Add 2 teaspoons salt and the asparagus. When the water returns to a boil, reduce the heat slightly and boil gently, uncovered, until tender when pierced with a sharp knife, 4–7 minutes, depending upon their size.

Meanwhile, in a small saucepan over medium-low heat, melt the butter. Add the lemon juice and capers, season to taste with pepper and cook, stirring gently, for 30–40 seconds. Taste and adjust the seasoning, adding salt, pepper, or lemon juice as needed.

When the asparagus spears are done, drain well and place on a serving platter or individual plates. Spoon the caper sauce over them and then scatter on the pine nuts. Using a vegetable peeler and holding the piece of Parmesan over the asparagus, shave off paper-thin slices; be generous with the cheese. Serve at once.

GREEN BEANS AND TUNA WITH BASIL

SERVES 4

A great combination of flavors, this dish has probably been a part of the antipasto table for more than a century. It makes an excellent first course, a luncheon main course, or a light supper when served with a soup and a fruit dessert.

⟫ Seek out young, small green beans and cook only until tender-crisp. Red bell pepper adds a pleasant touch of color and flavor.

⟫ For the dressing, I've used fresh lemon juice instead of vinegar because it goes better with the tuna and gives the whole dish a nice freshness. I've also found that the flavors are distributed better by tossing the beans with the lemon juice before adding the oil. The dish will be at its best if assembled at the last minute and served at room temperature.

1 lb (500 g) young, tender green beans, trimmed and cut into 3–4-inch (7.5–10-cm) lengths

1 small red bell pepper (capsicum), cut in half lengthwise, seeded and deribbed

salt

⅓ cup (2 oz/60 g) diced sweet red (Spanish) onion

2 tablespoons finely chopped fresh basil leaves

1 tablespoon fresh lemon juice, plus extra to taste

freshly ground pepper

3 tablespoons extra-virgin olive oil, plus extra to taste

1 can (6½ oz/200 g) solid-pack tuna in olive oil, preferably imported Italian, drained

1–2 tablespoons capers (depending upon your taste), rinsed and well drained

Fill a large saucepan three-fourths full of water and bring to a rapid boil over high heat. Add the green beans, bell pepper halves, and 2 teaspoons salt. Quickly bring back to a boil and cook, uncovered, until the beans are just tender but still firm, 4–5 minutes. Drain well.

⟫ Place the beans in a large bowl. Cut the pepper halves lengthwise into strips ½ inch (12 mm) wide. Add to the beans, along with the red onion and 1 tablespoon of the basil. Sprinkle with the 1 tablespoon lemon juice and a little salt and pepper to taste. Toss to coat the beans well with the lemon juice. Drizzle with the 3 tablespoons olive oil and toss again.

⟫ In a separate bowl, break the tuna into small chunks. Add the capers and the remaining 1 tablespoon basil. Season to taste with lemon juice, olive oil, pepper, and a little salt, if needed. Toss gently to blend.

⟫ Arrange the beans on a serving platter or individual plates and mound the tuna mixture in the center. Serve at once.

"Once you have become a basil addict it is hard to do without it; Mediterranean vegetables need basil as a fish needs water, and there is no substitute."

–Elizabeth David

SHRIMP-FILLED ARTICHOKES WITH MUSTARD DRESSING

SERVES 4

It is important to coat the cut surfaces of the artichoke with lemon juice so they do not turn brown. Cook the artichokes just until they are tender; any longer and they will be soft and soggy. Drain them well, bottoms up, on paper towels inside the still-hot pot in which they were cooked (you'll rid them of more liquid this way). For the best flavor, do not refrigerate the artichokes before serving.

❧ *Look for large but young artichokes with closely fitting leaves that look green and fresh. Too many artichokes are harvested past their prime and tend to be tough and fibrous.*

1 lemon, plus 2 tablespoons fresh
   lemon juice
4 large but young artichokes
2 tablespoons coriander seeds
2 bay leaves
salt
1 lb (500 g) small shrimp (prawns),
   peeled (leave tail fin attached)
   and deveined (see page 289)
2 teaspoons Dijon mustard
2 tablespoons chopped fresh basil
⅔ cup (5 fl oz/160 ml) extra-virgin
   olive oil
freshly ground pepper

Cut the lemon in half and squeeze the juice into a bowl. Trim the artichokes (see page 291). As each one is trimmed, brush the cut surfaces with the lemon juice. Spread open the center and, using a small spoon, scoop out the choke (thistlelike core).

❧ Make a bouquet garni: Place the coriander seeds and 1 of the bay leaves in the center of a 6-inch (15-cm) square of cheesecloth (muslin). Gather together the edges, forming a sachet, and tie with kitchen string.

❧ Fill a large saucepan three-fourths full of water and bring to a rapid boil. Add the bouquet garni, 2 teaspoons salt, and any lemon juice remaining in the bowl. Add the artichokes, stem end down, allowing them to float. Reduce the heat slightly, cover partially and boil until the stem end is tender when pierced with a sharp knife, about 20 minutes. Using tongs, transfer the artichokes upside down (stem end up) to a plate. Discard the pan contents and place a double layer of paper towels on the bottom. Place the artichokes on the towels, stem end up, cover partially, and set aside to cool.

❧ Fill a small saucepan half full of water and bring to a boil. Add 1 teaspoon salt and the remaining bay leaf. Reduce the heat to medium-low and simmer for 5 minutes. Add the shrimp, reduce the heat to low, cover and gently poach until pink and opaque, about 2 minutes. Drain and set aside to cool slightly.

❧ In a large bowl, make a dressing by combining the 2 tablespoons lemon juice, ⅛ teaspoon salt, and the mustard, stirring until the salt dissolves. Add the basil, olive oil, and pepper to taste. Whisk until well blended; taste and adjust the seasoning. Add the shrimp and toss to coat well.

❧ Transfer the artichokes to a serving platter, stem ends down. Spread open the centers. Using a slotted spoon, transfer the shrimp to the centers, dividing them equally. Pour the dressing into 4 individual bowls and serve alongside for dipping the artichoke leaves. Serve the artichokes warm or at room temperature.

CELERY ROOT WITH MUSTARD MAYONNAISE

SERVES 4

The French call this refreshing first-course salad céleri-rave rémoulade. This makes an excellent lunch dish or dinner first course when there is a shortage of fresh salad vegetables.

If by chance the mayonnaise mixture separates when you begin to add oil, start over again with another egg yolk. If the mixture separates when half or more of the oil has been beaten in, the mayonnaise can be saved by putting another egg yolk in a clean bowl and vigorously beating in a little of the separated mixture until emulsified and smooth, then beating in the rest of the mixture a little at a time. Then beat in the rest of the oil plus additional oil until very thick.

FOR THE MUSTARD MAYONNAISE:

1 egg yolk, at room temperature

1 tablespoon Dijon mustard

⅛ teaspoon salt

dash of cayenne pepper

½ cup (4 fl oz/125 ml) light olive oil
   or vegetable oil

2 tablespoons fresh lemon juice

1–2 tablespoons heavy (double) cream

1 celery root (celeriac), about 1 lb
   (500 g)

To make the mustard mayonnaise, in a bowl, combine the egg yolk, mustard, salt, and cayenne pepper. Using a whisk, beat until well blended. Add a little oil and whisk vigorously until an emulsion forms. Add a little more oil and again whisk vigorously to ensure the emulsion is stabilized. Then continue to add oil, a little at a time, beating vigorously after each addition until it is absorbed. When all of the oil has been beaten in, the sauce should be very thick. Add the lemon juice and whisk to mix well. Whisk in 1 tablespoon cream. Add more cream as needed to attain a creamy sauce. Taste and adjust the seasoning. Set aside.

❧ Using a sharp paring knife, peel the celery root, removing all of the brown skin. Then, using the medium holes on a handheld shredder, shred the celery root. Immediately put the shredded celery root into a bowl and add about one-half of the mustard mayonnaise. Mix well. Add more of the mayonnaise as necessary to coat the celery root lightly.

❧ Spoon onto individual plates and serve immediately. ⊞ ❧

ASPARAGUS WITH ORANGE HOLLANDAISE SAUCE

SERVES 4

Hollandaise, the classic sauce for dressing warm asparagus in France, is usually flavored with lemon. The orange juice used in this recipe is a nice change of pace and goes particularly well with the vegetable.

❧ *Keep in mind these few simple tips: Make the sauce over simmering water instead of over direct heat; too much heat will only cook the egg yolk rather than thicken the sauce. A bowl rather than the top pan of a double boiler contributes to a smoother whisking of the sauce. And finally, I find that softened butter blends in more readily than the more commonly used melted butter.*

FOR THE ORANGE HOLLANDAISE SAUCE:
2 egg yolks
3 tablespoons fresh orange juice
6 tablespoons (3 oz/90 g) unsalted
   butter, cut into slices ¼ inch (6 mm)
   thick, at room temperature
salt and freshly ground pepper

1½ lb (750 g) asparagus spears
2 teaspoons salt
1 orange

To make the sauce, place the egg yolks and 2 tablespoons of the orange juice in a heatproof bowl or the top pan of a double boiler. Set the bowl or pan over (but not touching) hot or barely simmering water in a saucepan or the bottom pan of the double boiler. Whisk continuously until warm and just beginning to thicken, about 1 minute. Add the butter, 1 slice at a time, whisking until fully absorbed before adding the next slice. When all of the butter is absorbed, continue to whisk until thickened, 2–3 minutes. Do not overcook.

❧ Remove the bowl or pan from the pan of hot water; season to taste with salt and pepper. If the sauce is too thick, stir in as much of the remaining 1 tablespoon orange juice as needed to thin to desired consistency. You should have about ¾ cup (6 fl oz/180 ml) sauce. Remove the bottom pan from the heat and let the water cool slightly. Then replace the hollandaise over the warm water and cover loosely with a paper towel (this prevents a skin from forming).

❧ Cut or break off the tough white ends from the asparagus spears. Trim all the spears to the same length. If the spears are large, use a vegetable peeler to peel away the tough skin as well, starting 2 inches below the tip.

❧ Select a large sauté pan or frying pan that will hold the asparagus in a single layer. Fill half full with water and place over high heat. Bring to a boil and add the salt and asparagus. Bring back to a boil, reduce the heat slightly and boil gently, uncovered, until just tender when pierced with a knife tip, 6–9 minutes, depending upon the size of the spears. Remove from the heat and drain well.

❧ To serve, immediately divide the asparagus among 4 warmed plates, arranging the spears in a row, and spoon the warm hollandaise sauce in a wide stripe across the middle of the asparagus. Using a zester or fine-holed shredder, and holding the orange over each serving, shred a little zest from the orange peel directly over the hollandaise on each serving (see page 287). Serve immediately. ⊞ ❧

"Scallops have the sweetest taste of any seafood, a most companionable taste that makes possible a wide, and sometimes surprising, variety of flavor harmonies."

—Marcella Hazan

SHRIMP AND SCALLOPS WITH MIXED HERBS AND BABY GREENS

SERVES 4

Using some of the larger-leaved herbs whole gives the dish a delightful extra dimension of flavor; you may want to try incorporating these herbs into your green salads as well.

❧ *The shrimp and scallops in this recipe are poached. If you prefer, grill or sauté them. For the grill, brush them first with olive oil. If sautéing them, heat 1 tablespoon each unsalted butter and olive oil in a sauté pan, then add the shellfish. Toss and turn until the shrimp are pink and the scallops are opaque, 2–3 minutes.*

1 cup (1 oz/30 g) flat-leaf (Italian) parsley leaves, stems removed, plus 2 tablespoons coarsely chopped parsley
1 cup (1 oz/30 g) small spinach leaves, carefully washed, stems removed, and leaves torn into small pieces
1 cup (1 oz/30 g) small watercress sprigs, carefully washed and trimmed
½ cup (½ oz/15 g) fresh basil leaves, torn into small pieces
¼ cup fresh cilantro (fresh coriander) leaves, stems removed
¼ cup fresh dill sprigs, feathery tops only, stems removed
2 tablespoons fresh lemon juice
salt
dash of cayenne pepper
½ cup (4 fl oz/125 ml) extra-virgin olive oil
1 clove garlic, minced
1 green (spring) onion, including some tender green tops, minced
1 bay leaf
¾ lb (375 g) sea scallops, cut into 1-inch (2.5-cm) pieces, or bay scallops, left whole

1 lb (500 g) small or medium-sized shrimp (prawns), peeled (leave tail fin attached) and deveined
12–16 crostini (recipe on page 283)

In a bowl, toss together the 1 cup (1 oz/30 g) parsley leaves, the spinach, watercress, basil, cilantro, and dill. Cover and set aside.

❧ In another bowl, make a dressing by combining the lemon juice, ⅛ teaspoon salt, and the cayenne pepper. Stir until the salt dissolves. Add the olive oil and whisk until blended. Stir in the garlic and green onion. Set aside.

❧ Fill a saucepan half full of water, add 1 teaspoon salt and the bay leaf, and bring to a boil over medium heat. Reduce the heat to medium-low and simmer for 5 minutes. Add the scallops, reduce the heat to low, cover, and gently poach until opaque, about 2 minutes. Using a slotted spoon, transfer the scallops to a colander to drain. Raise the heat to medium-low so the water simmers steadily and add the shrimp. Again reduce the heat to low, cover and poach until pink and opaque, about 2 minutes. Using a slotted spoon, transfer the shrimp to the colander to drain completely. Then place the scallops and shrimp in a bowl, drizzle on half of the dressing and toss until well coated. Let cool.

❧ Drizzle the remaining dressing over the greens and toss to coat. Arrange the greens around the perimeter of a serving platter. Spoon the scallops and shrimp in the center and sprinkle with the chopped parsley. Serve immediately with the warm crostini.

VEGETABLES WITH THREE SAUCES

SERVES 4

Crudités, the most popular of all first courses in France, are assortments of raw vegetables that have been cut, sliced, or shredded to make them easy to eat. I have taken the liberty here of blanching two of the vegetables—cauliflower and green beans—for better flavor, color, and texture.

1 fennel bulb, trimmed, old or bruised
    leaves removed
½ lb (250 g) young green beans,
    trimmed and cut in half if long
ice water to cover
1 small head cauliflower, cut into florets,
    large florets halved
1 slender English (hothouse) cucumber
1 tablespoon tarragon white wine
    vinegar
salt and freshly ground pepper
⅔ cup (5 fl oz/160 ml) extra-virgin
    olive oil
1 tablespoon red wine vinegar
1 teaspoon Dijon mustard
½ cup (4 fl oz/125 ml) sour cream
2 teaspoons chopped fresh dill
½–1 tablespoon fresh lemon juice
3 young carrots, about ½ lb (250 g)
    total weight, peeled and shredded
½ lb (250 g) cherry tomatoes,
    stems removed
3 sprigs each of any 3 of the following
    fresh herbs: tarragon, mint, dill, flat-leaf
    (Italian) parsley, basil, and lemon thyme

Cut the fennel bulb in half lengthwise through the narrow side. Cut each half crosswise into slices ⅛ inch (3 mm) thick. Set aside. Place the green beans in a bowl, add ice water to cover, and set aside to crisp for 10–15 minutes.
❧ Fill a saucepan three-fourths full with water and bring to a boil. Using

tongs, transfer the green beans to the boiling water; reserve the ice water. Boil, uncovered, until bright green but still crisp, 3–4 minutes. Using the tongs, return the beans to the ice water. Add the cauliflower florets to the boiling water and boil until about half tender, 3–4 minutes. Drain; set aside to cool. Drain the green beans; set aside.

❧ Peel the cucumber and cut lengthwise into quarters, then cut each quarter in half lengthwise. If the seeds are large, use a small knife to remove the seed core. Cut the strips into 2–2½-inch (5–6-cm) lengths. Set aside.

❧ Make the 3 sauces: In a small bowl, whisk together the tarragon vinegar, ⅛ teaspoon salt, and pepper to taste. Gradually add ⅓ cup (2½ fl oz/80 ml) of the olive oil, whisking well. Set aside. In another small bowl, whisk together the red wine vinegar, mustard, and salt and pepper to taste. Gradually add the remaining ⅓ cup (2½ fl oz/80 ml) olive oil, whisking well. Set aside. In a third small bowl, whisk together the sour cream, chopped dill, lemon juice, and salt and pepper to taste.

❧ To serve, arrange the shredded carrots, fennel, and the bowl of tarragon vinaigrette on a serving dish. On a second dish, arrange the green beans, cauliflower, and the mustard vinaigrette. On a third dish, arrange the tomatoes, cucumber strips, and the dill cream sauce. Garnish each dish with the herb sprigs. F ❧

PÂTÉ MAISON
SERVES 4-6

My interest in French country-style pâté recipes started in the mid-1960s, when I saw a brown-glazed earthenware terrine that the famed Elizabeth David had made for her shop in London. Elizabeth, whose recipes were much less rich and time-consuming than others found in most cookbooks of the time, gave me a recipe to go with it. This one is, in fact, simply a well-seasoned, finely textured meat loaf to be eaten cold. Once cooked, it will keep for about 4 days in the refrigerator.

½ lb (250 g) boneless veal, chicken, or turkey, cut into 1-inch (2.5-cm) pieces
½ lb (250 g) bacon slices, cut into 1-inch (2.5-cm) pieces
1 clove garlic, cut in half
1 shallot, cut in half
¼ lb (125 g) smoked ham, cut into 1-inch (2.5-cm) pieces
salt and freshly ground pepper
1 egg
tiny pinch of ground cinnamon
1 tablespoon Cognac or other good-quality brandy
1 bay leaf

Position a rack in the middle of an oven and preheat to 400°F (200°C).

❧ In a food processor fitted with the metal blade, combine the veal or poultry, bacon, garlic, and shallot and process until minced. Add the ham, salt and pepper to taste, egg, cinnamon, and brandy and process until the ham is finely chopped.

❧ Transfer to a rectangular terrine or loaf pan with a 2-cup (16 fl oz/500 ml) capacity, packing it in firmly. Smooth the top with a rubber spatula, and press the bay leaf gently into the meat mixture.

❧ Bake, uncovered, until the pâté has pulled away from the sides of the dish or pan and the top is nicely browned, about 45 minutes.

❧ Remove from the oven, let cool, cover, and refrigerate for 1 day to allow the flavors to develop. Cut into slices to serve. F ❧

BRUSCHETTA TRIO

SERVES 4–6

If you've ever joined the noontime crowd at a bar in the business section of an Italian city, you know what many Italians eat for lunch—bruschetta, a sandwich with a difference. A thick slice of rustic country bread is grilled or toasted and, while still hot, rubbed with a cut piece of garlic, drizzled with fruity olive oil, and topped with a wide variety of flavorful fare.
❧ *For the tomato-topped bruschetta, seek out sun-ripened tomatoes and fresh young basil. The cheese bruschetta is best with an Italian-style ricotta, which has a creamier texture and better taste than most American versions; you'll find it in specialty-food stores or high-quality markets.*

1 red bell pepper (capsicum)

1 yellow bell pepper (capsicum)

2 tablespoons extra-virgin olive oil, plus extra for drizzling

2 cloves garlic, minced, plus 2 cloves garlic, cut in half

salt and freshly ground pepper

4 ripe plum (Roma) tomatoes

1 tender celery stalk, cut into small dice (½ cup/2½ oz/75 g)

3 green (spring) onions, including some tender green tops, chopped

2 tablespoons chopped fresh basil

1 cup (8 oz/250 g) ricotta cheese, preferably Italian style, drained of any liquid

½ cup (¾ oz/20 g) coarsely chopped flat-leaf (Italian) parsley

1 teaspoon fresh lemon juice, plus 1 lemon

12 slices coarse country Italian or French bread, each about ½ inch (12 mm) thick and 3½–4 inches (9–10 cm) in diameter

Roast and peel the bell peppers (see page 290). Cut lengthwise into strips ¼ inch (6 mm) wide. Set aside.
❧ In a saucepan over medium-low heat, warm the 2 tablespoons olive oil. Add the 2 minced garlic cloves and sauté gently, stirring, for 30–40 seconds. Add the bell peppers and sauté until just tender, 5–6 minutes. Season to taste with salt and pepper, transfer to a bowl, and cover to keep warm.
❧ Core the tomatoes and cut in half crosswise. Gently squeeze out the seeds. Cut into small dice and place in a separate bowl. Add the celery, green onions, and basil, and season to taste with salt and pepper. Stir to blend. Set aside at room temperature.
❧ In another bowl, combine the ricotta cheese, parsley, and the 1 teaspoon lemon juice. Stir to mix well and season to taste with salt and pepper. Set aside at room temperature.
❧ When ready to serve, preheat a broiler (griller). Place the bread slices on a baking sheet and place under the broiler. Toast, turning once, until lightly golden, about 1½ minutes on each side. Remove the bread from the broiler and immediately rub 1 side of each slice with the cut side of a garlic clove. Drizzle or brush the garlic-rubbed sides evenly and lightly with olive oil.
❧ To serve, top 4 of the warm bread slices with the bell pepper slices. Top 4 of the slices with the tomato mixture. Top the final 4 slices with the ricotta cheese mixture. Using a zester or small shredder (see page 287), shred the zest (yellow part only) from the skin of the lemon directly over the bruschetta topped with the ricotta mixture. Place on plates and serve immediately.

$\mathscr{S}$OUPS

A bowlful of soup can often take on the role of main course as easily as it can begin a meal. Add a simple salad to refreshing Zucchini Soup (page 41), made with the summertime squash prevalent in American gardens, and you have a light-yet-satisfying supper. Partner Italian Minestrone (page 55) with crusty bread and well-aged cheese, and it becomes a robust winter meal.

Depending on their ingredients and preparation, soups can be elegant and refined or rustic and humble. On the following pages, you'll find this variety illustrated by a delightful array of classics, including France's elemental Leek and Potato Soup (page 59); a Fresh Tomato and Bread Soup with Basil (page 47) that captures the magic of the Italian countryside; and an American-style chicken soup (page 44) just like Grandma might have made.

TOMATO-LEEK SOUP WITH DILL

SERVES 4

If you raise tomatoes in your backyard and end up with a bumper crop during the summer, or simply find vine-ripened tomatoes at an unbeatable price in your local market, this is a recipe to remember.
Be sure to rinse the leeks thoroughly to rid them of any sand or grit lodged between the leaves, following the instructions in the recipe. If leeks are unavailable, use 2 cups (8 oz/250 g) coarsely chopped yellow onion.

This is one soup that truly benefits from using a food mill for puréeing. If you like to cook soup, I strongly advise you to make the small investment in a food mill, which simplifies the preparation of many different puréed soups. In the case of this recipe, passing the soup through a food mill produces an even consistency while removing the tomatoes' skins and seeds and any tough leek fibers. If you don't have a food mill and want to use a food processor or blender instead, force the soup through a medium-mesh sieve after puréeing.

2 medium leeks
3 tablespoons extra-virgin olive oil or vegetable oil
2 cloves garlic, coarsely chopped
2 tablespoons water
2 lb (1 kg) ripe plum (Roma) tomatoes, cored and coarsely chopped
1 potato, preferably baking variety, peeled and coarsely chopped
1 tablespoon chopped fresh dill, plus chopped fresh dill for garnish
½ teaspoon salt
⅛ teaspoon red pepper flakes
½ lemon
½ cup (4 fl oz/125 ml) sour cream

Trim the leeks, leaving some of the tender green tops intact. Make a lengthwise slit along each leek to within about 2 inches (5 cm) of the root end. Place under running water to wash away any dirt lodged between the leaves. Cut crosswise into slices ½ inch (12 mm) thick. You should have about 2 cups (8 oz/250 g). Set aside.
In a large saucepan over low heat, warm the oil. Add the garlic and sauté gently for 2 minutes. Add the leeks, raise the heat to medium and sauté, stirring, until soft, 3–4 minutes. Add the water, stir, cover, and cook over medium-low heat for 4–5 minutes longer. Do not allow to boil dry; add water as necessary.
Add the tomatoes, potato, the 1 tablespoon dill, salt, and red pepper flakes to the pan. Cook uncovered over medium heat, stirring constantly, until the juices start to release, 2–3 minutes. Then cover and cook, stirring occasionally, until the tomatoes are soft and the leeks and potato are tender when pierced with a fork, 15–20 minutes longer.
Remove from the heat. Pass the soup though a food mill (see page 292): Fit the food mill with the medium disk and rest the mill over a large bowl. Ladle the soup solids and liquids into the mill and turn the handle to purée. Alternatively, force the soup through a coarse-mesh sieve. Return the puréed soup to the pan and place over medium heat. Bring to a simmer. Squeeze a little juice from the lemon half into the soup, taking care to keep seeds out. Taste and adjust the seasoning. If a thinner soup is desired, add water.
Ladle the soup into warmed individual bowls. Float 2 tablespoons sour cream on top of each serving. Garnish with chopped dill. A

SCALLOP CREAM SOUP

SERVES 6 AS A FIRST COURSE, 4 AS A MAIN COURSE

I enjoyed this soup several times in Paris many, many years ago and devised my own recipe for it when I returned home. It goes very well before a simple main course such as grilled lamb chops with asparagus, or quickly seared veal slices with spinach. Or serve it as a main course for a weekend lunch or supper, accompanied by a green salad of young, tender lettuces.

❧ *The soup goes together quickly and simply. Just remember that you should have the other courses prepared beforehand, so you can give it your full attention, thus ensuring that the scallops are perfectly poached and that the soup thickens without curdling.*

2 tablespoons unsalted butter

2 tablespoons minced shallots (about
  2 small shallots)

1 small yellow onion, minced (about
  ½ cup/2½ oz/75 g)

2 tablespoons all-purpose (plain) flour

3 cups (24 fl oz/750 ml) milk, heated

1 bay leaf

2 fresh thyme sprigs

3 or 4 small, young carrots, peeled and
  thinly sliced (about 1 cup/4 oz/125 g)

1 lb (500 g) sea scallops or bay
  scallops, trimmed

1 cup (8 fl oz/250 ml) bottled
  clam juice

½ cup (4 fl oz/125 ml) dry white wine

1 cup (8 fl oz/250 ml) heavy
  (double) cream

3 egg yolks

salt and freshly ground pepper

1 lemon, cut crosswise into thin slices

chopped fresh parsley or thyme
  for garnish

In a large saucepan over medium-low heat, melt the butter. Add the shallots and sauté for 1 minute. Add the onion and sauté until translucent, 4–5 minutes. Add the flour and stir until well blended. Cook, stirring, for a few seconds without browning. Gradually add the milk, stirring. Raise the heat to medium and stir until the mixture comes to a boil and is thickened and smooth, 3–4 minutes. Add the bay leaf, thyme and carrots, cover partially, and cook gently until the carrots are tender, 15–20 minutes; do not allow to boil. Discard the bay leaf and thyme.

❧ Meanwhile, if using sea scallops, cut into small pieces or thin slices; leave bay scallops whole. In a small saucepan, combine the clam juice and wine and bring to a boil. Reduce the heat to low and add the scallops. Cover and poach very gently until just opaque, about 2 minutes. Using a slotted spoon, transfer the scallops to a plate and set aside. Reserve the poaching liquid.

❧ When the carrots are tender, add the poaching liquid to the milk mixture and remove from the heat. In a bowl, combine the cream and egg yolks and beat until blended. Slowly add about 1 cup (8 fl oz/250 ml) of the hot milk mixture to the yolk-cream mixture, stirring constantly until well blended, then add to the soup. Cook over medium-low heat, stirring constantly, until the soup coats the spoon and thickens, 5–6 minutes; do not allow it to boil. Add the scallops and season to taste with salt and pepper. Ladle into warmed bowls. Float lemon slices on each bowl and sprinkle with parsley or thyme. Serve at once. F ❧

"The quality of the soup should foretell that of the entire meal."

—Madame Seignobos

ONION SOUP

SERVES 4

Nothing tastes better on a cold winter day than a bowl of hot onion soup with its cap of melted cheese concealing a floating baguette slice. All you need for a complete meal is a green salad, a glass of red wine, and more bread to sop up the stock.

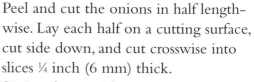 *Make sure that the bowls you use for serving the soup are flameproof. In France, onion soup is served in individual glazed earthenware crocks.*

1½–2 lb (750 g–1 kg) yellow onions
¼ cup (2 oz/60 g) unsalted butter
1 tablespoon all-purpose (plain) flour
5 cups (40 fl oz/1.25 l) chicken stock, heated
1 tablespoon molasses
2 fresh parsley sprigs
2 fresh thyme sprigs
1 bay leaf
salt and freshly ground black pepper
pinch of cayenne pepper
2–3 tablespoons dry sherry
8–12 slices French baguette
1 cup (4 oz/125 g) shredded Gruyère cheese

Peel and cut the onions in half lengthwise. Lay each half on a cutting surface, cut side down, and cut crosswise into slices ¼ inch (6 mm) thick.

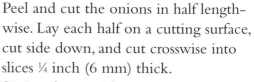 In a large, wide saucepan over medium heat, melt the butter. Add the onions and sauté, stirring occasionally, until they are evenly golden, 20–30 minutes.

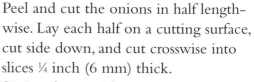 Sprinkle the flour over the onions; stir and cook until evenly distributed, 1–2 minutes. Raise the heat to medium-high and gradually add the chicken stock, stirring constantly. Continue to stir until the mixture comes to a boil and is smooth and thickened, 3–4 minutes. Add the molasses and stir until blended.

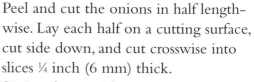 Gather the parsley and thyme sprigs and bay leaf together into a bunch, fold over the stems and tie securely with kitchen string to form a bouquet garni. Add to the pan. Reduce the heat to low, cover partially and simmer gently until the onions are very tender, 30–40 minutes. Season to taste with salt and black pepper and with the cayenne.

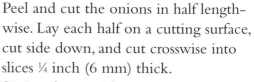 At serving time, preheat a broiler (griller). Warm 4 deep flameproof soup bowls.

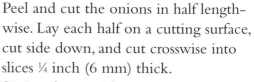 Remove the bouquet garni from the soup and discard. Stir in sherry to taste. Place the soup bowls on a heavy-duty baking sheet or a broiler pan and ladle the soup into the bowls. Float 2 or 3 baguette slices on top of each bowl. Generously sprinkle the cheese on the bread slices. Place under the broiler, with the cheese topping about 4 inches (10 cm) from the heat source, and broil (grill) until the cheese melts and starts to turn golden, 4–5 minutes. Serve at once. F

ZUCCHINI SOUP

SERVES 4

This simple summertime soup makes a pleasant start to a meal. It is rather thick, so add more milk or chicken stock if you prefer it thinner. Freshly grated nutmeg brings out the flavor of most green vegetables; if you haven't used it before, give it a try. You can also add a finely shredded carrot to the soup if you like, or add 8–12 small peeled and deveined shrimp (prawns) during the last 4–5 minutes of cooking.

≫ *It's worth the little extra time to salt and drain the shredded zucchini. The step removes a slight edge of bitterness. Don't worry about the salt: most of it washes away in the squeezing and rinsing.*

1½–2 lb (750 g–1 kg) small
    zucchini (courgettes)
salt
2 tablespoons unsalted butter
2 yellow onions, diced (2 cups/
    8 oz/250 g)
2 cups (16 fl oz/500 ml) chicken stock
freshly grated nutmeg
2 teaspoons finely chopped fresh mint
3 cups (24 fl oz/750 ml) milk
freshly ground pepper
½ teaspoon fresh lemon juice, or to taste
4 thin lemon slices

Trim the zucchini and shred on a medium-holed shredder; you should have 6–7 cups. Alternatively, use the shredding disk of a food processor. In a colander set over a bowl, layer half of the zucchini. Sprinkle with salt, then top with the remaining zucchini and again sprinkle with salt. Set aside for 25–30 minutes to drain off the bitter liquid.

≫ Pick up the drained zucchini by small handfuls and squeeze out the released juice. Return the zucchini to the colander and rinse under cold running water to wash out the salt. Again, squeeze out the moisture by handfuls, then set aside.

≫ In a large saucepan over medium-low heat, melt the butter. Add the onions and sauté, stirring, until translucent, 3–4 minutes. Add the chicken stock, cover, and simmer until the onions are tender, 15–20 minutes. Transfer the onions and liquid to a food processor fitted with the metal blade or to a blender; purée until smooth.

≫ Return the onion purée to the pan and add the zucchini, a pinch of nutmeg, and 1 teaspoon of the mint. Bring to a simmer, cover, and simmer for 6–8 minutes. Add the milk and season with salt, if needed, pepper, and the ½ teaspoon lemon juice or more to taste. Heat until very hot but do not allow to boil. Taste and adjust the seasoning again.

≫ Ladle into warmed individual bowls. Sprinkle with the remaining mint and garnish each serving with a slice of lemon.

WHITE BEAN SOUP

SERVES 4–6

A bowl of robust bean soup makes a good supper dish on a cold winter evening. Various versions of this soup have been part of American cooking since colonial times; in fact, the U.S. Senate dining room is famous for its white bean soup. Easy to make, this soup is a big help to those on a busy schedule. Feel free to substitute small white (navy) beans for the Great Northern beans.

❧ *Presoaking is such a fixture of recipes using dried beans that few people question the step. But new methods of drying beans for commercial sale now make overnight soaking unnecessary. I find that most dried beans can be treated in one of two ways: Soak them for 3–4 hours in cold water to cover before draining and cooking in fresh water. Or bring the beans and hot tap water to cover to a simmer, remove from the heat, cover, and let stand for 1–1½ hours before draining and continuing with the recipe.*

2 cups (1 lb/500 g) dried Great
   Northern beans
1 smoked ham shank or ham hock,
   ¾–1 lb (375–500 g)
1 small yellow onion stuck with
   3 whole cloves
1 bay leaf
3 fresh oregano or thyme sprigs
3 large fresh parsley sprigs
1 celery stalk with leaves, cut into
   2 or 3 pieces
½ lb (250 g) ripe plum (Roma)
   tomatoes
1 carrot, peeled and sliced
   (½ cup/2 oz/60 g)

1 sweet red (Spanish) onion or other
   sweet onion, diced (1 cup/4 oz/125 g)
1 teaspoon salt
freshly ground pepper

Sort through the beans, discarding any impurities or discolored beans. Rinse the beans, drain, and put into a large pot. Add hot tap water to cover by 2–3 inches (5–7.5 cm). Bring just to a simmer and remove from the heat. Cover and let soak for 1–1½ hours. Drain, rinse, and drain again.

❧ Return the beans to the pot and add 6 cups (48 fl oz/1.5 l) hot tap water. Rinse the ham shank or hock and add to the pot along with the yellow onion pierced with cloves. To assemble a bouquet garni, gather together the bay leaf, oregano or thyme sprigs, and parsley sprigs. Sandwich the bouquet between the 2 or 3 celery pieces and tie securely with kitchen string. Add to the pot. Bring just to a boil, reduce the heat to low, cover, and simmer for 45 minutes.

❧ Meanwhile, core and peel the tomatoes (see page 289): Bring a saucepan three-fourths full of water to a boil. Core the tomatoes and then cut a shallow X in the opposite end. Put them into the boiling water for 20–30 seconds to loosen the skins. Using a slotted spoon, transfer the tomatoes to a bowl of cold water. Using your fingers or a paring knife, immediately remove the skins. Cut in half crosswise and carefully squeeze out the seeds. Cut into small chunks; you should have about 1 cup (6 oz/185 g). Set aside.

❧ At the end of the 45-minute cooking time for the beans, remove the yellow onion and the bouquet garni and discard. Remove the ham shank or hock and, when cool enough to handle, cut the meat from the bone, removing and discarding any fat. Discard the bone and chop or shred the meat into small pieces. Return to the pot along with the tomatoes, carrot, and ½ cup (2 oz/60 g) of the sweet onion. Add the salt and freshly ground pepper to taste. Cover and simmer until the beans are completely tender, about 30 minutes longer.

❧ Taste and adjust the seasoning. Serve in large individual bowls with the remaining sweet onion sprinkled evenly over the top. A ❧

CHICKEN SOUP WITH CELERY AND LEMON

SERVES 4

This chicken soup reminds me of the ones my grandmother made when I was a child, especially when I had to stay home from school with a cold. To add even more citrus flavor, float a thin slice of lemon on top of each serving with the parsley and celery leaves.

For a fresh-tasting, clear soup, it is important to remove all the scum that rises to the surface when you bring the chicken thighs to a boil, and then to skim off the fat when the soup is done. If you have the time to make the chicken stock from scratch, do so. Just combine 1–2 pounds (500 g–1 kg) chicken parts (wings, backs, and necks); 1 carrot, 1 onion, and 1 celery stalk, all cut into chunks; a bay leaf; a pinch of dried thyme; salt and pepper; and water to cover. Simmer for 1 hour, skimming regularly, and strain.

But if time is short, don't hesitate to use a commercial variety of broth, preferably one with a good chicken flavor. You can freshen up canned broth by simmering it with a chunk each of onion, celery, and carrot for 15–20 minutes, then straining. Be aware, however, that some commercial broths are salty and you may not need to salt the soup further.

1 small bunch celery
2 tablespoons unsalted butter
1 yellow onion, diced
 (1 cup/4 oz/125 g)
4 chicken thighs, 1¼–1½ lb (625–750 g)
 total weight
3 cups (24 fl oz/750 ml) chicken stock
3 cups (24 fl oz/750 ml) water
1 bay leaf
4 or 5 fresh thyme sprigs
2 or 3 fresh parsley sprigs

4 lemon zest strips, each 3–4 inches
 (7.5–10 cm) long by 1 inch (2.5 cm)
 wide (see page 287)
¼ teaspoon salt, or to taste
freshly ground pepper
juice of 1 lemon
chopped fresh parsley

Remove the large outer stalks from the celery bunch and set aside for another use; use only 4 or 5 medium-sized inner stalks and the small ones in the center. Reserve some leaves for garnish. Separate the stalks and slice thinly, including the remaining leaves. You should have about 2 cups (8 oz/250 g). Set aside.

In a large saucepan over medium-low heat, melt the butter. Add the onion and sauté, stirring, until translucent, 3–4 minutes. Stir in the celery and set aside.

Rinse the chicken thighs and place in another saucepan. Add the chicken stock and the water. Bring to a boil and, using a skimmer or kitchen spoon, remove the scum from the surface. Transfer the chicken and its liquid to the pan holding the onions and celery.

To assemble a bouquet garni, gather together the bay leaf, thyme sprigs, parsley sprigs, and lemon zest strips and tie securely with kitchen string. Add to the pan along with the salt and pepper to taste and bring to a boil. Reduce the heat to low, cover, and simmer until the chicken and vegetables are tender, about 45 minutes.

Discard the bouquet garni. Using a kitchen spoon, skim off the fat from the surface. Stir in half of the lemon juice, taste, and add more if needed, along with more salt and pepper if needed. Serve in warmed individual bowls with a whole thigh in each bowl. Garnish with parsley and celery leaves. Alternatively, transfer the thighs to a plate, remove the skin and bones, cut up the meat and return it to the soup before serving.

SPINACH AND RICE SOUP

SERVES 4

I first had a version of this soup years ago in a small country restaurant in Tuscany. I've added chickpeas (garbanzo beans) to enhance the texture. They call for about 2 hours of soaking and cooking and can be prepared several hours in advance. That done, the soup actually takes very little time to prepare.

❧ *I specify Arborio rice here, the rice used to make risotto, as the soup needs the creaminess that comes from this type of rice when cooked.*

½ cup (3½ oz/105 g) dried chickpeas
    (garbanzo beans)
6 cups (48 fl oz/1.5 l) chicken stock
1 cup (8 fl oz/250 ml) dry white
    wine or water
2 bunches spinach, 1½–2 lb
    (750 g–1 kg) total weight
¼ cup (2 fl oz/60 ml) water
1 tablespoon olive oil
1 small yellow onion, finely chopped
    (about ½ cup/2 oz/60 g)
1 clove garlic, finely chopped
    (about 1 teaspoon)
½ cup (3½ oz/105 g) Italian Arborio
    rice or medium-grain white rice
salt and freshly ground pepper
freshly grated nutmeg

Sort through the chickpeas, discarding any discolored ones or impurities. Rinse the chickpeas, drain, and place in a bowl. Add hot tap water to cover by 2 inches (5 cm) and let soak for 1 hour. Drain, rinse again, and place in a saucepan with hot tap water to cover by 1 inch (2.5 cm). Place over medium-high heat and bring to a boil. Reduce the heat to medium-low, cover, and simmer until tender, about 1 hour. Drain and set aside.

❧ In a saucepan over medium heat, combine the chicken stock and the 1 cup (8 fl oz/250 ml) wine or water. Heat to just under a boil. Reduce the heat to low and keep warm.

❧ Pick over the spinach, discarding any old or damaged leaves, and wash well. Remove the stems. Gather the leaves together in bundles and chop coarsely. Place in a large sauté pan or saucepan and add the ¼ cup (2 fl oz/ 60 ml) water. Cover, place over medium heat, and cook, stirring a couple of times to cook evenly, until the spinach wilts, 1–2 minutes. Transfer to a colander and, using a kitchen spoon, press against the spinach to remove all the liquid. Set aside.

❧ In a large pot or saucepan over medium-low heat, warm the olive oil. Add the onion and garlic and sauté gently, stirring, until translucent, 4–5 minutes. Add the rice and stir until the rice is coated with the oil, 2–3 minutes.

❧ Stirring constantly, slowly pour in the hot stock mixture. Then add the spinach and chickpeas and bring to a simmer. Cover partially and simmer gently over low heat, stirring occasionally, until the rice is cooked just until al dente (tender but firm to the bite), 20–25 minutes. Season to taste with salt and pepper and a little nutmeg. If the soup is too thick, add a little water to achieve the proper consistency.

❧ To serve, ladle into warmed bowls and serve immediately.

FRESH TOMATO AND BREAD SOUP WITH BASIL

SERVES 4

This rustic soup depends so much upon the full flavor of fresh tomatoes that it is tastiest made in summer, when good vine-ripened tomatoes are available. Fresh basil is necessary, too; the dried variety has little distinctive flavor. It is best to use Arborio rice, as it thickens the soup slightly, and the slice of lightly toasted, olive oil–brushed country bread is a delicious addition to each bowl.

I especially like this soup for a Saturday or Sunday brunch, followed by a simple green salad topped with quickly sautéed or grilled shrimp (prawns)—and more bread alongside.

3 lb (1.5 kg) ripe plum (Roma)
    tomatoes

3 tablespoons olive oil, plus extra
    for brushing on bread

1 yellow onion, chopped (1 cup/
    4 oz/125 g)

3 cloves garlic, minced

¼ cup firmly packed, finely shredded
    fresh basil leaves

¼ teaspoon sugar

pinch of red pepper flakes

salt and freshly ground black pepper

¼ cup (2 oz/60 g) Italian Arborio rice
    or medium-grain white rice

6–7 cups (48–56 fl oz/1.5–1.75 l)
    chicken stock, heated

4 slices coarse country Italian or French
    bread, each about ½ inch (12 mm)
    thick and 3½–4 inches (9–10 cm)
    in diameter

Core and peel the tomatoes (see page 289). Cut the tomatoes in half crosswise and carefully squeeze out the seeds. Chop the tomatoes; you should have about 6 cups (2¼ lb/1.1 kg).

In a large saucepan over medium-low heat, warm the 3 tablespoons olive oil. Add the onion and garlic and sauté gently, stirring, until translucent, 6–7 minutes. Add the tomatoes, half of the basil leaves, the sugar, red pepper flakes, and salt and black pepper to taste. Stir in the rice, cover partially, and simmer until the tomatoes start to break down, 8–10 minutes. Add 6 cups (48 fl oz/1.5 l) of the chicken stock, re-cover partially, and simmer until the rice is almost tender, 10–15 minutes longer.

Remove one-third of the soup from the pan. Fit a food mill with the fine disk and rest it over a bowl. Ladle the removed soup into the mill and turn the handle to purée. Alternatively, purée in a food processor with the metal blade or in a blender. Return the purée to the pot, stir well, cover partially, and continue to barely simmer over low heat, stirring occasionally to prevent sticking, until the rice is tender, another 8–10 minutes. Add the remaining 1 cup (8 fl oz/250 ml) chicken stock if the soup seems too thick. Taste and adjust the seasoning.

Meanwhile, preheat an oven to 325°F (165°C). Brush each bread slice on one side with olive oil and arrange on a baking sheet, oiled side up. Place in the oven until the bread is warm, a few minutes.

To serve, place a warm bread slice in each of 4 large, warmed shallow soup bowls. Ladle the hot soup over the bread. Garnish with the remaining shredded basil and serve at once.

"Plain fare gives as much pleasure as a costly diet, while bread and water confer the highest possible pleasure when they are brought to hungry lips."

—Epicurus

EASY VEGETABLE SOUP

SERVES 4

You can vary the ingredients in this versatile soup recipe according to whatever is in season, freshest, or most reasonably priced at the market. Better yet, choose the vegetables you like the best. Just be sure they go well together. Green peas can replace the green beans, and turnips can replace the carrots. Feel free to add zucchini (courgettes), bell pepper (capsicum), chickpeas (garbanzo beans), or pasta.

Nothing could be better or easier to make than this soup. But cutting up the vegetables ahead of time makes the recipe that much easier. Don't cook the soup too long after you've added all the vegetables: the freshness of their flavor is most important here.

1 lb (500 g) ripe plum (Roma) tomatoes

2 tablespoons unsalted butter

1 yellow onion, diced (1 cup/4 oz/125 g)

2 cups (16 fl oz/500 ml) chicken stock

4 cups (32 fl oz/1 l) water

1 bay leaf

3 fresh oregano sprigs

2 fresh parsley sprigs

2 lemon zest strips, each 2 inches (5 cm) long by 1 inch (2.5 cm) wide (see page 287)

½ cup (2 oz/60 g) thinly sliced carrot

1 lb (500 g) red new potatoes, unpeeled, cut into 1-inch (2.5-cm) cubes

½ cup (2½ oz/75 g) diced celery, including the leaves

½ teaspoon salt, or to taste

freshly ground pepper

1 ear of yellow corn, husk and silk removed, trimmed of any defects

¼ lb (125 g) small green beans, trimmed and sliced 1 inch (2.5 cm) thick on the diagonal (1 cup)

Core and peel the tomatoes (see page 289). Bring a saucepan three-fourths full of water to a boil. Core the tomatoes and then cut a shallow X in the opposite end. Put them into the boiling water for 20–30 seconds to loosen the skins. Using a slotted spoon, transfer to a bowl of cold water. Using your fingers or a paring knife, immediately remove the skins. Cut in half crosswise and carefully squeeze out the seeds. Cut into small pieces. Set aside.

In a large saucepan over medium-low heat, melt the butter. Add the onion and sauté, stirring, until translucent, 3–4 minutes. Add the chicken stock and water. To assemble a bouquet garni, gather together the bay leaf, oregano sprigs, parsley sprigs, and lemon zest strips and tie securely with kitchen string. Add to the pan along with the tomatoes, carrot, potatoes, celery, and the salt and pepper to taste. Bring just to a simmer over medium-high heat, then reduce the heat to low, cover, and simmer for 20 minutes.

Firmly hold the ear of corn, stem end down, on a cutting surface and, using a sharp knife, carefully cut off the kernels. Add the kernels to the soup along with the green beans and continue to simmer, covered, for another 15 minutes.

Remove and discard the bouquet garni. Taste and adjust the seasoning. Serve very hot.

CANNELLINI BEAN SOUP

SERVES 4–6

This simple white bean soup is one of Italy's finest, and the addition of pasta makes it especially satisfying. I cook the pasta separately and then add it at serving time to ensure that the pasta is cooked properly—neither underdone nor overcooked.

If you can't find Italian cannellini beans—usually sold in Italian markets or specialty-food stores—use Great Northern beans instead. Search out good Italian romano cheese, too. If fresh oregano is unavailable, substitute 1 teaspoon dried.

5 cups (2¼ lb/1.1 kg) drained, cooked cannellini beans (recipe on page 282)

1 red bell pepper (capsicum)

3 tablespoons olive oil

3 cloves garlic, chopped

1 yellow onion, diced (1 cup/4 oz/125 g)

1 carrot, peeled and diced (½ cup/ 2½ oz/75 g)

1 celery stalk, diced (½ cup/2½ oz/75 g)

2 teaspoons chopped fresh oregano

6 cups (48 fl oz/1.5 l) chicken stock

salt and freshly ground pepper

1 cup (3½ oz/105 g) dried spinach fusilli (spiral) pasta

½ cup (2 oz/60 g) freshly grated romano cheese

Cook the beans as directed. Drain and set aside.

Roast and peel the bell pepper (see page 290). Cut lengthwise into strips ½ inch (12 mm) wide, then cut the strips in half crosswise. Set aside.

In a large, deep saucepan over medium-low heat, warm 2 tablespoons of the olive oil. Add the garlic and sauté, stirring, for 30–40 seconds. Add the onion and sauté gently, stirring, until translucent, 4–5 minutes. Add the carrot, celery, and oregano and sauté, stirring, until they begin to soften, 4–5 minutes.

Raise the heat to medium-high and add the reserved beans, bell pepper, and chicken stock. Bring to a simmer, reduce the heat to medium-low, cover, and simmer until the vegetables are tender, about 20 minutes. Season to taste with salt and pepper.

Remove 3 cups (24 fl oz/750 ml) of the soup from the pan. Fit a food mill with the fine disk and rest it over a bowl. Ladle the removed soup into the mill and turn the handle to purée. Alternatively, purée in a food processor fitted with the metal blade or in a blender. Return the purée to the pot, stir well and simmer over low heat for 4–5 minutes to blend the textures. Watch carefully that the bean purée does not scorch.

Fill a saucepan three-fourths full of water and bring to a boil over medium-high heat. Add the pasta, 2 teaspoons salt, and the remaining 1 tablespoon olive oil. Cook until the pasta is al dente (tender but firm to the bite), 5–6 minutes, or according to the package instructions. Drain and keep warm.

To serve, ladle the soup into warmed bowls and add cooked pasta to each bowl. Sprinkle with the romano cheese and serve at once.

"There are many ways to love a vegetable. The most sensible way is to love it well-treated."

−M.F.K. Fisher

CARROT SOUP WITH CORIANDER

SERVES 4

Coriander, an intriguing Middle Eastern spice popular in France, adds excellent flavor to carrots. Fresh leaves of cilantro (coriander in its fresh form) make the soup even livelier. Sherry, stirred in just before serving, and a garnish of crème fraîche, a thick, slightly soured French-style cultured cream found in specialty-food shops, contribute further dimensions of flavor.

The potato acts as a necessary thickening agent. Alternatively, you could use 1 cup (5 oz / 155 g) cooked white rice. For a special garnish, make thin carrot curls with a vegetable peeler.

10–12 carrots, 1–1½ lb (500–750 g)
   total weight
1 baking potato, 8–9 oz (250–280 g)
2 oz (60 g) shallots (3 or 4 shallots)
6 tablespoons (3 oz/90 g)
   unsalted butter
¾ teaspoon ground coriander
3 cups (24 fl oz/750 ml) chicken stock
½ teaspoon sugar
¼ teaspoon salt
1 cup (8 fl oz/250 ml) milk, or as needed
freshly ground pepper
2–3 tablespoons dry sherry
about ½ cup (4 fl oz/125 ml) crème
   fraîche or sour cream
4 tablespoons chopped fresh cilantro
   (fresh coriander)

Peel the carrots and cut crosswise into pieces ½ inch (12 mm) thick. Peel the potato and cut into small cubes. Cut the shallots crosswise into thin slices. Set aside.

In a large saucepan over medium-low heat, melt the butter. Add the shallots and sauté, stirring occasionally, until softened, 2–3 minutes; do not allow to brown. Add the carrots, potato, and coriander and sauté, stirring a couple of times, for 2–3 minutes. Add the chicken stock, sugar, and salt. Raise the heat to medium and bring to a simmer. Reduce the heat to low, cover partially, and gently simmer until the vegetables are soft when pierced with the tip of a knife, 20–25 minutes.

Remove from the heat and let cool slightly. Working in batches, ladle into a food processor fitted with the metal blade or into a blender. Process to form a smooth purée. Return the purée to the saucepan and add the 1 cup (8 fl oz/250 ml) milk and pepper to taste. Place over medium heat and heat until just beginning to simmer. Taste and adjust the seasoning. If too thick, add more milk. Just before serving, stir in the sherry to taste.

Ladle into warmed soup bowls. Top each bowl with 1–2 spoonfuls crème fraîche or sour cream and a generous sprinkling of cilantro.

LENTIL, TOMATO, AND MINT SOUP

SERVES 4–6

I first encountered this soup of lentils and tomatoes flavored with fresh mint years ago in Rome. I was intrigued with its un-expectedly delicious combination of tastes, which probably shows the influence of North African cooking from the days of the Roman Empire. The mint contributes a marvelously light, refreshing flavor; do not substitute dried mint, which simply cannot compare.

❧ *The soup is so satisfying that all you need is good crusty bread and a green salad to make a splendid lunch.*

2 cups (14 oz/440 g) dried lentils
6 cups (48 fl oz/1.5 l) water
salt
3 lb (1.5 kg) ripe plum (Roma)
　tomatoes
3 tablespoons olive oil
2 yellow onions, chopped
　(2–2½ cups/8–10 oz/250–315 g)
¼ cup (⅓ oz/10 g) chopped fresh mint,
　plus extra for garnish
4 cups (32 fl oz/1 l) chicken stock,
　or as needed
freshly ground pepper

Sort through the lentils, discarding any discolored ones or impurities. Rinse the lentils, drain, and place in a large saucepan with the water. Place over medium-high heat, add 2 teaspoons salt, and bring just to a boil. Reduce the heat to medium-low, cover partially, and simmer until the lentils are tender, about 30 minutes. Drain and set aside.

❧ While the lentils are cooking, core, peel, and seed the tomatoes (see page 289). Chop the tomatoes coarsely; you should have 5½–6 cups (2–2¼ lb/ 1–1.1 kg). Set aside.

In a large saucepan over medium-low heat, warm the olive oil. Add the onions and sauté gently, stirring, until translucent, 6–7 minutes. Add the tomatoes and the ¼ cup mint and cook gently, uncovered, until the tomatoes break down and the juices are released, 10–15 minutes longer.

Stir in the chicken stock and the reserved lentils, cover partially, and barely simmer over medium-low heat until the flavors are well blended and everything is tender, 10–15 minutes longer. Add more chicken stock or water if the soup seems too thick. Season to taste with salt and pepper.

To serve, ladle into warmed bowls and sprinkle with chopped mint.

SPLIT PEA SOUP

SERVES 4

With roots firmly planted in the peasant cooking of such European countries as France, Germany, and Holland, split pea soup came to America with the early settlers. It remains a favorite on both sides of the Atlantic, and I have enjoyed it many times in small bistros in Paris and in towns north of the city. I recommend serving it as a simple, satisfying evening meal.

You'll note that sausage is included in the recipe, just as I have found it so often in France. You can, of course, make a vegetarian version by leaving it out. In either case, serve the soup with crusty French bread.

3 ripe tomatoes, 10–12 oz (315–375 g) total weight
1 large leek
1½ cups (10½ oz/330 g) dried split peas
1 tablespoon olive oil or vegetable oil
1 carrot, peeled and diced (½ cup/2½ oz/75 g)

1 celery stalk, diced (½ cup/2½ oz/75 g)
½ lb (250 g) smoked sausages such as andouille or other flavorful smoked sausages made of pork, veal, chicken, or turkey
6 cups (48 fl oz/1.5 l) chicken stock or water
½ teaspoon salt
3 fresh parsley sprigs
3 fresh thyme sprigs
1 bay leaf
2 orange zest strips (see page 287), each 2 inches (5 cm) long by 1 inch (2.5 cm) wide and each stuck with 1 whole clove
freshly ground pepper

Core, peel, and seed the tomatoes (see page 289). Chop coarsely; you should have about 1½ cups (9 oz/280 g). Set aside. Trim the leek, leaving about 1 inch (2.5 cm) of the tender green tops, then rinse it (see page 291). Cut crosswise into ¼-inch (6-mm) slices. Set aside. Sort through the split peas, discarding any damaged peas or small stones. Rinse, drain, and set aside.

In a large saucepan over medium-low heat, warm the oil. When hot, add the leek slices and sauté until they begin to wilt, 3–4 minutes. Add the carrot and celery and sauté for 2–3 minutes longer. Add the split peas, tomatoes, whole sausages, stock or water, and salt and stir well. Gather the parsley and thyme sprigs, bay leaf, and orange zest strips into a bunch, fold over the stems, and tie securely with kitchen string to form a bouquet garni. Add to the pan. Raise the heat and bring to a boil. Reduce the heat to low, cover partially and simmer until the split peas and vegetables are tender, 40–50 minutes.

Let cool slightly. Using tongs, transfer the sausages to a plate.

Remove and discard the bouquet garni. Working in batches, ladle the soup into a food processor fitted with the metal blade or into a blender. Pulse to form a coarse purée and return to the pan. Cut the sausages crosswise into ¼-inch (6-mm) slices and return to the pan. Place over medium heat; bring to a simmer, stirring constantly. Reduce the heat to low and simmer gently for a few minutes. Add pepper to taste and adjust the seasoning.

Ladle into warmed soup bowls and serve at once.

MINESTRONE

SERVES 4–6

*Every region of Italy has its own version
of this hearty vegetable soup, and as you
travel the country you find that the choice
of vegetables varies along with the inclusion
of pasta, dried beans, or rice—alone or in
pairs. I've included macaroni and cannellini
beans. I recommend cannellini beans
because they have good flavor and texture.
You can, however, substitute Great Northern
or small white lima beans. And if fresh
oregano is not available, use ½ teaspoon dried.*
⤷ *For the soup to be at its best, the
vegetables must be cooked in the prescribed
sequence, so that the longer-cooking vegetables go in first. Once the pasta has been
added, the soup should continue cooking
only until the pasta is al dente (tender
but firm to the bite).*

¾ cup (5 oz/155 g) dried
  cannellini beans
2 cups (16 fl oz/500 ml) hot tap water
1½ lb (750 g) ripe plum (Roma)
  tomatoes
2 tablespoons unsalted butter
1 large yellow onion, cut into ½-inch
  (12-mm) dice (about 1½ cups/
  6 oz/185 g)
2 carrots, peeled and cut into ½-inch
  (12-mm) dice (about 1 cup/5 oz/155 g)
2 celery stalks, cut into ½-inch (12-mm)
  dice (about 1 cup/5 oz/155 g)
3 or 4 small potatoes, preferably yellow-
  fleshed such as Yellow Finn or Yukon
  gold, or russet, peeled and cut into
  ¾-inch (2-cm) dice
2 or 3 fresh oregano sprigs
6 cups (48 fl oz/1.5 l) chicken stock
4 or 5 green Swiss chard leaves,
  carefully washed, stems removed, and
  leaves cut into strips ¼ inch (6 mm)
  wide (about 1½ cups/3 oz/90 g
  firmly packed)

1 cup (3½ oz/105 g) elbow macaroni
  or other short dried pasta
salt and freshly ground pepper
8–10 fresh basil leaves, cut into
  fine shreds
1 cup (4 oz/125 g) freshly grated
  Italian Parmesan cheese, preferably
  Parmigiano-Reggiano

Sort through the beans, discarding any
discolored ones or impurities. Rinse
the beans, drain, and place in a saucepan
with hot tap water to cover by 2 inches
(5 cm). Place over medium-high heat
and bring to a boil. Immediately remove
from the heat, cover, and let stand for
1 hour. Drain, rinse, and drain again.
Return the beans to the pan and add
the 2 cups (16 fl oz/500 ml) hot tap
water. Place over medium-high heat
and bring to a simmer. Reduce the
heat to medium-low, cover, and simmer
until the beans are tender, 1–1½ hours.
Set aside.
⤷ While the beans are cooking, core
and peel the tomatoes (see page 289).
Cut the tomatoes in half crosswise
and carefully squeeze out the seeds.
Chop the tomatoes; you should have
2½–3 cups (15–18 oz/470–560 g).
Set aside.
⤷ In a large saucepan over medium-
low heat, melt the butter. Add the onion
and sauté until translucent, 6–7 minutes.
Add the carrots and celery and sauté
until beginning to soften, 4–5 minutes.
Add the potatoes, tomatoes, oregano,
and stock, raise the heat, and bring
to a simmer. Reduce the heat to
medium-low, cover, and simmer until
the potatoes are almost tender,
about 20 minutes.

⤷ Add the chard and the cannellini
beans and their liquid and stir well.
Cover and simmer over medium-low
heat until the chard is tender, about
15 minutes longer. Add the pasta, cover
and simmer until the pasta is tender,
about 15 minutes longer. Season to taste
with salt and pepper.
⤷ To serve, ladle into warmed bowls.
Sprinkle with the basil and cheese.

VEGETABLE SOUP WITH TOMATO-BASIL SAUCE

SERVES 4

Tomato-basil sauce gives this vegetable soup its special aroma and flavor. The sauce is known in France as pistou, *although it is more commonly made without the addition of tomatoes. You may notice a similarity to Italy's pesto sauce, a good example of how many preparations found in the south of France are common to other Mediterranean countries, with only slight variations in ingredients.*

Fresh basil is absolutely necessary for the sauce; the dried herb just does not have the same flavor. If you cannot find fresh oregano or marjoram for the soup, however, you can substitute ½ teaspoon of the dried herb.

1 lb (500 g) ripe tomatoes
½ bunch large-leaved spinach, about
    ½ lb (250 g)
2 tablespoons olive oil
1 yellow onion, cut into ¼-inch (6-mm)
    dice (about 1 cup/4 oz/125 g)
1 lb (500 g) baking potatoes, peeled and
    cut into ½-inch (12-mm) dice (about
    2 cups/10 oz/315 g)
3 or 4 carrots, peeled and cut into
    ½-inch (12-mm) dice (1–1½ cups/
    5–7½ oz/155–235 g)
2 tablespoons coarsely chopped fresh
    parsley, preferably flat-leaf (Italian)
leaves from 3 fresh oregano or
    marjoram sprigs, chopped
6 cups (48 fl oz/1.5 l) chicken stock,
    or as needed
salt and freshly ground pepper
tomato-basil sauce (recipe on page 285)
3 small zucchini (courgettes), trimmed
    and cut into ½-inch (12-mm) dice
½ lb (250 g) small green beans, trimmed
    and cut into 2-inch (5-cm) lengths

Core, peel, and seed the tomatoes (see page 289). Chop coarsely; you should have about 2 cups (12 oz/375 g). Set aside.

Rinse the spinach thoroughly. Pick over and discard any old or damaged leaves and remove the stems and discard. Gather the leaves into a stack and, using a sharp knife, cut crosswise into strips ½ inch (12 mm) wide. You should have about 2 cups (4 oz/125 g), packed. Set aside.

In a large saucepan or stew pot over medium-low heat, warm the olive oil. When hot, add the onion and sauté, stirring occasionally, until translucent, 6–8 minutes. Add the tomatoes, potatoes, carrots, parsley, and oregano or marjoram and cover. Let steam for 4–5 minutes. Add 6 cups (48 fl oz/1.5 l) chicken stock and salt and pepper to taste. Raise the heat to medium and bring to a simmer. Reduce the heat to low, cover partially, and simmer gently until the potatoes and carrots are almost tender, 15–20 minutes.

Meanwhile, prepare the tomato-basil sauce.

When the vegetables are almost tender, add the zucchini and green beans, plus more chicken stock if needed to cover the vegetables. Continue to simmer until the beans are just tender, 8–10 minutes. Add the spinach and simmer for another few minutes until it wilts. Taste and adjust the seasoning.

Ladle into warmed soup bowls and top each serving with a spoonful of tomato-basil sauce. Serve any remaining sauce in a bowl at the table.

"My cook, who makes the best pistou I have ever tasted, says it does not matter what vegetables you put in pistou, as long as there are plenty of them."

—Waverley Root

CREAM OF MUSHROOM SOUP

SERVES 4

I've adapted this lovely first-course soup from one that was made for me years ago by my friend Cheryl Schultz, in Dallas, Texas. What impressed me about the recipe then, and still does, is how well it highlights the flavor of the mushrooms—just as a classic French bistro soup should. The potato imparts to the soup all the thickening it needs, and the splash of Madeira provides a special bouquet.

Melting a little Brie cheese on top at serving time adds elegance and richness. Make sure you select a cheese that is ripe and soft, and have it at room temperature so that it will begin to melt the moment you add it. Select mushrooms with tightly closed caps; there should be no gills showing.

1 lb (500 g) small, firm fresh mushrooms, preferably brown
¼ cup (2 oz/60 g) unsalted butter
2 tablespoons chopped shallots (about 2 small shallots)
1 small white sweet onion, chopped (about ½ cup/2½ oz/75 g)
1 white potato, peeled and cut into ½-inch (12-mm) dice (about 1 cup/ 5 oz/155 g)
2 cups (16 fl oz/500 ml) chicken stock
salt
1 cup (8 fl oz/250 ml) heavy (double) cream
2–3 tablespoons Madeira wine, preferably imported
freshly grated nutmeg
freshly ground pepper
2 oz (60 g) Brie cheese, rind removed and sliced into 10–12 thin pieces
chopped fresh basil

Using a soft brush or clean kitchen towel, brush off any soil or other impurities from the mushrooms. Do not rinse in water. Trim the stems and chop the mushrooms coarsely; set aside.

Marin a sauté pan or large saucepan over medium-low heat, melt the butter. Add the shallots and onion and simmer, stirring occasionally, until soft and translucent, 5–6 minutes. Add the mushrooms, increase the heat to medium, and sauté, stirring and tossing, until the mushrooms begin to release their liquid, 8–10 minutes; do not allow the onion to brown. Add the potato, chicken stock, and salt to taste, cover partially, and simmer until the mushrooms and potato are soft, 15–20 minutes, adjusting the heat if necessary to maintain a simmer.

Remove from the heat and let cool slightly. Working in batches, ladle the soup into a food processor fitted with the metal blade or into a blender. Process the soup to form a smooth purée. Return the purée to the pan and add the cream. Place over medium-low heat and bring almost to a simmer; do not allow to boil. Add the Madeira to taste, a little nutmeg, and a little pepper. Taste and adjust the seasoning.

Ladle into warmed soup plates or bowls. Float 2 or 3 pieces of the cheese on the surface of each bowl of soup. Sprinkle with chopped basil and serve.

LEEK AND POTATO SOUP

SERVES 4

One of the most comforting of all hot soups, leek and potato is also one of the most delicious when served cold—as the classic recipe called vichyssoise—on a warm day. I have added carrot to the traditional recipe to enhance the color and flavor.

❧ *I call for a food mill to purée the soup. This simple kitchen tool gives it a more substantial texture than if it were puréed in a food processor or blender, but you can certainly use those machines if you like.*

1 lb (500 g) leeks (about 3 medium)
2 tablespoons unsalted butter
1 lb (500 g) baking potatoes,
   peeled and cubed
2 carrots, peeled and sliced
salt and freshly ground pepper
¼ cup (2 fl oz/60 ml) heavy (double)
   cream if serving hot or ½ cup (4 fl oz/
   125 ml) cream if serving cold
4 thin lemon slices
fresh chives

Following the directions on page 291, trim the leeks, leaving about 1 inch (2.5 cm) of the tender green tops, then rinse them. Cut crosswise into slices ½ inch (12 mm) thick.

❧ In a large saucepan over medium-low heat, melt the butter. When foaming, add the leeks and sauté, stirring occasionally, until they have wilted a little, 3–4 minutes. Add the potatoes and carrots, then add water just to cover the vegetables. Raise the heat to medium and bring to a boil. Reduce the heat to low and simmer, uncovered, until the vegetables are tender when pierced with the tip of a knife, about 30 minutes.

❧ Fit a food mill with the medium disk and rest the mill over a large bowl. Using a ladle or a large spoon and working in batches, transfer the cooked vegetables and their liquid to the food mill and turn the handle to purée.

❧ If serving the soup hot, return the puréed vegetables to the saucepan and season to taste with salt and pepper. Return the saucepan to medium-low heat, stir in ¼ cup (2 fl oz/60 ml) cream and heat to just under a boil. Add a little water if the purée is too thick. Taste and adjust the seasoning.

❧ Ladle into warmed bowls and float a lemon slice on top of each serving. Using scissors, cut the chives into pieces ¼ inch (6 mm) long and sprinkle the chives on the lemon slice. Serve at once.

❧ To serve cold, do not return the purée to the saucepan. Instead, cover the bowl and refrigerate until well chilled. When ready to serve, season to taste with salt and pepper and stir in ½ cup (4 fl oz/125 ml) cream, mixing well. Taste and adjust the seasoning. Ladle into chilled individual bowls. Float a lemon slice on top of each serving and garnish with the chives as directed above.

ROASTED RED PEPPER SOUP

SERVES 4

Make this colorful soup during the summer, when red bell peppers (capsicums) are most abundant in the market. You can serve it cold as well as hot; it tastes even better after being refrigerated overnight. Turn any leftovers into a rich cream soup by stirring in an equal quantity of milk or cream and seasoning to taste.

&/~ *The method given for roasting and peeling peppers is easiest when you're preparing more than two or three; but several other methods exist, including blistering their skins directly over a gas flame or an electric burner. If you're rushed for time, you can skip the roasting and peeling of the peppers. Simply halve, stem, and seed them, cut them into medium pieces, and add them to the saucepan with the onions. In this case, don't purée the vegetables in a food processor or blender; instead, pass them, along with their cooking liquid, through a food mill fitted with a medium or fine disk (see page 292). A food mill produces a coarse, even purée while eliminating most of the pepper skins.*

2–2½ lb (1–1.25 kg) red bell peppers (capsicums) (6 or 7)

3 tablespoons extra-virgin olive oil or vegetable oil

1 large yellow onion, chopped (1½ cups/6 oz/185 g)

1 cup (8 fl oz/250 ml) chicken stock

2 cups (16 fl oz/500 ml) water

1 teaspoon salt, or to taste

pinch of red pepper flakes or cayenne pepper

1 tablespoon fresh lemon juice

8–10 fresh basil leaves, shredded

⅓–½ cup (3–4 fl oz/80–125 ml) heavy (double) cream

Roast and peel the bell peppers (see page 290): Preheat a broiler (griller) or an oven to 500°F (260°C). Cut the peppers in half lengthwise and remove the stems, seeds, and ribs. Lay the peppers, cut side down, on a baking sheet. Place under the broiler or in the oven. Broil (grill) or roast until the skins blister and blacken. Remove from the broiler or oven and cover with aluminum foil. Let steam until cool enough to handle, 10–15 minutes. Then, using your fingers or a knife, peel off the skins. Chop the peppers into medium pieces; set aside.

&/~ In a large saucepan over medium-low heat, warm the oil. Add the onion and sauté, stirring occasionally, until translucent, 3–4 minutes; do not allow to brown. Add the chicken stock, the water, salt, and red pepper flakes or cayenne pepper. Cover partially and bring to a boil. Reduce the heat to low and simmer until the onion is tender, 15–20 minutes. Add the roasted peppers and cook for 10 minutes longer.

&/~ Place a colander over a large bowl. Drain the peppers and onion in the colander, reserving the liquid. Working in batches, transfer the peppers and onion to a food processor fitted with the metal blade or to a blender. Pulse a few times to achieve a textured purée.

&/~ Return the purée and the reserved liquid to the saucepan and reheat over medium heat. Cook, stirring, for 3–4 minutes. Stir in the lemon juice and cook for 1 minute longer. Taste and adjust the seasoning. Stir in about one-third of the shredded basil.

&/~ Ladle the soup into warmed individual bowls. Float 1–2 tablespoons cream on each serving and then sprinkle with the remaining basil. Serve immediately.

A &/~

"Anybody who is conscientious enough to follow simple directions can learn to cook."

–James Beard

$\mathcal{S}$ALADS

The best salads are those that speak of the seasons and of the simple enjoyment offered by fresh ingredients at their peak. These pleasures are provided by such classic preparations as a French Endive and Mushroom Salad with Mustard Dressing (page 80) or an Italian Escarole Salad with Pear and Prosciutto (page 78). But a good salad doesn't have to be based on greens, especially in summer, when a flavorful Corn and Red Pepper Salad (page 65) celebrates America's summertime harvest.

Of course, the ease of preparing salads excites many cooks around the world to try more complex combinations of tastes, textures, and colors. Consider the Mango and Melon Salad (page 83), which bespeaks France's fascination with the tropics; an Italian Blood Orange, Fennel, and Olive Salad (page 81), with its sophisticated contrasts of sweet, savory, tangy, and salty flavors; or the innovative light version presented here for Caesar Salad (page 74), with its dressing that alluringly combines garlic, anchovies, lemon juice, and Parmesan cheese.

BROILED SHRIMP AND SPINACH SALAD
SERVES 4

Light salads combining hot seafood or chicken with fresh greens are some of California's best contributions to American cooking. Add a good soup and a simple fruit dessert and you have a perfect weekend lunch or weekday supper.
Seek out the baby spinach leaves (usually prewashed) that are now being grown especially for use in salads. Otherwise, pick out a bunch of spinach that has lots of small, tender leaves, and take care to wash them thoroughly.
As most raw shrimp for sale today were flash-frozen at the time of the catch, I find it best to peel the shrimp and then soak them in salted water for 10–15 minutes to freshen them and eliminate any strong odor. After soaking, rinse well in fresh water before use.

1 lb (500 g) shrimp (prawns) in the shell (about 24)
2⅛ teaspoons salt, or to taste
½ lb (250 g) young, small green beans, trimmed
½ lb (250 g) baby spinach leaves, or one bunch young, tender spinach
1½ tablespoons fresh lemon juice
⅓ cup (3 fl oz/80 ml) extra-virgin olive oil
2 teaspoons minced fresh dill
freshly ground pepper
1 tablespoon minced green (spring) onion, including some tender green tops

Preheat a broiler (griller).
Peel, devein, and butterfly the shrimp as directed on page 289. Place the shrimp in a bowl and add water to cover. Add 1 teaspoon of the salt, stir to dissolve, and let stand for 10 minutes. Drain, rinse, and drain again; dry on paper towels. Set aside.
Bring a saucepan three-fourths full of water to a boil. Add the green beans and 1 teaspoon salt and bring back to a boil. Cook until tender but still crisp, 4–5 minutes. Drain and immediately plunge into cold water to stop the cooking. Drain again and set aside.
Rinse the baby spinach leaves, if necessary, and dry. If using bunch spinach, pick over the leaves, discarding tough and large ones, and remove the stems. Wash and dry well. If the leaves are large, tear them into small pieces. Place the spinach in a bowl.
To make the vinaigrette, in a small bowl, combine the lemon juice and the remaining ⅛ teaspoon salt and stir to dissolve. Add the olive oil, dill, and pepper to taste and whisk until blended. Stir in the green onion and set aside.
Arrange the shrimp in a small broiling pan without a rack or in a flameproof baking dish. Brush the shrimp with a little of the vinaigrette and place under the broiler about 3 inches (7.5 cm) from the heat. Broil (grill) until the shrimp turn pink, turning once, 3–4 minutes. Remove from the broiler and add the remaining vinaigrette and the green beans to the pan or dish. Stir to coat the shrimp and beans with the vinaigrette. Using tongs, transfer the shrimp and beans to a plate.
Pour the warm vinaigrette over the spinach and toss quickly. Divide the spinach among individual plates and arrange the shrimp and green beans on top. Serve at once. A

ESCAROLE SALAD WITH BACON

SERVES 4

Very light and simple, this salad makes a nice introduction to a hearty bistro-style main course such as Roast Tarragon Chicken (recipe on page 131).

If you cannot find escarole, chicory (curly endive) may be substituted. Be sure to seek out good smoked lean bacon, preferably freshly cut from a slab by the butcher. If you like, thinly sliced mushrooms or radishes may be added to the salad.

For the best-flavored dressing, use an aged sherry vinegar or a raspberry white wine vinegar with a good, fresh raspberry flavor and color. Be sure to try the dressing before you add it to the lettuce, and adjust the oil and vinegar proportions to your taste. If your sherry vinegar is not that strong, or if you use raspberry vinegar, you may need to add more vinegar.

1 large or 2 small heads escarole
　(Batavian endive)
6 oz (185 g) thickly sliced smoked
　lean bacon (about 6 slices)

FOR THE DRESSING:

1 tablespoon sherry vinegar or
　1–1½ tablespoons raspberry vinegar
⅛ teaspoon salt
freshly ground pepper
4–5 tablespoons (2–3 fl oz/60–80 ml)
　extra-virgin olive oil

Separate the leaves from the heads of escarole, discarding any old or damaged leaves and the core. Rinse and dry well. Tear the leaves into small pieces and place in a bowl, cover with plastic wrap, and refrigerate to crisp for 30–40 minutes.

Cut the bacon crosswise into pieces ½ inch (12 mm) wide. Place in a heavy frying pan over medium heat and fry, stirring and tossing, until lightly browned, 3–4 minutes. Using a slotted spoon, transfer to paper towels to drain. Pour off the fat from the pan, wipe clean with a paper towel, and set aside.

To make the dressing, in a small bowl, combine the vinegar, salt, and pepper to taste and stir until the salt dissolves. Gradually add 4 tablespoons (2 fl oz/60 ml) olive oil, whisking until well blended. Add another 1 tablespoon olive oil if needed to balance the flavors of the dressing. Taste and adjust the seasoning.

Remove the escarole from the refrigerator and spoon the dressing over the top. Toss until the leaves are evenly coated. Return the bacon to the reserved pan and place over medium heat to warm.

Divide the escarole among 4 plates and sprinkle with the warm bacon pieces. Serve at once.

CORN AND RED PEPPER SALAD

SERVES 4

Bright in both color and flavor, this salad makes a good accompaniment to cold meats or grilled chicken or fish. When tomatoes are ripe and plentiful, try serving it in large tomato shells: slice off the tops of the tomatoes, scoop out their seeds and membranes, and spoon in the salad.

If you have never tasted tarragon-flavored wine vinegar, I suggest you sample this delicately perfumed seasoning; it's available in better food markets and most specialty-food stores. The best version is made with champagne vinegar; those made with white wine vinegar are preferable to those made with red wine vinegar. Try the vinegar on green salads, chicken, and vegetables.

I think it is best to cook the ears of corn before cutting off their kernels. The kernels cook better and stay moister.

1 large red bell pepper (capsicum)
1⅛ teaspoons salt
4 ears of yellow corn, husks and silk removed, trimmed of any defects
2 tablespoons minced green (spring) onion, including some tender green tops
1 tablespoon white tarragon vinegar
3 tablespoons extra-virgin olive oil
freshly ground pepper
romaine (cos) or butter (Boston) lettuce

Roast and peel the bell pepper (see page 290): Preheat a broiler (griller) or an oven to 500°F (260°C). Cut the bell pepper in half lengthwise and remove the stem, seeds, and ribs. Lay the pepper halves, cut side down, on a baking sheet. Place under the broiler or in the oven. Broil (grill) or roast until the skin blisters and blackens. Remove from the broiler or oven and cover with

aluminum foil. Let steam until cool enough to handle, 10–15 minutes. Then, using your fingers or a knife, peel off the skin. Cut the pepper lengthwise into strips ¼ inch (6 mm) wide and then cut the strips in half crosswise. You should have about 1 cup (5 oz/155 g). Set aside.

Bring a large pot three-fourths full of water to a boil. Add 1 teaspoon of the salt and the corn to the boiling water, cover partially, and boil for 5 minutes. Remove the corn and immediately plunge into cold water to stop the cooking. When cool enough to handle, firmly hold each ear of corn, stem end down, on a cutting surface. Using a sharp knife, carefully cut off the kernels. You should have approximately 3 cups (18 oz/560 g).

Place the corn kernels, pepper strips, and green onion in a bowl and stir together. In a small bowl, stir together the vinegar and the remaining ⅛ teaspoon salt until the salt dissolves. Add the olive oil and freshly ground pepper to taste and whisk until well blended. Pour the dressing over the corn mixture and stir until well blended. Taste and adjust the seasoning. At this point the corn mixture can be covered and refrigerated for 1–2 hours.

To serve, arrange lettuce leaves on a serving plate or 4 individual plates and place the corn mixture in the center.

A

CHICORY AND GOAT CHEESE SALAD

SERVES 4

Goat's milk cheese, long a favorite on European tables, has only recently become popular in America. Many European countries produce distinctive goat cheeses, from Greece's feta to Italy's caprini. French-style chèvres may now be found in many cheese shops, in both imported and domestic versions. Be sure to select a soft, fresh variety for this recipe.

❧ *Walnut white wine vinegar is, as its name implies, a white wine vinegar infused with the essence of walnuts, producing an excellent flavor that goes well in salad dressings. Several brands are imported from France and may be found in specialty-food shops and in the international sections of large food stores. Tarragon white wine vinegar can be substituted.*

½ cup (2 oz/60 g) walnut pieces, broken into small pieces or coarsely chopped
1 tablespoon walnut white wine vinegar
⅛ teaspoon salt
freshly ground pepper
6 tablespoons (3 fl oz/90 ml) extra-virgin olive oil
1 or 2 heads chicory (curly endive), depending upon size
1 slice coarse country bread or whole wheat (wholemeal) bread
¼ lb (125 g) fresh goat cheese, preferably chèvre, cut into 4 equal slices

Position a rack in the middle of an oven and preheat to 325°F (165°C). Spread the walnut pieces on a baking sheet. Place in the oven and bake until they begin to change color, 6–8 minutes. Watch carefully so they do not burn. Remove from the oven and set aside to cool.

❧ In a small bowl, combine the walnut vinegar, salt, and pepper to taste and stir until the salt dissolves. Gradually add 4 tablespoons (2 fl oz/60 ml) of the olive oil, whisking until well blended. Taste and adjust the seasoning. Set aside.

❧ Separate the leaves from the heads of chicory, discarding any old or damaged leaves. Rinse and dry thoroughly. Tear the leaves into bite-sized pieces and put into a large bowl. Set aside.

❧ Preheat a broiler (griller). Remove the crust from the bread slice and discard. Tear the bread into small pieces and place in a food processor fitted with the metal blade or in a blender. Process to form fine, soft crumbs. Transfer to a saucer. In a separate saucer, place the remaining 2 tablespoons olive oil. Carefully holding 1 slice of cheese at a time, place in the olive oil, turning to coat on all sides. Then place in the bread crumbs and turn to coat thoroughly with the crumbs. Place on a baking sheet and set aside.

❧ Whisk the reserved dressing again until blended and spoon over the lettuce. Toss and turn the leaves until well coated. Divide among 4 plates.

❧ Slip the cheese slices into the broiler about 4 inches (10 cm) from the heat source and broil (grill) until the tops are golden and the cheese has softened, 1–2 minutes. Using a spatula, carefully transfer each slice to the center of a lettuce-lined plate. Sprinkle with the walnut pieces and serve at once.

freshly ground pepper

½ cup (4 fl oz/125 ml) extra-virgin
    olive oil

2–3 teaspoons honey

Halve each avocado and remove the
pit. Peel the halves and cut each lengthwise into 5 or 6 slices.

꙳ Halve the papaya(s) and remove
the seeds. Peel the papaya halves and
then cut lengthwise into thin slices.

꙳ Peel the cucumber(s), cut in half
crosswise and then slice in half lengthwise. Using a melon baller or small
spoon, scoop out the seeds and discard.
Cut crosswise into slices ½ inch
(12 mm) thick.

꙳ Separate the lettuce leaves from
the head and pick out 8 of the best
ones; save the remaining leaves for
another use. Wash and dry well.

꙳ Remove the zest from the limes
(see page 287): Using a zester or a
fine-holed shredder, and holding each
lime over a saucer, shred the zest (green
part only) from the skin. Cut each lime
in half and squeeze the juice from all
4 lime halves; you will need 2 tablespoons. Set aside.

꙳ On individual plates, make an
attractive arrangement of the lettuce
and the avocado, papaya, and cucumber
slices, dividing them evenly. Sprinkle
the shredded lime zest over the top.

꙳ In a small bowl, combine the
2 tablespoons lime juice, the salt, and
pepper to taste. Stir well to dissolve the
salt. Add the olive oil and 2 teaspoons
honey and whisk until well blended.
Taste and adjust the seasoning, adding
more honey if desired.

꙳ Spoon the dressing over the salad
or pass in a bowl at the table. A ꙳

TROPICAL SALAD WITH LIME DRESSING

SERVES 4

*California-grown avocados are the best
choice for this refreshing salad. The Haas
avocado, with bumpy green-black skin, is
available in summer; Fuerte avocados, with
smooth green skins, are available in winter.
Simply holding an avocado in your hand
will tell you if the flesh is turning soft
beneath the skin, a sign of ripeness. Unless
you plan to make the salad immediately,
select avocados that are just beginning
to ripen and feel only slightly soft. All
avocados bruise easily, especially when
close to being ripe; choose ones with no
visible bruises.*

꙳ *If you have never eaten English (hothouse) cucumbers, I urge you to try them.
Much milder in flavor than other cucumbers, they have thinner skins and very
small seeds. In fact, you don't even have
to peel them or remove the seeds if you
want to skip that step.*

꙳ *When making the vinaigrette, dissolve
the salt in the lime juice before adding
the oil, as the oil prevents the salt from
dissolving fully.*

2 ripe avocados

1 large or 2 small, ripe papayas

1 English (hothouse) cucumber,
    or 1 or 2 regular cucumbers

1 head romaine (cos) lettuce

2 limes

⅛ teaspoon salt

GARDEN GREENS AND CITRUS SALAD

SERVES 4

Tender, crisp little salad leaves give this recipe a pleasing variety of tastes, colors, and shapes. Many food stores today carry prewashed, mixed, and ready-to-eat assortments, sold in bulk or prepacked in plastic bags. They're incredibly good and will make you a confirmed salad lover.

I also encourage you to seek out a fruit-flavored vinegar for the dressing. I do not mean vinegars made from fruit, most notably pear vinegar, which are regional specialties of the northeastern and northwestern United States. Rather, I am talking about infusions of raspberries, peaches, or other fruits in mild wine vinegars—delicious additions to salad dressings and to sauces for chicken, pork, and veal. Such vinegars are becoming increasingly available in food stores and specialty shops.

½ cup (2 oz/60 g) coarsely chopped pecans or walnuts

1 orange

1 pink grapefruit

8–10 oz (250–315 g) small garden lettuces, or a combination of romaine (cos), butter (Boston), and chicory (curly endive) lettuces

1 tablespoon peach vinegar or other fruit-flavored vinegar

⅛ teaspoon salt

freshly ground pepper

⅓ cup (3 fl oz/80 ml) extra-virgin olive oil

2 teaspoons honey

½ cup (3 oz/90 g) crumbled feta cheese, preferably made from sheep's milk

2 or 3 thin slices sweet red (Spanish) onion or other sweet onion, separated into rings

Preheat an oven to 325°F (165°C). Spread out the nuts on a baking sheet and bake until they begin to change color, 6–8 minutes. Watch carefully so they do not burn. Remove from the oven and set aside to cool.

Peel and section the orange (see page 290): Peel the orange, cutting away all of the white pith. Using a sharp, thin-bladed knife, cut along both sides of each segment, against the membranes, to release the whole segments. Peel and section the grapefruit in the same manner. Set aside.

If using small garden lettuces, pick over and discard any old leaves. Wash and dry well (if lettuces are not purchased already washed). If using other lettuces, discard tough outer leaves, wash and dry thoroughly, and tear into bite-sized pieces. Place in a large bowl.

In a small bowl, stir together the vinegar, salt, and pepper to taste until the salt dissolves. Add the olive oil and honey and whisk until well blended. Taste and adjust the seasoning. Drizzle the dressing over the lettuces and toss to coat well.

Divide the lettuces among individual plates. Arrange the orange and grapefruit segments among the leaves. Sprinkle on the feta cheese and nuts, scatter the onion rings over the surface, and serve. A

MEDITERRANEAN TUNA SALAD

SERVES 4

This is my own version of salade niçoise, a French salad that enjoys universal appeal. I have added fresh dill, an excellent complement to the tuna. For surrounding the salad, I chose mesclun, the classic Provençal mixture of baby lettuces and herbs, available in well-stocked produce shops or food stores; you can substitute any small lettuces you like.

I know that grilled fresh tuna often appears in Niçoise salads on restaurant menus today. But I still prefer to use canned tuna, which has the best and most traditional flavor for this dish. Look for tuna packed in olive oil.

½ lb (250 g) young green beans, trimmed and cut in half crosswise
ice water to cover
salt
1 lb (500 g) small, ripe tomatoes
1 cucumber, 9–10 oz (280–315 g)
1 small green bell pepper (capsicum), seeded, deribbed, and cut into ½-inch (12-mm) squares
4 small green (spring) onions, including some tender green tops, chopped
3–4 tablespoons coarsely chopped fresh dill
2 cans (6½ oz/200 g each) solid-pack tuna in olive oil, drained and flaked into small chunks

FOR THE DRESSING:
1 tablespoon fresh lemon juice
1 tablespoon white wine vinegar
salt and freshly ground pepper
½ cup (4 fl oz/125 ml) extra-virgin olive oil

¼ lb (125 g) mesclun or other small lettuces, carefully rinsed and dried
4 eggs, hard boiled, peeled, and quartered lengthwise
8 anchovy fillets in olive oil, drained, rinsed, and cut in half crosswise
20–24 tiny Niçoise olives or 12–16 small Italian or Spanish black olives

Place the green beans in a bowl, add ice water to cover, and set aside for 10–15 minutes. Fill a saucepan three-fourths full of water and bring to a boil. Add 2 teaspoons salt. Transfer the beans to the pan (reserve the ice water). Boil until bright green but still crisp, 3–4 minutes. Return the beans to the ice water. When cool, drain and set aside.

Core the tomatoes, cut into wedges, and put into a bowl. Peel the cucumber, cut in half lengthwise, and, using a melon baller or small spoon, scoop out the seeds and discard. Cut crosswise into slices ¼ inch (6 mm) thick and add to the tomatoes. Add the bell pepper, green onions, dill, tuna, and green beans.

To make the dressing, in a small bowl, combine the lemon juice, vinegar, ⅛ teaspoon salt, and pepper to taste. Stir until the salt dissolves. Gradually add the olive oil, whisking until blended. Spoon half of the dressing over the vegetables and toss. Taste and adjust the seasoning. Pour the remaining dressing into a bowl.

Divide the lettuces among 4 plates. Spoon the vegetables on top. Place 4 egg quarters on each plate and top each quarter with 1 anchovy fillet half. Divide the olives among the salads, then serve. Pass the remaining dressing.

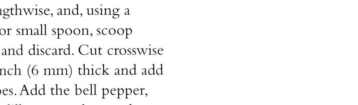

"Salad refreshes without weakening and comforts without irritating."

–Jean-Anthelme Brillat-Savarin

CHICKEN SALAD WITH APPLE AND WALNUTS

SERVES 4

Taking the basic ingredients of the famous Waldorf salad—apples, celery, and walnuts—and combining them with strips of freshly sautéed chicken breast makes a delightful contemporary salad. By substituting a light vinaigrette made with fresh lemon juice—which keeps the apples from discoloring—for the Waldorf's traditional mayonnaise-based dressing, you get the kind of fresh-tasting, light lunch that many people crave.

🔊 *If you have never tried walnut oil, this is a great opportunity to taste it. But seek out a good oil pressed from lightly toasted nuts, light in color and flavor. Some walnut oils are dark and strong tasting, and if that is all you can find, I suggest using a mild olive oil instead. Once opened, the walnut oil should be refrigerated.*

½ cup (2 oz/60 g) coarsely chopped
   walnuts
1 large or 2 small bunches watercress
1 large tart apple such as Granny Smith
½ lemon, plus 1 tablespoon fresh
   lemon juice
salt and freshly ground pepper
¼ cup (2 fl oz/60 ml) good-quality
   toasted walnut oil (see note)
4 chicken breast halves, 8–9 oz
   (250–280 g) each, skinned and boned
   (5–6 oz/155–185 g when boned)
   (see page 286)
2 tablespoons unsalted butter
2 tablespoons extra-virgin olive oil
2 or 3 celery stalks with leaves,
   preferably the tender center stalks,
   thinly sliced crosswise (½–¾ cup/
   2–3 oz/60–90 g)

Preheat an oven to 325°F (165°C). Spread the walnuts on a baking sheet and bake until they begin to change color, 6–8 minutes. Watch carefully so they do not burn. Set aside to cool.

🔊 Wash the watercress carefully. Discard the main stems and any yellow or old leaves. You should have about 6 cups (6 oz/185 g). Dry well, place in a salad bowl, cover with a damp kitchen towel, and refrigerate for 20–30 minutes.

🔊 Peel, quarter, and core the apple. Cut the quarters in half crosswise and then thinly slice lengthwise. Place in a bowl. Squeeze the juice from the ½ lemon over the top to keep them from turning brown. Toss to coat well. Set aside.

🔊 In a small bowl, stir together the 1 tablespoon lemon juice, ⅛ teaspoon salt, and pepper to taste until the salt dissolves. Whisk in the walnut oil until well blended. Set aside.

🔊 Remove all fat from the chicken breasts. Rinse the breasts and dry with paper towels. Place each breast between 2 sheets of plastic wrap and, using a rolling pin, flatten to an even thickness. Season with salt and pepper. In a large sauté pan (preferably nonstick) over medium-high heat, melt the butter with the olive oil. When hot, add the chicken breasts and sauté, turning once, until lightly browned and opaque throughout when pierced with a sharp knife, 3½–4 minutes on each side. Transfer to a plate and keep warm.

🔊 Add the celery, apple, and half of the walnuts to the watercress. Whisk the dressing again, pour over the salad, and toss well. Divide among 4 individual plates. Slice the warm chicken breasts crosswise into strips ½ inch (12 mm) wide and arrange over the salads. Sprinkle with the remaining walnuts and serve. A 🔊

CAESAR SALAD

SERVES 4

So many versions of Caesar salad exist today that it's hard to tell what is authentic. I still like the flavor of the one reputed to be the original, as created by the Tijuana chef César Cárdenas: a salad of crisp romaine lettuce and garlic croutons coated with a tart dressing of lemon juice, garlic, Parmesan cheese, and anchovy bound in a light emulsion with coddled (lightly boiled) egg.

But so many people are concerned about eating eggs today, not to mention almost-raw ones, that I've left the egg out of this version and have instead used plain yogurt to create the creamy emulsion. One thing I wouldn't dream of changing, though, is the anchovy; many versions omit it, but I like a good anchovy flavor in my Caesar salad, as well as the taste of imported Parmesan. Be sure to seek out high-quality anchovies, as some brands can be overly strong in flavor.

It's also important to make fresh croutons. There's nothing worse in a salad than stale bread cubes. Sautéing the croutons in good olive oil with garlic is quick and easy.

1 or 2 heads romaine (cos) lettuce, depending upon size, preferably with small leaves

3 or 4 slices French or Italian bread, each ⅜ inch (1 cm) thick

3 tablespoons extra-virgin olive oil, plus ½ cup (4 fl oz/125 ml)

2 cloves garlic

salt

6–8 good-quality anchovy fillets in olive oil, drained

1½ teaspoons dry mustard

2 tablespoons fresh lemon juice

1½ tablespoons plain yogurt

½ cup (2 oz/60 g) freshly grated Parmesan cheese

freshly ground pepper

Break off the leaves from the lettuce stalk, discarding the bruised ones and reserving large outer leaves for another use. Separate the smaller inner leaves and wash and dry well. Break into halves or thirds. Place in a salad bowl, cover with a damp kitchen towel, and refrigerate for 20–30 minutes to crisp.

Remove the crusts from the bread slices and discard. Cut the bread into ½ inch (12 mm) cubes. You should have approximately 2 cups (4 oz/125 g).

In a large frying pan over low heat, warm the 3 tablespoons olive oil. Using the flat side of a chopping knife, smash 1 of the garlic cloves and add to the oil. Sauté for 1–2 minutes. Add the bread cubes and fry, stirring and tossing, until crisp and golden on all sides, 4–5 minutes. Discard the garlic. Sprinkle the bread cubes with a little salt. Using a slotted spoon, transfer to paper towels to drain. Set aside to cool.

Chop the remaining garlic clove and combine with the ½ cup (4 fl oz/125 ml) olive oil in a blender. Purée until smooth. In a small bowl, and using a fork, mash the anchovies until they form a paste. Add to the oil and garlic in the blender along with the mustard, lemon juice, and yogurt. Blend at high speed until a smooth emulsion forms. Add 2 tablespoons of the Parmesan cheese and blend again. Season with a little salt, remembering that anchovies are salty, and a little pepper.

Add three-fourths of the dressing to the lettuce and toss to coat well. Add about half of the remaining cheese and toss again. Taste and add more dressing or more seasonings to taste. Sprinkle with the toasted croutons and the remaining cheese. Serve immediately.

A

BEET AND ORANGE SALAD

SERVES 4

I was served a salad somewhat like this about thirty years ago in a restaurant in Vallauris, near Nice. Ever since then, I have been creating variations on that memorable dish.

🌿 *If you do not like to eat beets, the French way of cooking them might change your mind. In France they are baked instead of boiled, which produces a much better flavor. In fact, vegetable markets there sell beets already baked. Do give this simple cooking method a try.*

4 or 5 beets, 2–2½ lb (1–1.25 kg) total weight

2 oranges, preferably seedless navel

1 fennel bulb, 12–14 oz (375–440 g)

1 or 2 bunches arugula, 7–8 oz (220–250 g) total weight, stems removed

FOR THE DRESSING:

2 tablespoons red wine vinegar

⅛ teaspoon salt

freshly ground pepper

1½ teaspoons Dijon mustard

⅓ cup (3 fl oz/80 ml) extra-virgin olive oil

4 tablespoons shredded fresh basil leaves

Position a rack in the middle of an oven and preheat to 450°F (230°C).

🌿 Cut off the tops of the beets, leaving about ½ inch (12 mm) of stem intact. Do not cut off the root ends or otherwise cut into the beets. Rinse well and pat dry. Enclose the beets in a large piece of foil and fold over the top to seal. Make a small slit in the top of the packet and place in a baking pan, folded side up.

🌿 Bake until tender when pierced with the tip of a sharp knife, 50–60 minutes

depending upon the size and age of the beets; test for doneness after about 45 minutes. Remove from the oven and open the packet partway to let the beets cool a little. When cool enough to handle, cut off the stem and root end from each beet. Using your fingers, or with the aid of a paring knife, peel off the skins; they should slip off easily. Set aside to finish cooling.

🌿 Peel and section the oranges (see page 290). Trim the root end and the stalks from the fennel bulb and remove any old or bruised outer leaves. Cut the bulb crosswise into thin slices. Add to the orange segments. Set aside.

🌿 Discard any old or bruised arugula leaves. Rinse carefully and dry well. If large, tear the leaves in half. Place in a separate bowl.

🌿 To make the dressing, in a small bowl, combine the vinegar, salt, and pepper to taste. Stir until the salt dissolves. Stir in the mustard until blended and thickened. Gradually add the olive oil, whisking until thickened. Adjust the seasoning. Drizzle about half of the dressing over the arugula and toss well. Set aside.

🌿 Thinly slice the beets crosswise. If large, cut in half. Add to the orange segments along with the basil. Drizzle with the remaining dressing and toss gently.

🌿 Arrange the arugula leaves on 4 salad plates, dividing them evenly. Spoon the beet-orange-fennel mixture over the top and serve at once. 🄵 🌿

ARUGULA SALAD WITH BLACK OLIVE CROSTINI

SERVES 4

A memorable first course for a dinner party, this salad may also be served for lunch along with a bowl of soup. The crostini make good hors d'oeuvres served with drinks as well.

In Italy the black olive purée that tops crostini usually includes anchovies, but I've found that sardines work equally well and appeal more to American tastes. The purée can be made a day ahead and refrigerated. Bring it to room temperature before using; assemble the crostini just before serving so they'll be at their most crisp.

Arugula leaves, with their slight edge of bitterness, are an excellent choice for the salad. If you can't find arugula, watercress is a good substitute. The most flavorful walnut oil for the dressing is the kind pressed from lightly toasted nuts. Refrigerate the oil once it has been opened.

2 tablespoons capers, drained
   and chopped
2 cloves garlic, chopped (1 teaspoon)
1 teaspoon chopped fresh oregano
1 tablespoon drained, boned, and
   mashed sardines
4 tablespoons extra-virgin olive oil
1 cup (5 oz/155 g) drained, pitted
   European black olives, such as Gaeta,
   Kalamata, or Spanish, chopped
1 lemon
12–16 crostini (recipe on page 283)
1–2 bunches arugula (rocket),
   8–9 oz (250–280 g) total weight
1 tablespoon white wine vinegar
⅛ teaspoon salt
1 tablespoon walnut oil (see note)
freshly ground pepper

In a food processor fitted with the metal blade or in a blender, combine the capers, garlic, oregano, sardines, and 2 tablespoons of the olive oil. Process until blended. Add the olives and process to form a coarse purée. Adjust the seasoning and transfer to a small bowl.

Using a zester or a fine-holed shredder, shred the zest (yellow part only) from the lemon directly onto the olive purée (see page 287). Set aside.

Prepare the crostini as directed and set aside to cool slightly.

Pick over the arugula and discard any old leaves and the stems. Rinse and dry thoroughly, tear into small pieces and place in a large bowl.

In a small bowl, combine the wine vinegar and salt. Stir to dissolve the salt. Sprinkle the vinegar over the greens and toss lightly until the leaves are coated. In the same small bowl, stir together the walnut oil and the remaining 2 tablespoons olive oil. While tossing the greens, drizzle on the oils. Continue to toss just until the leaves are lightly coated. Season to taste with pepper.

To serve, divide the greens among salad plates. Spread the crostini generously with the olive purée and place 3 or 4 crostini on the side of each plate. Serve immediately.

"The whole Mediterranean, the sculpture, the palms, the gold beads, the bearded heroes, the wine, the ideas, the ships, the moonlight, the winged gorgons, the bronze men, the philosophers—all of it seems to rise in the sour, pungent smell of these black olives between the teeth. A taste older than meat, older than wine. A taste as old as cold water."

—Laurence Durrell

"To remember a successful salad is generally to remember a successful dinner; at all events, the perfect dinner necessarily includes the perfect salad."

—George Ellwanger

ESCAROLE SALAD WITH PEAR AND PROSCIUTTO

SERVES 4

Here is a salad that you might find served by the shore at Portofino in late summer. It makes an excellent first course, either for a dinner party or a weekend lunch.
If escarole is unavailable, substitute chicory (curly endive), oak-leaf lettuce, or some other flavorful lettuce variety. If you cannot find fresh tarragon, use fresh mint. Be generous with the tarragon or mint, as they are both mild flavors.
Comice pears are large, round fruits with short necks and greenish yellow skins blushed with red. They are sweet and juicy, and I find they are the best choice to serve with prosciutto. You could, however, substitute Red Bartlett (Williams'), Anjou, or Royal Riviera pears.

1 large head escarole (Batavian endive)
3 or 4 fresh tarragon sprigs
1 tablespoon fresh lemon juice, plus
   juice of 1 lemon
⅛ teaspoon salt
1 teaspoon Dijon mustard
freshly ground pepper
¼ cup (2 fl oz/60 ml) extra-virgin
   olive oil
2 firm but ripe pears, preferably
   Comice (see note)
16 thin, lean prosciutto slices
¾ cup (4½ oz/140 g) ripe red seedless
   grapes, stems removed

Separate the leaves from the head of escarole, discarding any old or damaged leaves. Wash carefully, dry well, and tear into large bite-sized pieces. Place in a bowl. Remove the leaves from the tarragon sprigs and tear or chop into small pieces. Add to the bowl with the escarole and toss to mix. Cover with a damp kitchen towel and refrigerate to crisp.
In a small bowl, combine the 1 tablespoon lemon juice and the salt. Stir to dissolve the salt. Stir in the mustard and pepper to taste. Add the olive oil and whisk until well blended. Taste and adjust the seasoning. Set aside.
Place the juice of 1 lemon in a large bowl. Cut the pears into quarters, remove the stems and cores, and then cut each quarter into 2 wedges. Place the pear wedges in the bowl with the lemon juice and toss carefully to coat all cut surfaces (this prevents them from darkening).
Carefully separate the prosciutto slices and then wrap a slice around each pear wedge.
Whisk the dressing again and pour it over the greens. Toss to mix well. Divide the greens among 4 salad plates. Scatter the grapes over the greens (if the grapes are large, you may want to cut them in half). Arrange 4 prosciutto-wrapped pear wedges on each plate, next to the salad. Serve at once.

ENDIVE AND MUSHROOM SALAD WITH MUSTARD DRESSING

SERVES 4

A salad of many different flavors, this colorful mixture is an excellent prelude to simple grilled meats. The dressing is a traditional French blend of red wine vinegar, olive oil, and Dijon mustard, a combination that complements herbs and greens.

Find as many of the fresh herbs as you can. When they are combined in a light salad such as this, the resulting bouquet of tastes and aromas is surprising. Select mushrooms with tightly closed caps; there should be no gills showing.

2 heads Belgian endives (chicory/wit-loof), 8–9 oz (250–280 g) total weight

4 green (spring) onions, including some tender green tops

½ lb (250 g) small, firm fresh mushrooms, preferably brown

1 bunch radishes, trimmed and cut into slices ¼ inch (6 mm) thick

1 bunch watercress, carefully rinsed and tough stems removed

½ cup (¾ oz/20 g) coarsely chopped mixed fresh herbs, such as basil, tarragon, dill, mint, and flat-leaf (Italian) parsley, in any combination

FOR THE DRESSING:

2 tablespoons red wine vinegar

⅛ teaspoon salt

freshly ground pepper

2 teaspoons Dijon mustard

½ cup (4 fl oz/125 ml) extra-virgin olive oil

Trim off any damaged leaves from the endives and discard. Cut the endives crosswise into slices ½ inch (12 mm) thick, discarding the solid heart. Place in a large bowl. Trim and slice the green onions crosswise into 1-inch (2.5-cm) pieces, then slice each piece lengthwise into thin slivers. Add to the bowl.

Using a soft brush or clean kitchen towel, brush off any soil or other impurities from the mushrooms. Do not rinse in water. Trim the stems and cut the mushrooms vertically into slices ¼ inch (6 mm) thick. Add to the bowl along with the radishes, watercress, and herbs. Toss to mix.

To make the dressing, in a small bowl, combine the vinegar, salt, and pepper to taste and stir until the salt dissolves. Stir in the mustard until blended. Gradually add the olive oil, whisking until well blended and thickened. Taste and adjust the seasoning.

Drizzle about three-fourths of the dressing over the salad. Toss until well mixed; taste and add more dressing if needed. Store any leftover dressing in a tightly covered container in the refrigerator for up to 3 days. Divide the salad among 4 plates and serve at once.

BLOOD ORANGE, FENNEL, AND OLIVE SALAD

SERVES 4

Quickly becoming a classic in Italy's more sophisticated restaurants, this salad is fresh tasting, light, and low in fat—three requisites for healthful eating. Blood oranges are the first choice, but you can use regular oranges as well. Fresh fennel is available almost everywhere now; look for smaller bulbs, which are more tender. And use Italian, Greek black olives, or French Niçoise olives. Cured in brine, these flavorful olives are all now widely distributed in the United States.

Although balsamic vinegar is becoming popular now, beware of large bottles at cheap prices, which offer little more than a lightly flavored wine vinegar. True balsamic vinegar, which is aged for many years, should have a mildly tart-sweet flavor and a rich, dark color.

1 head chicory (curly endive)

4 or 5 fresh cilantro
   (fresh coriander) sprigs

2 small fennel bulbs, 1–1½ lb
   (500–750 g) total weight

4 or 5 blood oranges, preferably seedless,
   1½–2 lb (750 g–1 kg) total weight

2 tablespoons balsamic vinegar

⅛ teaspoon salt

⅓ cup (3 fl oz/80 ml) extra-virgin
   olive oil

1 teaspoon honey

1–2 teaspoons fresh orange juice

freshly ground pepper

16–20 small European black olives,
   such as Gaeta, Kalamata, or Niçoise

Separate the leaves from the head of chicory, discarding any old or damaged leaves. Wash carefully, dry well, and tear into bite-sized pieces. Place in a bowl. Remove the leaves from the cilantro sprigs and tear or chop into small pieces. Add to the bowl with the chicory and toss to mix. Cover with a damp kitchen towel and refrigerate to crisp.

Trim off any stems and bruised stalks from the fennel bulbs. Cut crosswise into paper-thin slices. Place in a separate bowl and set aside.

Cut a thick slice off the top and bottom of each orange, exposing the fruit beneath the peel. Working with 1 orange at a time, place upright on a cutting surface and, holding the orange firmly, thickly slice off the peel in wide strips, cutting off the pith and membrane with it to reveal the fruit sections. Cut the oranges crosswise into slices ¼ inch (6 mm) thick. Remove any seeds and discard. Place the orange slices in yet another bowl and set aside.

In a small bowl, combine the balsamic vinegar and salt. Stir to dissolve the salt. Add the olive oil, honey, and orange juice and whisk until well blended. Add pepper to taste. Taste and adjust the seasoning.

To serve, whisk the dressing again and drizzle half of it over the fennel. Toss to coat well. Arrange the fennel in a mound in the center of a platter or individual plates. Arrange the chicory around the fennel, then arrange the orange slices over the chicory. Drizzle the remaining dressing over the orange slices and chicory. Scatter the olives over the top. Serve immediately.

MANGO AND MELON SALAD

SERVES 4

The French have long been attracted to the fruits of the tropics and the Far East, and they use them to great advantage in their recipes. I think you'll be intrigued by how well the mint, green onion, and walnut marry with the fruits in this exotic combination. If you cannot find walnut-infused white wine vinegar, imported from France, feel free to substitute a good-quality, mild white wine vinegar.

1 red bell pepper (capsicum)
½ cup (2 oz/60 g) walnut pieces,
   coarsely chopped
1 head romaine (cos) lettuce
2 oranges, preferably seedless navel
2 ripe mangoes

FOR THE DRESSING:
2 tablespoons walnut white
   wine vinegar
⅛ teaspoon salt
freshly ground pepper
⅓ cup (3 fl oz/80 ml) extra-virgin
   olive oil
½ ripe cantaloupe, peeled, seeded, and
   cut into 1-inch (2.5-cm) cubes
2 green (spring) onions, including
   some tender green tops, chopped
2 tablespoons chopped fresh mint,
   plus mint sprigs for garnish
12–16 Niçoise olives or Italian or
   Spanish black olives

Roast, peel and seed the bell pepper (see page 290). Cut lengthwise into strips ¼ inch (6 mm) wide. Set aside.

 Position a rack in the middle of an oven and preheat to 325°F (165°C). Spread the walnuts on a baking sheet. Place in the oven and bake until they begin to change color and are fragrant, 6–8 minutes. Set aside to cool.

 Separate the lettuce leaves, discarding any old or damaged leaves and the core. Rinse carefully and dry well. Set aside 8 good leaves for garnishing and tear the other leaves into bite-sized pieces. Place in a large bowl and set aside.

 Peel and section the oranges (see page 290). Set aside. Peel each mango, then slice off the flesh in one piece from each side of the flat pit. Cut into 1-inch (2.5-cm) pieces. Slice the flesh from around the pit edges as well. Set aside.

 To make the dressing, in a small bowl, combine the walnut vinegar, salt, and pepper to taste and stir until the salt dissolves. Gradually add the olive oil, whisking until well blended. Taste and adjust the seasoning.

 To the bowl holding the lettuce, add the cantaloupe, green onions, chopped mint, bell pepper, walnuts, and mangoes. Whisk the dressing again and drizzle over the fruit. Toss gently until well mixed.

 For each salad, place 2 of the reserved lettuce leaves on opposite sides of a plate. Spoon the fruit mixture between the leaves. Garnish each salad with 3 or 4 orange segments, 3 or 4 olives, and mint sprigs. Serve at once.

"Friends are like melons. Shall I tell you why? To find one good you must a hundred try."

—Claude Mermet

Main Courses

SEAFOOD

The recipes in this section celebrate both the similarities and the differences prevalent in Italian, French, and American seafood preparations. Italians tend to approach seafood with eloquent simplicity, baking salmon (page 90) on a bed of Swiss chard or sautéing fresh tuna (page 96) with mint and coriander. The French add a touch of elegance with dishes such as Halibut with Hollandaise (this page) served on a bed of mushrooms and lightly gratinéed, or delicate sole fillets (page 103) embellished with shallots, wine, and grapes.

American cooks present a melting pot of influences in their typical seafood dishes. Crab Cakes (page 114) incorporate Italian bread crumbs and French Dijon mustard. Sautéed Scallops with Spinach (page 107) gain character from the signature fortified wines of Portugal or Sicily. Yet, as distinctive as each of these recipes may be, they share the common goal of preserving seafood's moistness and delicacy.

HALIBUT WITH HOLLANDAISE

SERVES 4

Quickly cooked fish fillets and mushrooms topped with a buttery hollandaise is one of the most venerable dishes of French cuisine. Other firm whitefish fillets such as sea bass or swordfish may be substituted.

If you have never made a hollandaise sauce before, I urge you to try it. You'll be surprised how easy it is to make (see my pointers in the note on page 29), and it truly does turn a plain dish into a special one. I prefer to use a bowl over simmering water rather than a double boiler for hollandaise. The sauce is easier to whisk and absorbs heat more slowly.

2 tablespoons chopped shallots
  (about 2 shallots)
½ lb (250 g) small, firm fresh mushrooms
4 halibut fillets, 6–7 oz (185–220 g)
  each and about 1 inch (2.5 cm) thick
¼ cup (2 fl oz/60 ml) dry white wine
salt and freshly ground pepper

FOR THE HOLLANDAISE SAUCE:

3 egg yolks, at room temperature
1½ tablespoons fresh lemon juice,
  plus extra if needed
¾ cup (6 oz/185 g) unsalted butter,
  cut into slices ¼ inch (6 mm) thick,
  at room temperature
chopped fresh parsley

Position a rack in the middle of an oven and preheat to 425°F (220°C). Butter a flameproof rectangular or oval baking dish that will accommodate the fish fillets comfortably in a single layer. Sprinkle the shallots evenly over the bottom.

Brush off any dirt from the mushrooms. Do not rinse in water. Cut into slices ¼ inch (6 mm) thick and spread over the shallots.

Rinse the halibut and pat dry with paper towels. Lay the fillets over the mushrooms and pour in the wine. Season to taste with salt and pepper. Cover and bake until opaque throughout when pierced with a sharp knife, 10–15 minutes.

Meanwhile, make the hollandaise: Place the egg yolks and 1½ tablespoons lemon juice in a heatproof bowl or the top pan of a double boiler. Set over (but not touching) barely simmering water in a saucepan or the bottom pan of the double boiler. Whisk until beginning to thicken, about 1 minute. Whisk in the butter, 1 slice at a time. Continue to whisk until thickened, 2–3 minutes; do not overcook. Remove from the pan of hot water and continue whisking until cooled slightly. Cover partially and keep warm. Do not discard the hot water.

When the fillets test done, carefully drain off the liquid from the baking dish into a small saucepan. Cover the dish to keep the fillets warm. Place the saucepan over high heat and boil until the liquid is reduced by about half, 2–3 minutes.

Preheat a broiler (griller). Reposition the hollandaise over the simmering water. Whisk in the reduced liquid, 1 tablespoon at a time, until thinned slightly; it will take no more than 2–3 tablespoons. Season to taste with salt and pepper and more lemon juice, if needed. Again drain off any liquid that has accumulated in the baking dish, then spoon the sauce over the fillets. Broil (grill) until lightly browned, 1–2 minutes. Sprinkle with parsley and serve immediately.

STEAMED MUSSELS

SERVES 4

On my many midwinter trips to Paris during the 1960s tracking down kitchen-ware for the first Williams-Sonoma shop, I always looked forward to a Metro ride out to the flea market on a Saturday, which meant I would have steamed mussels—moules marinières—at Chez Louisette, a small, popular restaurant in one of the market alleyways. The hot, aromatic bowlful of shellfish, served with crusty bread to soak up the juices, brought me absolute bliss.

I have never forgotten this dish, and have never tasted mussels as good—that is, until developing, testing, and writing this recipe took me back to the sixties.

3½–4 lb (1.75–2 kg) mussels,
   preferably medium-sized
¼ cup (2 oz/60 g) unsalted butter
¼ cup (1¼ oz/37 g) minced shallots
   (about 4 shallots)
1 small bay leaf
1 tablespoon chopped fresh thyme
1 cup (8 fl oz/250 ml) dry white wine
6 tablespoons chopped fresh parsley
salt and freshly ground pepper
crusty French bread

Scrub the mussels thoroughly under running water, removing any beards clinging to the shells. Discard any mussels that do not close to the touch.
In a large pot over medium-low heat, melt the butter. When foaming, add the shallots and sauté, stirring, until translucent, 2–3 minutes. Add the bay leaf, thyme, and wine, raise the heat to medium-high and cook for about 2 minutes. Add the mussels, sprinkle 4 tablespoons of the parsley over the mussels, and sprinkle to taste with salt and pepper. Cover and steam, shaking

the pan to toss about the mussels once or twice, until the mussels open, about 5 minutes.

⫸ Using a slotted spoon, transfer the mussels to 4 warmed soup plates or bowls, dividing them equally. Discard any mussels that have not opened. Spoon the broth over the mussels and sprinkle with the remaining 2 table-spoons chopped parsley. Serve with crusty French bread to sop up the juices, and provide small bowls at the table for discarding the shells. Ⓕ ⫸

Spanish Rice with Shrimp

Serves 4

I suppose Spanish rice had its beginning in the American Southwest. Certainly by the first half of the 20th century it was popular throughout the United States. I like to think of it as a simple paella: the shrimp, ham, and bell pepper transform it into a one-dish meal. If you'd like a little more spice in your rice, add one or two mild fresh chili peppers, seeded and chopped, with the garlic and onion.

¾–1 lb (375–500 g) small or medium-sized shrimp (prawns) in the shell
salt
1½ lb (750 g) ripe plum (Roma) tomatoes
4 tablespoons (2 fl oz/60 ml) extra-virgin olive oil, or as needed
3 oz (90 g) cooked ham, cut into small strips (¾ cup)
2 or 3 cloves garlic, depending upon your taste and the size of cloves, minced
1 yellow onion, diced (1 cup/4 oz/125 g)
1 celery stalk, diced (½ cup/2½ oz/75 g)

1 green bell pepper (capsicum), seeded, deribbed, and diced (1 cup/5 oz/155 g)
1 cup (8 fl oz/250 ml) water
pinch of cayenne pepper
1 cup (7 oz/220 g) medium-grain white rice
chopped fresh flat-leaf (Italian) parsley or curly-leaf parsley
lemon wedges (optional)

Position a rack in the middle of an oven and preheat the oven to 350°F (180°C). Butter a shallow 2-qt (2-l) baking dish.
⫸ Peel and devein the shrimp as directed on page 289. Put the shrimp in a bowl with water to cover. Add 1 tea-spoon salt, stir to dissolve, and let stand for 10 minutes to freshen the shrimp. Drain, rinse, and drain again. Set aside.
⫸ Meanwhile, core, peel, and seed the tomatoes as directed on page 289. Chop coarsely; you should have about 3 cups (18 oz/560 g). Set aside.
⫸ In a large sauté pan or frying pan over medium-high heat, warm 2 table-spoons of the oil. Add the shrimp and sauté quickly, stirring and tossing, just until they turn pink, about 5 minutes. Transfer to a plate and set aside.
⫸ Add the ham to the same pan and place over medium-low heat. Adding more oil if needed, sauté, stirring, 2–3 minutes. Then add the garlic and onion and sauté, stirring, until trans-lucent, 3–4 minutes longer. Add the celery, bell pepper, and tomatoes, stir well, and cook uncovered, stirring occa-sionally, until the tomatoes start to break down, another 6–8 minutes. Stir in the water, ½ teaspoon salt and the cayenne pepper. Transfer to a bowl and set aside.
⫸ Heat the remaining 2 tablespoons oil in the same pan over medium heat.

Add the rice and cook, stirring, until translucent, 2–3 minutes. Return the tomato mixture to the pan along with the shrimp and cook over low heat, stirring occasionally, about 8 minutes. Taste and adjust the seasonings.
⫸ Transfer the rice mixture to the prepared baking dish, cover loosely with aluminum foil and bake for 15 minutes. Remove the foil and continue to bake until the rice is just tender, another 10–15 minutes.
⫸ Remove from the oven, re-cover with the foil and let stand for 10 min-utes. Garnish with parsley and serve. Pass a bowl of lemon wedges, if desired. Ⓐ ⫸

"Fish is held out to be one of the greatest luxuries of the table and not only necessary, but even indispensable at all dinners where there is any pretence to excellence or fashion."

—Mrs. Isabella Beeton

BAKED SALMON ON CHARD

SERVES 4

Baking salmon on top of Swiss chard keeps the fish moist and eases the removal of the delicate fillets from the baking dish.
Fresh cucumber relish, quickly and easily prepared, is an especially good accompaniment to the salmon. Use the freshest-looking cucumber you can find. An English (hothouse) cucumber would be best, as it is particularly mild and has very small seeds and a thin skin.
If fresh dill is unavailable, substitute 1 teaspoon dried dill. For the best results, prepare the relish an hour ahead to allow time for the flavors to develop.

FOR THE CUCUMBER RELISH:

1 cucumber, preferably English (hothouse)
½ red bell pepper (capsicum), seeded, deribbed, and cut into ¼-inch (6-mm) dice (about ½ cup/2½ oz/75 g)
2 or 3 green (spring) onions, including some tender green tops, finely chopped (about 2 tablespoons)
1 teaspoon chopped fresh dill
¼ cup (2 fl oz/60 ml) white cider vinegar
2½ tablespoons sugar
⅛ teaspoon salt

2–3 tablespoons extra-virgin olive oil
8 green Swiss chard leaves
salt
4 salmon fillets, 6–7 oz (185–220 g) each, skin removed
freshly ground pepper

About 1 hour before serving, make the cucumber relish: Peel the cucumber and cut in half lengthwise. Using a small spoon or melon baller, scoop out the seeds and discard. Cut the cucumber into ¼-inch (6-mm) dice; you should have about 1½ cups (7½ oz/235 g).
In a bowl, combine the cucumber, bell pepper, green onions, and dill. In a separate small bowl, combine the cider vinegar, sugar, and salt. Stir until the sugar and salt dissolve. Add the sweetened vinegar to the cucumber mixture and stir well. Taste and adjust the seasoning. Set aside at room temperature for 50–60 minutes, stirring frequently.
Position a rack in the middle of an oven and preheat to 425°F (220°C).
Select a baking dish that will accommodate the salmon fillets comfortably in a single layer. Brush the bottom of the dish with some of the olive oil.
Rinse the chard leaves. Trim the white stems from the chard, including the first 2 inches (5 cm) that protrude into the leaves. Discard the stems. Fold the leaves in half crosswise, sprinkle them with water and arrange in 4 stacks of 2 leaves each in the bottom of the dish. Sprinkle the chard with a little salt and lay a salmon fillet, skinned side down, on each chard stack. Brush the salmon with olive oil and sprinkle to taste with salt and pepper.
Bake, uncovered, until the salmon flesh is opaque throughout when pierced with the tip of a knife, 12–15 minutes.
Using a spatula, carefully transfer the fillets with their chard leaves to warmed plates. Top each fillet with 3–4 spoonfuls of the cucumber relish. Serve at once.

HALIBUT WITH TOMATOES AND PINE NUTS

SERVES 4

During summer, when tomatoes are at their best, you'll find some version of this simple fish dish in almost every restaurant in Italy. Fish and tomatoes have a strong affinity. With garlic and dill, the result is even better.

Select a particularly full-flavored, fruity extra-virgin olive oil for this dish. If you have good fresh coarse country bread, place a slice on each plate to help soak up the ample juices. Other flaky whitefish, such as bass, sea bass, or snapper, can be substituted for the halibut.

¼ cup (1½ oz/45 g) pine nuts

2 lb (1 kg) ripe plum (Roma) tomatoes

3 tablespoons olive oil, preferably a flavorful oil

3 cloves garlic, chopped (about 1 tablespoon)

1 bay leaf

2 tablespoons chopped fresh dill or 1 tablespoon dried dill

1 cup (8 fl oz/250 ml) dry white wine or water

½ teaspoon salt

freshly ground pepper

4 halibut fillets, 6–7 oz (185–220 g) each

coarsely chopped fresh flat-leaf (Italian) parsley for garnish

1 lemon, cut into wedges

In a heavy frying pan over medium heat, toast the pine nuts, stirring, until lightly colored and fragrant, 1–2 minutes. Set aside.

Core and peel the tomatoes (see page 289). Cut the tomatoes in half crosswise and carefully squeeze out the seeds. Chop the tomatoes coarsely; you should have 4–4½ cups (1½–1¾ lb/ 750–875 g).

In a large sauté pan or deep frying pan over medium-low heat, warm the olive oil. Add the garlic and sauté gently, stirring, until it just starts to change color, 1–2 minutes. Add the bay leaf, dill, and tomatoes and cook gently, uncovered, until the tomatoes start to break down and release their juices, 8–10 minutes. Stir in the wine or water, salt, and pepper to taste. Continue to cook, uncovered, until the tomatoes have broken down and are tender, about 10 minutes longer. Taste and adjust the seasoning; it should be highly seasoned.

Carefully lay the fish fillets on top of the tomatoes in a single layer. Cover and barely simmer over low heat until the fish flesh is opaque throughout when pierced with the tip of a sharp knife, 12–15 minutes, depending upon the thickness of the fish. Plan on about 10 minutes per inch (2.5 cm) at the thickest part of the fish; do not overcook.

To serve, carefully transfer the fillets to warmed plates. Spoon the tomato sauce over the top and around each fillet. Garnish with the toasted pine nuts and parsley and arrange lemon wedges alongside. Serve immediately.

BAKED SHRIMP WITH DILL

SERVES 4

As most raw shrimp available in fish markets were flash-frozen at the time of the catch, I prefer to soak them in salted water for 10–15 minutes to freshen them and rid them of any fishy odor. After soaking, rinse well in fresh water before use. Butterflying the shrimp not only makes a more attractive presentation but also helps to cook them faster. Serve with crusty French or Italian bread, adding only a green salad to make a good weekend lunch or supper.

❧ *If fresh dill is unavailable, use 1–2 teaspoons dried, placing the herb in the palm of one hand and using the thumb of the other to crush it, to release all the flavor. If you like the flavor of dill, feel free to increase the measure.*

1 lb (500 g) shrimp (prawns) in the
  shell (about 24)

1⅛ teaspoons salt

1 or 2 cloves garlic, depending upon
  taste and size of cloves, minced

2 tablespoons minced green (spring)
  onion, including some tender
  green tops

2 tablespoons chopped fresh parsley

1 tablespoon chopped fresh dill

2 tablespoons fresh lime juice

freshly ground pepper

3–4 tablespoons extra-virgin olive oil

Position a rack in the middle of an oven and preheat the oven to 450°F (230°C). Oil a large, shallow baking dish, preferably a round dish 10 inches (25 cm) in diameter.

❧ Peel, devein, and butterfly the shrimp (see page 289): Peel the shrimp, leaving the last segment of shell with tail fin intact. Using a small, sharp knife, make a slit along the shrimp's curved back about halfway through to expose the black veinlike intestinal tract, then remove and discard. Continue slitting down into the meat just far enough so that, with your fingertips, you can open the shrimp and flatten it easily. Be careful not to cut all the way through.

❧ Place the shrimp in a bowl and add water to cover. Add 1 teaspoon of the salt, stir to dissolve, and let stand for 10 minutes. Drain, rinse, and drain again; dry on paper towels. Arrange the shrimp in the prepared baking dish, placing them close together in concentric circles and with cut part down and spread out and tails up.

❧ Sprinkle the garlic, green onion, parsley, and dill evenly over the shrimp. In a small bowl, stir together the lime juice, the remaining ⅛ teaspoon salt, and pepper to taste, mixing well to dissolve the salt. Whisk in the olive oil and sprinkle evenly over the shrimp.

❧ Bake until the shrimp are pink, 8–10 minutes. Do not overbake, as they will toughen. Serve at once. A ❧

FISH STEW WITH COUSCOUS

SERVES 4

While I love the classic bouillabaisse, it can be time-consuming to make. I have found that some of France's simpler fish stews, such as this one borrowed from Algiers, are exceptionally good.

Frozen fish stock, now available at better food markets, can be excellent; do take advantage of it. If you cannot find an acceptable product and do not care to make stock yourself, feel free to substitute bottled clam juice.

Because I prefer the taste and texture of dried chickpeas, (garbanzo beans) I make sure to cook them well in advance. If time is a problem, though, you can use canned ones. You will need 1 cup (7 oz/220 g). Rinse them before adding to the stew.

½ cup (3½ oz/105 g) dried chickpeas
  (garbanzo beans)
1 lb (500 g) ripe plum (Roma)
  tomatoes
2 tablespoons olive oil
1 tablespoon minced garlic (2 or
  3 cloves)
1 sweet white onion, chopped
  (¾–1 cup/4–5 oz/125–155 g)
1 cup (4 oz/125 g) thinly sliced carrot
  (2 or 3 carrots)
1 cup (4 oz/125 g) thinly sliced celery
  (about 3 stalks)
1½ teaspoons ground turmeric
2 teaspoons ground cumin
⅛ teaspoon red pepper flakes
pinch of ground cloves
2 cups (16 fl oz/500 ml) fish stock
  (see note)
1 cup (8 fl oz/250 ml) water
2 zucchini (courgettes), cut crosswise
  into slices ¼ inch (6 mm) thick
½ cup (3 oz/90 g) golden raisins
  (sultanas)

salt and freshly ground black pepper
2 lb (1 kg) assorted whitefish fillets
  such as sea bass, halibut, and snapper
couscous (recipe on page 283)

Sort through the chickpeas, discarding any damaged peas or small stones. Rinse and drain. Place in a saucepan and add water to cover by 2 inches (5 cm). Bring to a boil, remove from the heat, cover, and let soak for 1 hour. Drain, rinse, and return to the pan. Again add water to cover by 2 inches (5 cm). Bring to a boil, reduce the heat to low, cover, and simmer until tender, about 1 hour. Drain.

Core, peel, and seed the tomatoes (see page 289). Chop coarsely.

In a large sauté pan over medium-low heat, warm the oil. When hot, add the garlic and sauté until it begins to change color, 30–40 seconds. Add the onion and sauté until translucent, 6–7 minutes. Add the chickpeas, tomatoes, carrot, celery, turmeric, cumin, red pepper flakes, cloves, fish stock, and water. Cover partially and simmer until barely tender, 20–25 minutes. Add the zucchini, raisins, and salt and black pepper to taste and simmer for 6–7 minutes longer. Adjust the seasoning.

Rinse the fish and cut into pieces 1 inch (2.5 cm) by 1½ inches (4 cm). Add to the stew, immersing them in the liquid. Cover and cook over very low heat until the fish is opaque throughout when pierced with a knife tip, 10–15 minutes.

About 15 minutes before serving, prepare the couscous and have ready.

Spoon the couscous into warmed deep plates and spoon the stew around it. Serve immediately. F

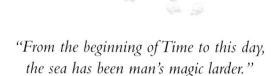

"From the beginning of Time to this day, the sea has been man's magic larder."

–André Simon

FRESH TUNA WITH MINT AND CORIANDER

SERVES 4

In Sicily, where tuna is a common catch, mint and coriander frequently season the fish, a sign of the culinary influence of North Africa.

Seek out only the very freshest tuna from a reputable seafood merchant. The fish should not have any strong flavor, only a fresh, clean ocean scent. Quick searing in a hot pan is all that is necessary to cook the tuna; left any longer on the heat, the fish is likely to dry out.

1 tablespoon unsalted butter

1 tablespoon olive oil

1 sweet white onion, diced (1–1¼ cups/4–5 oz/125–155 g)

4 tuna steaks, each 6–7 oz (185–220 g) and ½ inch (12 mm) thick

salt and freshly ground pepper

¼ cup (2 fl oz/60 ml) white wine vinegar

¼ cup (2 fl oz/60 ml) water

¼ cup chopped fresh mint, plus extra mint leaves for garnish

⅛ teaspoon ground coriander

In a large sauté pan or frying pan over medium-low heat, melt the butter with the olive oil. When hot, add the onion and sauté gently, stirring, until translucent, 8–10 minutes. Using a slotted spoon, transfer all of the onion to a plate, leaving as much of the oil in the pan as possible. Set the onion aside.

Raise the heat to high. When very hot but not smoking, add the tuna steaks and sear quickly, turning once, until lightly golden, about 2 minutes on each side. Season lightly with salt and pepper to taste and carefully transfer to a warmed serving platter or to individual warmed plates. Cover to keep warm.

Reduce the heat to medium-low. Return the onion to the pan and add the wine vinegar and water. Simmer for a few seconds, then add the chopped mint and the coriander. Simmer for a few seconds longer and season to taste with salt and pepper.

Spoon the onion mixture over the tuna steaks and garnish with the mint leaves. Serve immediately.

BAKED SALMON FILLET WITH SPINACH

SERVES 4

Salmon lends itself very well to baking, especially when fillets are layered with vegetables that flavor the fish while keeping it moist. Either of the hollandaise sauces on pages 29 and 86 will marry well with this dish. Any leftover salmon makes an excellent cold salad.

 For this recipe, order the very end of the tail section of salmon from your fishmonger. This is the section between the cavity opening and the tail that has only the central bone structure, eliminating any chance of stray bones in the flesh. It yields two halves that are perfect for layering with the filling. Ask your fishmonger to fillet and skin the salmon for you.

1 bunch spinach, about 1 lb (500 g)

3 tablespoons unsalted butter

2 tablespoons minced green (spring) onion, including some tender green tops (2 or 3 onions)

salt and freshly ground pepper

freshly grated nutmeg

1 tail end piece salmon, about 2 lb (1 kg), skinned and boned (see note)

1 lemon

chopped fresh parsley

parsley sprigs, dill sprigs, or green (spring) onions for garnish

Position a rack in the center of an oven and preheat to 425°F (220°C). Butter the bottom of a rectangular or oval baking dish that will hold the salmon comfortably.

 Remove the stems from the spinach and discard. Discard any old or bruised leaves. Rinse the spinach thoroughly and place in a large saucepan with just the water clinging to the leaves. Cover and place over medium heat. Cook, turning once or twice, just until the leaves are wilted, about 2 minutes. Transfer to a colander and drain, pressing out any excess water with a large spoon. Fluff up with a fork, place on a clean cutting surface, and, using a sharp knife, chop finely. Set aside.

 In a small saucepan over medium-low heat, melt 2 tablespoons of the butter. Add the green onion and sauté gently, stirring, until translucent, 1–2 minutes. Add the spinach and stir to incorporate. Season to taste with salt, pepper, and nutmeg. Remove from the heat and set aside.

 Rinse the salmon tail piece, then pat dry with paper towels. You should have 2 matching fillets.

 Lay 1 salmon fillet in the baking dish, skinned side down. Arrange the spinach evenly on top. Place the other fillet on top, skinned side up. Cut the remaining 1 tablespoon butter into small pieces and dot the top of the salmon with them. Sprinkle to taste with salt and pepper. Bake until the salmon is opaque throughout when pierced with the tip of a sharp knife, about 20 minutes.

 Using a spatula, transfer the salmon to a warmed serving plate. Cut the lemon into 4 or 5 thin slices and arrange them in a row down the center of the salmon. Sprinkle with chopped parsley. Garnish the plate with parsley sprigs, dill sprigs, or green onions. To serve, cut the salmon into 4 equal pieces and transfer to warmed plates.

F

BROILED SWORDFISH WITH GREEN OLIVES

SERVES 4

Fish cooked or garnished with olives and oregano is a popular dish of southern Italy and most likely illustrates the influence of nearby Greece.

Fresh oregano, of course, is your best choice, but if it is unavailable, substitute 2 teaspoons of the dried herb, using your thumb to crush it in the palm of your hand to release its essential oils and thus its flavor.

Find a good brand of green olives packed in brine. Those imported from Italy, Spain, or Greece will have the crispest texture and the brightest, cleanest flavor.

2 lemons

⅛ teaspoon salt

¼ cup (2 fl oz/60 ml) extra-virgin olive oil

1 tablespoon minced fresh oregano, plus 4 oregano sprigs for garnish (optional)

2 tablespoons fine fresh bread crumbs

freshly ground pepper

4 swordfish steaks, each 6–7 oz (185–220 g) and ¾ inch (2 cm) thick

10–12 green olives in brine, preferably Italian, Greek, or Spanish, pitted and thinly sliced

Using a zester or fine-holed shredder, shred the zest (yellow part only) from 1 of the lemons directly onto a small plate (see page 287). Set aside.

Squeeze the juice from the lemon into a small bowl; you should have about 2 tablespoons. Add the salt and stir to dissolve. Add the olive oil, the 1 tablespoon oregano, bread crumbs, and pepper to taste. Whisk until well blended.

If there is any skin on the swordfish steaks, remove it with a sharp knife. In a glass or porcelain dish that will accommodate the steaks comfortably in a single layer, spoon in half of the lemon-oil mixture to cover the bottom. Arrange the fish steaks in the dish and spoon the other half of the lemon-oil mixture over the steaks. Marinate at room temperature for 20–25 minutes, turning over the steaks a couple of times.

Preheat a broiler (griller) with the broiling pan and rack in place. Remove the steaks from the dish, reserving the marinade, and place on the rack of the broiling pan. Place under the broiler and broil (grill) until the flesh is opaque throughout when pierced with the tip of a sharp knife, 4–5 minutes on each side, depending upon the thickness of the fish. Plan on about 10 minutes per inch (2.5 cm) at the thickest part of the fish; do not overcook.

Meanwhile, transfer the reserved marinade to a small saucepan and place over low heat until hot. Cut the remaining lemon lengthwise into quarters; set aside.

When the swordfish steaks are done, carefully transfer to warmed plates. Top with the hot marinade. Scatter the green olive slices over the fish and sprinkle with the lemon zest. Garnish with the oregano sprigs, if desired, and lemon wedges and serve immediately.

"While it is desirable now and then to experiment with sauces most fish steaks and fillets are best when broiled and basted with some sharp basting liquid and brought to the table with a crisp and slightly browned surface."

—Angelo Pellegrini

"We have a saying in Italy that good love starts in your stomach. You never see anyone go through the best day of his or her life on an empty stomach."

–Pino Luongo

SEAFOOD STEW

SERVES 4

With so many regions of Italy facing the sea, recipes for fish stew abound, each with its own distinctive personality. Arguably the two things most of these recipes have in common, however, are the presence of tomatoes and the utter simplicity of their presentation. The simple version I offer here includes fennel, which has a fresh anise flavor that naturally complements seafood. Wait until the fennel is cooked tender before you add the fish, since the latter requires just a few minutes of cooking.

꩜ *Good coarse country Italian or French bread is an absolute necessity for soaking up the flavorful juices.*

1 lb (500 g) ripe plum (Roma) tomatoes

2 small fennel bulbs, 1½–2 lb (750 g–1 kg) total weight, stems removed

3 tablespoons extra-virgin olive oil, plus extra for brushing on bread

3 cloves garlic, chopped (about 2 teaspoons)

2 bay leaves

1 tablespoon fresh lemon juice

1 cup (8 fl oz/250 ml) dry white wine

2 cups (16 fl oz/500 ml) bottled clam juice

4 cups (32 fl oz/1 l) water

2 teaspoons salt

pinch of red pepper flakes

12–14 mussels in the shell, well scrubbed

2 lb (1 kg) assorted whitefish such as sea bass, halibut, red snapper, and sole, in any combination, cut into 2-inch (5-cm) pieces

½ lb (250 g) small shrimp (prawns), peeled (leave tail fin attached), and deveined (see page 289)

4 slices coarse country bread, each about ½ inch (12 mm) thick

coarsely chopped fresh flat-leaf (Italian) parsley for garnish

Core and peel the tomatoes (see page 289). Cut in half crosswise and squeeze out the seeds. Chop the tomatoes coarsely; set aside.

꩜ Trim the root end of each fennel bulb and remove any stalks. Cut the bulbs in half lengthwise and then cut each half lengthwise into 4 wedges; set aside.

꩜ In a large saucepan or pot over medium-low heat, warm the 3 tablespoons olive oil. Add the garlic and sauté until it just begins to change color, 1–2 minutes. Add the tomatoes, fennel, and bay leaves and cook, uncovered, until the tomatoes start to release their juices, 8–10 minutes. Stir in the lemon juice, wine, clam juice, water, salt, and red pepper flakes. Cover partially and cook over low heat until the fennel is almost tender, 20–25 minutes.

꩜ Meanwhile, discard any mussels that do not close to the touch.

꩜ When the fennel is almost tender, add the fish pieces, cover, and barely simmer over low heat for 10 minutes. Add the mussels and shrimp and continue to barely simmer until the fish is opaque throughout when pierced with a sharp knife, the shrimp are pink, and the mussels are open, another 5–6 minutes. Discard any mussels that did not open. Taste and adjust the seasoning.

꩜ Meanwhile, preheat an oven to 325°F (165°C). Brush each bread slice with oil and arrange on a baking sheet, oiled side up. Warm in the oven, a few minutes.

꩜ To serve, place a warm bread slice in each of 4 deep, warmed soup bowls. Ladle the stew over the bread and garnish with chopped parsley. Serve at once. ꩜

FILLETS OF SOLE WITH MUSTARD-HORSERADISH SAUCE

SERVES 4

Fillet of sole has always been one of the easiest fishes to find in the market. Although it has a wonderfully delicate texture, it also is fairly bland. I've found that the fish stands up well to stronger seasonings, such as the mustard and horseradish used here. Other mild-flavored whitefishes—sea bass, halibut, red snapper—can also be prepared this way.

❧ *Just a few ingredients go into the dish, but all of them play key roles, so pay close attention to their quality. Seek out mushrooms that are small and firm, without the brown filaments on the under-sides of the caps that indicate they are old. Make your own fresh bread crumbs from an Italian or French loaf. Use freshly grated Parmesan cheese, preferably imported. And the plain prepared horseradish found in the refrigerated section of your food store will have a far superior flavor to the one found bottled in the condiments aisle.*

2 or 3 slices French or Italian bread
½ lb (250 g) small fresh mushrooms
¼ cup (2 oz/60 g) unsalted butter
1 large or 2 small shallots, chopped
   (2 tablespoons)
juice of 1 lemon (about 3 tablespoons)
3–4 tablespoons Dijon mustard
1–1½ tablespoons prepared horseradish
¼ cup (1 oz/30 g) freshly grated
   Parmesan cheese
½ cup (4 fl oz/125 ml) sour cream
salt and freshly ground pepper
4 sole fillets, 6–7 oz (185–220 g) each

Position a rack in the lower part of an oven and preheat the oven to 425°F (220°C). Butter a flameproof baking

dish that will accommodate the fish fillets in a single layer without crowding.

❧ Remove the crusts from the bread and discard. Cut or tear the bread into small pieces and put into a food processor fitted with the metal blade or into a blender. Pulse a few times to make coarse crumbs; you should have 1–1½ cups (2–3 oz/60–90 g). Set aside.

❧ Clean the mushrooms by brushing them with a soft-bristled brush or a paper towel; do not wash. Slice thinly and set aside.

❧ In a sauté pan over medium-low heat, melt the butter. Add the shallots and sauté, stirring, for 1 minute. Raise the heat to medium, add the mushrooms, and cook, stirring and tossing, until the mushrooms are just wilted, 2–3 minutes. Set aside.

❧ In a bowl, stir together the lemon juice, mustard, horseradish, Parmesan cheese, and sour cream until well blended. Add to the mushrooms, return to the heat, and bring just to a simmer. Stir to blend and season to taste with salt and pepper.

❧ Rinse the sole fillets and pat dry with paper towels. Place in the prepared baking dish in a single layer and spoon the sauce over the fillets. Sprinkle the bread crumbs evenly over the top. Bake until the fish is opaque throughout when pierced with a sharp knife, 10–20 minutes; the timing depends upon the thickness of the fillets.

❧ Preheat a broiler (griller). Slip the baking dish under the broiler and broil (grill) to brown the top lightly, 1–2 minutes. Serve at once. A ❧

FILLETS OF SOLE WITH GRAPES

SERVES 4

An elegant classic of French cooking, this is probably one of the easiest dishes to prepare at the last minute. The secret to success lies in having everything laid out before the cooking begins. Bear in mind, too, that the dish is finished under the broiler, so take care not to overcook the fish fillets when sautéing them.

❧ *Other thin whitefish fillets such as red snapper or sand dab can be used in place of the sole. Make sure that the grapes you select are sweet; sometimes grapes are picked too soon and can be on the sour side.*

4 sole fillets, 6–7 oz (185–220 g) each
½ cup (2½ oz/75 g) all-purpose
    (plain) flour
salt and freshly ground pepper
3 tablespoons unsalted butter
1 tablespoon olive oil or vegetable oil
¼ cup (1¼ oz/37 g) chopped shallots
    (about 4 shallots)
¾ cup (6 fl oz/180 ml) dry white wine
    or white vermouth
1½ cups (9 oz/280 g) white seedless
    grapes
fresh dill sprigs

Preheat a broiler (griller).
❧ Rinse the fish fillets and pat dry with paper towels. Place the flour, ¼ teaspoon salt, and ⅛ teaspoon pepper on a plate and mix together. Lightly dredge the fillets in the flour mixture, coating evenly on both sides and shaking off the excess.
❧ In a large sauté pan or frying pan over medium-high heat, melt the butter with the oil. When foaming, add the fillets, in 2 batches if necessary to prevent crowding, and sauté, turning once, until starting to turn golden, about 2 minutes on each side. Using a slotted spatula, transfer the fillets to a warmed flameproof baking dish that will hold them in a single layer; keep warm.
❧ Add the shallots to the same pan, reduce the heat to low, and sauté, stirring, until translucent, 1–2 minutes. Pour off any excess fat, but reserve the shallots in the pan. Add the wine or vermouth and bring to a boil over medium-high heat. Boil until reduced by about one-third, scraping up any browned bits on the pan bottom. Add the grapes and continue to boil until the liquid is reduced a little more, 1–2 minutes. Season to taste with salt and pepper and pour over the fillets, distributing the grapes and shallots evenly over and around the fish pieces.
❧ Place under the broiler, with the top of the fillets about 4 inches (10 cm) from the heat source. Broil (grill) until the top is just beginning to brown and the sauce is bubbly, 2–3 minutes. Garnish with dill sprigs and serve immediately. F ❧

BAKED SEA BASS IN PARCHMENT

SERVES 4

No matter where one lives in Italy, the sea is nearby, so it is only natural that Italians love fish. One of their favorite ways to prepare it is wrapped in parchment (baking) paper and baked, a method that not only yields moist, tender results, but is also quick and easy. Aluminum foil can be used in place of the parchment.

❧ *A little garlic or onion is usually tucked into the parcel along with herbs, lemon, and, if the fish is not an oily variety, a little olive oil. For this recipe I've chosen sea bass, which comes out moist and flaky. You can substitute any mild-flavored, non-oily fish, such as halibut, haddock, bass, snapper, sole, or turbot.*

❧ *This dish is excellent served with Baked Stuffed Tomatoes with Basil (see page 225).*

extra-virgin olive oil
2 or 3 large cloves garlic (depending
    upon your taste), thinly sliced
2–4 very small fresh rosemary sprigs
    (depending upon your taste),
    plus extra sprigs for garnish
1½–2 lb (750 g–1 kg) sea bass fillet,
    in one piece, skin removed
salt and freshly ground pepper
2 tablespoons capers, rinsed and drained
chopped fresh flat-leaf (Italian) parsley
    for garnish
lemon wedges

Position a rack in the middle of an oven and preheat to 425°F (220°C). Cut a piece of parchment (baking) paper or aluminum foil that will enclose the fish fillet comfortably.

❧ Lay the sheet of parchment or foil on a flat surface. Brush an area in the center, about the size of the fish, with olive oil. Sprinkle with half of the garlic slices and top with 1 or 2 rosemary sprigs. Lay the fish on top and brush the top of the fish with olive oil. Sprinkle with the remaining garlic slices and top with 1 or 2 rosemary sprigs. Sprinkle to taste with salt and pepper.

❧ Enclose the fish in the parchment or foil by folding in the sides and then folding the edges together, sealing well. Place the packet on a baking sheet. Bake until the flesh is opaque throughout when pierced with the tip of a knife, 15–20 minutes, depending upon the thickness of the fish. Plan on about 10 minutes per inch (2.5 cm) at the thickest part of the fish; do not overcook. To check for doneness, open the corner of the packet and pierce the fish with the tip of a sharp knife; if not yet ready, reseal and bake a few minutes longer.

❧ Remove the packet from the oven, then open it up and carefully transfer the fish to a warmed serving platter. Top with the capers and parsley. Arrange the lemon wedges and rosemary sprigs around the fish. Spoon the juices from the packet over the fish and serve at once. I ❧

"Fish must swim thrice—once in the water, a second time in the sauce, and a third time in wine in the stomach."

–John Ray

CURRIED SHRIMP WITH RICE

SERVES 4

The French love of exotic seasonings and fruits, which dates back to their colonial era, is evident in this Parisian bistro recipe. The relish, a combination of fresh mango, green onion, cilantro, and lime, perfectly balances the aromatic flavors of the curried shrimp.
🌙 *Be sure to use fresh curry powder. If a container has been sitting in your cupboard for more than six months, it probably has lost much of its punch. Buy a fresh supply from a source that is likely to have a good turnover of the product, such as an ethnic market. Cans of coconut milk and bags or boxes of jasmine rice, a fragrant long-grain white rice grown in Thailand, can also be purchased at ethnic markets, as well as in specialty-food shops and the international section of many large food stores.*

1 large mango
2 or 3 green (spring) onions, including some tender green tops, coarsely chopped
leaves from 2 or 3 fresh cilantro (fresh coriander) sprigs, coarsely chopped
1 lime
cayenne pepper
1½ lb (750 g) small or medium fresh shrimp (prawns), peeled and deveined
salt
1¾ cups (14 fl oz/430 ml) water
2 cups (14 oz/440 g) jasmine rice or other long-grain white rice, rinsed
2 tablespoons unsalted butter
1 tablespoon olive oil
1 or 2 garlic cloves, peeled and finely chopped
1 sweet white onion, chopped (about 1 cup/5 oz/155 g)
1½ tablespoons curry powder
¾ cup (6 fl oz/180 ml) dry white wine
1 cup (8 fl oz/250 ml) coconut milk

Peel the mango, then slice off the flesh in one piece from each side of the flat pit. Cut into ½-inch (12-mm) cubes. Slice the flesh from the edges of the pit as well. Place in a small bowl and add the green onions and cilantro. Remove the zest from the lime (see page 287), shredding it directly over the mango. Cut the lime in half and squeeze the juice from 1 half over the fruit. Add a dash of cayenne, toss, and adjust the seasoning. Set aside.
🌙 Put the shrimp in a bowl with water to cover. Add 1 teaspoon salt, stir to dissolve, and let stand for 10 minutes. Drain, rinse, and drain again. Set aside.
🌙 In a saucepan, bring the water to a boil. Add the rice and ¼ teaspoon salt and stir twice. Reduce the heat to low, cover and cook until the water is

absorbed, about 20 minutes. Let stand, covered, for 10 minutes off the heat.
🌙 Meanwhile, in a sauté pan over medium-low heat, melt the butter with the oil. Add the garlic and sauté for a few seconds. Add the onion and sauté until translucent, 4–5 minutes. Add the curry powder, stir, and sauté for 1 minute. Raise the heat to medium, add the wine, and cook until the onion is tender and the liquid is reduced by one-third, 8–10 minutes. Add the coconut milk, bring to a simmer, and add the shrimp. Reduce the heat to low, cover, and cook until the shrimp are red and opaque, 2–3 minutes. Season with salt, cayenne, and lime juice.
🌙 Spoon the rice onto the center of warmed plates. Place the shrimp mixture along one side and the mango relish along the other, then serve. 🄵 🌙

SAUTÉED SCALLOPS WITH SPINACH

SERVES 4

Scallops and spinach are a classic combination of tastes, textures, and colors—an ideal light main course for lunch or supper.

Buy your scallops from a reliable seafood market. I find large sea scallops easier to sauté, but use the smaller bay scallops if you prefer. If the sea scallops you purchase are very large or thick, slice them in half horizontally to make two thinner rounds from each scallop. They will take only 1–2 minutes to cook on each side. Be careful not to overcook them, as they quickly lose their delicate tenderness. The scallops are ready just at the moment they turn opaque and are lightly tinged with brown.

1 or 2 bunches spinach, 1–1½ lb (500–750 g) total weight
½ lb (250 g) ripe plum (Roma) tomatoes
3 tablespoons unsalted butter
2 tablespoons minced shallot
salt and freshly ground pepper
pinch of freshly grated nutmeg
1 lb (500 g) sea scallops, cut in half horizontally if large
1 tablespoon extra-virgin olive oil
1–2 tablespoons Madeira, Marsala, or port wine
lemon wedges

Pick over the spinach, discarding any old leaves, and remove the stems. Wash well and put into a bowl with a little water. Set aside.

Core, peel, and seed the tomatoes as directed on page 289. Finely chop; you should have about 1 cup (6 oz/185 g). Set aside.

In a saucepan over medium-low heat, melt 1 tablespoon of the butter. Add the shallot and sauté, stirring, until translucent, 1–2 minutes. Add the tomatoes, raise the heat to medium-high and cook rapidly, stirring, until thickened, 8–10 minutes. Season to taste with salt and pepper. Set aside and cover to keep warm.

Transfer the spinach to a large saucepan with just the water clinging to the leaves. Sprinkle with a little salt and the nutmeg, cover and place over medium-high heat. Cook, turning the leaves over once or twice so they cook evenly, until just wilted, 2–3 minutes. Immediately drain in a colander and press out the water with the back of a wooden spoon. Fluff up the leaves with a fork. Set aside and cover to keep warm.

Rinse the scallops and dry with paper towels. In a large sauté pan or frying pan (preferably nonstick) over medium-high heat, melt the remaining 2 tablespoons butter with the olive oil. When bubbling, add the scallops in batches and sauté, turning once, until beginning to brown, 1–2 minutes on each side. Transfer to a warmed plate and keep warm. Add the tomatoes to the pan and heat to a simmer. Stir in the Madeira or other wine; taste and adjust the seasoning. Return the scallops to the pan and heat through to serving temperature.

Arrange the spinach around the perimeter of a warmed serving dish. Spoon the scallops and tomato sauce into the center. Garnish with lemon wedges. A

BAKED SEA BASS WITH TOMATO AND FENNEL

SERVES 4

Any other whitefish, such as halibut or red snapper, can be substituted for the sea bass, but do not use an oily fish. Take a few moments to run your fingertips over the fillets; pull out any remaining little bones you detect, using tweezers if necessary, so you and your guests won't have to deal with them at the table. You can also use one large piece of fish weighing about 1½ pounds (750 g) instead of the fillets.

2 or 3 slices French or Italian bread
1½ lb (750 g) ripe plum (Roma)
 tomatoes
4 tablespoons (2 oz/60 g) unsalted
 butter
1 small yellow onion, diced
 (½ cup/2 oz/60 g)
salt and freshly ground pepper
1 fennel bulb, about 1 lb (500 g)
2 tablespoons water
1 lemon, cut in half, plus
 1 whole lemon
4 sea bass fillets, about 6–8 oz
 (185–250 g) each
1 tablespoon fennel seeds

Position a rack in the lower part of an oven and preheat to 425°F (220°C). Butter a flameproof baking dish that will hold the fish fillets in one layer.

Remove the crusts from the bread. Cut the bread into small pieces and put into a food processor fitted with the metal blade or into a blender. Pulse a few times to make coarse crumbs (1–1½ cups/2–3 oz/60–90 g). Set aside.

Core, peel, and seed the tomatoes as directed on page 289. Chop coarsely; you should have about 3 cups (18 oz/ 560 g). In a saucepan over medium-low heat, melt 2 tablespoons of the butter. Add the onion and sauté until translucent, about 2 minutes. Add the tomatoes, raise the heat to medium, and cook, stirring, until softened, 3–4 minutes longer. Season to taste with salt and pepper; set aside.

Trim off any stems and bruised stalks from the fennel. Thinly slice the bulb vertically, then cut vertically into thin strips. In a saucepan over low heat, melt the remaining butter. Add the fennel, a pinch of salt, and the water. Cover and cook over low heat until just tender, 10–15 minutes; do not allow to become dry. Uncover, raise the heat, and cook away most of the liquid. Let cool slightly.

Scatter half of the fennel in the prepared dish. Rinse and dry the fish fillets. Using 1 lemon half, squeeze juice on both sides of each fillet, sprinkle with salt and pepper, and place atop the fennel. Distribute the remaining fennel over the fillets. Spoon on the tomato mixture and sprinkle with the bread crumbs. Squeeze the other lemon half over the top and scatter on the fennel seeds.

Bake, uncovered, until the fish is opaque throughout when pierced with a knife, 15–20 minutes; the timing depends upon the thickness of the fish.

Preheat a broiler (griller). Slip the baking dish under the broiler and broil (grill) until lightly browned, 1–2 minutes. Using a zester or a fine-holed shredder, shred the zest from the remaining whole lemon as directed on page 287, distributing it evenly over the fish. Serve immediately. A

BROILED SWORDFISH STEAKS WITH BASIL, OLIVE OIL, AND CAPERS

SERVES 4

Satisfyingly meaty and yet mild in flavor, swordfish is understandably one of the most popular fish in the United States. Fortunately, it is caught along both the Atlantic and Pacific coasts and is available almost everywhere. Usually cooked by broiling (grilling), the dense flesh requires frequent basting to keep it from becoming dry; care must also be taken not to overcook it.

✺ *Prepare the sauce in advance so that you can serve the fish immediately. If you can't find fresh basil, don't use dried, which doesn't approach the flavor of the fresh herb; instead, substitute about 1 teaspoon fresh or dried dill.*

4 tablespoons (2 fl oz/60 ml) fresh
  lemon juice
salt and freshly ground pepper
½ cup (4 fl oz/125 ml) extra-virgin
  olive oil
2 tablespoons chopped fresh basil
4 swordfish steaks, 7–8 oz (220–250 g)
  each, ¾–1 inch (2–2.5 cm) thick
¼ cup (¾ oz/20 g) minced green
  (spring) onion, including some tender
  green tops
¼ cup (2 oz/60 g) well-drained
  capers, rinsed

Preheat a broiler (griller).

✺ In a small bowl, combine 1 tablespoon of the lemon juice and 1 or 2 pinches each of salt and pepper and stir until the salt dissolves. Add ¼ cup (2 fl oz/60 ml) of the olive oil and 1 tablespoon of the basil; stir well. Rinse the swordfish steaks and pat dry with paper towels. Brush both sides of each fish steak with some of the olive oil mixture and place on the rack of a broiler pan.

✺ Place under the broiler about 2 inches (5 cm) from the heat source. Broil (grill), basting with the remaining olive oil mixture a couple of times, until the fish is opaque throughout when pierced with a sharp knife, 5–6 minutes on each side.

✺ Meanwhile, in a small bowl, combine the remaining 3 tablespoons lemon juice and 1 or 2 pinches each of salt and pepper; stir until the salt dissolves. Add the remaining ¼ cup (2 fl oz/60 ml) olive oil, the remaining 1 tablespoon basil, the green onion, and capers. Stir to mix well.

✺ When the fish steaks are done, transfer to warmed plates and spoon the olive oil–caper sauce over the fish. Pass any remaining sauce in a bowl at the table. A ✺

"Our lives are not in the lap of the gods, but in the lap of our cooks."

−Lin Yutang

POACHED SALMON STEAKS WITH CUCUMBERS

SERVES 4

Poaching is one of the easiest ways to prepare salmon and one of the most attractive ways to serve it— not to mention being low in fat and calories. The poaching liquid, a quickly made court bouillon of water, wine, and aromatic vegetables, contributes a delicate flavor and can be made 1 hour in advance of poaching the fish. You can also use it to cook sea bass, halibut, or sole fillets or steaks. Whichever fish you use, take care not to overcook it.

Cucumbers make a perfect accompaniment to salmon, and the method used in this recipe is an excellent way to prepare them. The light salting draws out some of their bitter juices and prevents the cucumbers from watering down the sour cream dressing. Although most of the salt drains away with the juices, you probably won't have to add more salt to the final cucumber mixture.

2 cucumbers

salt

⅓ cup (3 fl oz/80 ml) sour cream

2 teaspoons minced fresh dill

4 cups (32 fl oz/1 l) water

½ cup (4 fl oz/125 ml) dry white wine

½ celery stalk, cut into chunks

1 carrot, cut into chunks

¼ yellow onion, cut into chunks

2 thick lemon slices, plus 1 lemon, cut into wedges, for garnish

4 peppercorns

3 fresh parsley sprigs

1 bay leaf

4 salmon steaks, 6–8 oz (185–250 g) each

Peel the cucumbers and cut in half lengthwise. Using a melon baller or a small spoon, scoop out the seeds and discard. Cut crosswise into slices ¼ inch (6 mm) thick. In a colander set over a bowl, layer half of the cucumber slices. Sprinkle with salt, then top with the remaining cucumber slices and again sprinkle with salt. Rest a small plate directly on the cucumbers; weight down the plate with a couple of food cans. Leave to drain in the refrigerator for 2–2½ hours. Dry the cucumber slices with paper towels and return them to the refrigerator.

In a small bowl, stir together the sour cream and dill. Cover and refrigerate.

In a large sauté pan or roasting pan with high sides that will hold the salmon steaks in one layer without crowding, combine the water, wine, celery, carrot, onion, 2 lemon slices, peppercorns, parsley, bay leaf, and 2 teaspoons salt. Bring to a simmer, cover, and simmer over low heat for 25–30 minutes.

Rinse the salmon steaks. Using kitchen string, tie each steak to hold its shape. Add the steaks to the simmering liquid, cover or partially cover, and simmer gently over low heat for 10 minutes. Check for doneness by inserting a knife into the salmon; the flesh should be opaque throughout. Do not overcook.

Just before serving, again dry the cucumber slices, then combine them with the sour cream mixture in a bowl. Mix until well blended.

Using a spatula or large slotted spoon, transfer the salmon steaks to individual plates. Add 1 or 2 spoonfuls of the cucumber mixture and a lemon wedge to each plate. Serve at once.

GRILLED SWORDFISH WITH TOMATO SAUCE

SERVES 4

This is a great way to serve fish in the summertime, when vine-ripened tomatoes are at their peak and the weather invites outdoor dining. If you don't have an outdoor grill, use a broiler (griller).

🍥 *Do not process the sauce too long in your food processor or blender. It is at its best when the texture is coarse.*

2 lb (1 kg) ripe tomatoes

5 tablespoons (3 fl oz/80 ml) olive oil

2 tablespoons chopped garlic
   (6 or 7 cloves)

1 yellow onion, chopped (about
   1 cup/5 oz/155 g)

¼ cup (2 fl oz/60 ml) red wine

salt and freshly ground pepper

3 tablespoons chopped fresh basil, plus
   whole leaves for garnish

4 swordfish steaks, 7–8 oz (220–250 g)
   each and 1 inch (2.5 cm) thick

Prepare a fire in a charcoal grill. Place the grill rack 4–6 inches (10–15 cm) above the heat and brush it with oil.

🍥 To make the sauce, core, peel, and seed the tomatoes (see page 289). Chop coarsely; you should have about 4 cups (1½ lb/750 g). In a saucepan over medium-low heat, warm 2 tablespoons of the olive oil. When hot but not smoking, add 1 tablespoon of the garlic and sauté, stirring, until it begins to change color, 30–40 seconds. Add the onion and continue to sauté, stirring occasionally, until translucent, 6–7 minutes. Raise the heat to medium, add the tomatoes, and cook, stirring, until they release some of their liquid, 6–7 minutes. Add the wine, reduce the heat to medium-low, and simmer until the liquid is reduced by half, 8–10 minutes.

Remove from the heat and let cool slightly.

🍥 While the sauce is cooking, place the swordfish steaks in a large dish in a single layer. In a small bowl, combine the remaining 3 tablespoons oil, 1 tablespoon garlic, 1 tablespoon of the basil, and a little salt and pepper. Stir well and brush on both sides of the fish steaks. Set aside for about 10 minutes.

🍥 Transfer the tomato mixture to a food processor fitted with the metal blade or to a blender and process, using a few pulses, to produce a coarse purée. Return the sauce to the saucepan and season to taste with salt and pepper. Stir in the remaining 2 tablespoons basil and return the pan to medium-low heat. Cook for a few minutes to blend the flavors, then taste and adjust the seasoning. Remove from the heat, set aside, and keep warm.

🍥 When the fire is ready, grill the fish, turning once or twice, until opaque throughout when pierced with a knife tip, 10–12 minutes total.

🍥 If the sauce has cooled, reheat it over medium-low heat. Place 3 or 4 spoonfuls of sauce on each warmed plate to make a bed for the fish. Place a swordfish steak on each bed of sauce and garnish with basil leaves. Serve at once.

CRAB CAKES

SERVES 4

Crab cakes are a permanent fixture in the cooking of America's eastern seaboard from New England to Georgia. An abundance of recipes from Baltimore and the Chesapeake Bay, Virginia, and elsewhere along the East Coast, each different from the others, all claim to be the most authentic.  *I've eaten lots of different versions of crab cakes. When done well, they're very special; but all too often they're indifferently prepared. The key to success lies in using fresh cooked crabmeat and lots of it, with just a little something extra to bind the mixture. The distribution of fresh crab has improved in recent years, and you can find it in good seafood markets all through the winter and spring. Most recipes use mayonnaise as a binder; I prefer to use cream mixed with egg and seasoned with fresh lemon juice, mustard, and cayenne pepper. A small amount of bread crumbs also helps lighten and bind the mixture; be sure to use your own freshly made crumbs from French or Italian bread.*

3 or 4 slices French or Italian bread
3 tablespoons unsalted butter
¼ cup (1 oz/30 g) minced green
   (spring) onion, including some tender
   green tops (3 or 4 onions)
1 lb (500 g) fresh cooked crabmeat,
   picked over to remove any shell
   fragments and cartilage
1 tablespoon chopped fresh parsley
⅓ cup (3 fl oz/80 ml) heavy
   (double) cream
2 eggs
2 tablespoons fresh lemon juice
1 tablespoon Dijon mustard
½ teaspoon salt, or to taste
cayenne pepper
½ cup (2½ oz/75 g) all-purpose
   (plain) flour

2 tablespoons vegetable oil
lemon wedges

Remove the crusts from the bread and discard. Cut or tear the bread into small pieces and put into a food processor fitted with the metal blade or into a blender. Pulse a few times to make coarse crumbs; you should have about 2 cups (4 oz/125 g). Place in a large bowl and set aside.
◑ In a small sauté pan over low heat, melt 1 tablespoon of the butter. Add the green onion and sauté until softened, 1–2 minutes. Add the green onion to the bread crumbs along with the crabmeat and parsley. Mix well.
◑ In a separate bowl, whisk together the cream and eggs until well blended. Whisk in the lemon juice, mustard, salt, and cayenne pepper to taste. Slowly add to the crab mixture, stirring continuously so that the bread crumbs are evenly moistened. Taste and adjust the seasoning.
◑ Form into 8 or 12 oval or round cakes about 1 inch (2.5 cm) thick. Put the flour on a plate or on a piece of waxed paper. Lightly and evenly coat each cake with the flour, shaking off any excess.
◑ In a large sauté pan or frying pan over medium-high heat, melt the remaining 2 tablespoons butter with the vegetable oil. When hot, sauté the cakes in batches, turning once, until lightly browned, 3–4 minutes on each side. Transfer to a warmed plate and keep warm until all the cakes are cooked.
◑ Serve immediately with lemon wedges. A ◑

$\mathcal{P}$OULTRY

"It tastes like chicken." How many times have you heard that expression when someone tries to describe an out-of-the-ordinary dish? Chicken, and other forms of poultry, are our culinary touchstones, always reliable and always pleasurable, as you'll find with the recipes that follow.

There is perhaps no more versatile main course ingredient than chicken. You can roast, bake, grill, broil, fry, sauté, braise, stew, steam, or poach it. And the results are delicious, with seasonings and sauces as simple or sophisticated as you like. Whether the dish is as elegant as a French Roast Tarragon Chicken (page 131), as rustic as Italian Sautéed Chicken Breasts with Parmesan Cheese (page 121), or as homey as an American Baked Chicken with Honey-Lemon Glaze (page 133), good eating is a certainty.

ROASTED ROSEMARY CHICKEN

SERVES 4

Seek out a fresh free-range chicken. They are not hard to find these days and have a wonderful flavor. Take care not to overcook the chicken. Start testing the breast and thigh for doneness after about 50 minutes of roasting. The breast naturally cooks in less time, so positioning the bird on its side for part of the roasting exposes the thighs to more heat, ensuring that the bird cooks more evenly. For a small chicken (3–4 lb/1.5–2 kg), a higher temperature works well. I always attain very moist results by roasting in a 425°F (220°C) oven. I like to serve the roasted chicken with golden polenta crostini (see page 226).

1 chicken, 3–4 lb (1.5–2 kg), preferably free-range
1 lemon, quartered
salt
3 cloves garlic, unpeeled
7 fresh rosemary sprigs
extra-virgin olive oil
freshly ground pepper
2 cups (16 fl oz/500 ml) water

Position a rack in the lower part of an oven and preheat to 425°F (220°C).
∂♪ Discard the giblets and neck, if any, from the chicken, or reserve for another use. Remove any fat from around the cavity. Rinse the chicken inside and out. Dry with paper towels. Rub the cavity with 1 of the lemon quarters and leave it in the cavity. Sprinkle the cavity lightly with salt. Using the flat side of a large knife, smash the garlic cloves and then peel them. Place inside the cavity along with the remaining 3 lemon quarters and 3 of the rosemary sprigs. Close the cavity with a small skewer or wooden toothpick.

∂♪ Place 1 of the remaining rosemary sprigs under each wing and 1 between each leg and the body of the chicken. Truss the chicken: using kitchen string, tie the legs together and then tie the legs and wings close to the body. Brush the chicken with olive oil and sprinkle with salt and pepper.
∂♪ Oil a rack in a roasting pan and place the chicken, on its side, on the rack. Add 1 cup (8 fl oz/250 ml) of the water to the pan. Place in the oven and roast for 20 minutes. Turn the chicken over onto its other side, brush with olive oil and roast for another 20 minutes. Turn the chicken breast side up, brush with oil again, and roast another 20 minutes, basting a couple of times with the pan juices. Check if the chicken is done by inserting an instant-read thermometer into the thickest part of the breast or thigh away from the bone. It should read about 165°F (74°C) in the breast or 180°F (82°C) in the thigh. Remove from the oven when it is within 2–3 degrees of the desired temperature, as it will continue to cook from its internal heat. (Alternatively, pierce the thigh joint with a knife tip; the juices should run clear.) Transfer to a warmed serving platter and cover loosely with aluminum foil for 10 minutes before carving.
∂♪ Using a spoon, skim the fat from the pan juices and discard. Place the pan over medium heat. Add the remaining 1 cup (8 fl oz/250 ml) water to the pan and heat, stirring to dislodge any browned bits from the pan bottom. Simmer for 1–2 minutes, continuing to stir. Season to taste with salt and pepper.
∂♪ Carve the chicken and spoon some of the pan juices over each serving.

"Poultry is the best and most delicious of the various matters with which man furnishes himself as food."

—Alexis Soyer

ROAST DUCK WITH PARSNIPS AND MARSALA

SERVES 4

Parsnips and Marsala are the perfect accompaniments to roast duck. The sweetness of the root vegetables blends perfectly with the wine in the sauce. Bring the duck to room temperature before roasting for the best results. Accompany with wild rice studded with chopped pecans and shallots.

1 duck, 4–5 lb (2–2.5 kg)
½ lemon
1 yellow onion, cut into quarters
4 or 5 fresh marjoram sprigs
salt
1 lb (500 g) parsnips
1 whole clove
1 bay leaf
2 cups (16 fl oz/500 ml) flavorful chicken broth
2 tablespoons dark brown sugar
¼ cup (2 fl oz/60 ml) dry Marsala

Position a rack in the center of an oven and preheat to 350°F (180°C).

Rinse the duck inside and out. Dry with paper towels. Rub the cavity with the lemon half, squeezing out some of the juice. Leave the lemon in the cavity and add 2 or 3 marjoram sprigs and sprinkle with ½ teaspoon salt. Put the duck, breast side down, on a rack in a roasting pan and place in the oven. Roast for 45 minutes. Turn over the duck and prick the skin on the breast all over to allow the fat to drain off. Roast for 45 minutes longer, pricking several times during roasting.

While the duck is cooking, peel the parsnips and cut crosswise into thin slices. In a saucepan, combine the parsnips, 1 teaspoon salt, and water to cover. Cover partially and bring to a boil over high heat. Reduce the heat to medium and cook until tender, 20–25 minutes. Drain and set aside.

Check if the duck is done: pierce the thigh with a knife tip; the juices should run pink for medium-rare. Alternatively, insert an instant-read thermometer into the thickest part of the thigh away from the bone. It should read about 180°F (82°C). If you prefer your duck well done, roast for 10–20 minutes longer. Be forewarned, however, for the meat will be dry. Remove the pan from the oven, then remove the duck from the pan, pouring off the accumulated liquid from the cavity into the pan. Place the duck on a warmed platter and keep warm.

Place the remaining 2 marjoram sprigs, the clove, and the bay leaf on a square of cheesecloth (muslin), bring the corners together, and tie securely with kitchen string to make a bouquet garni. Using a spoon, skim the fat from the pan juices and discard. Place the pan over medium heat and stir to dislodge any browned bits from the pan bottom. Add the chicken broth, brown sugar, Marsala, and bouquet garni and bring to a boil. Let boil until slightly reduced and thickened, 2–3 minutes. Taste and adjust the seasoning, then add the reserved parsnips and cook for 1 minute to heat through.

Using poultry shears, cut the duck into quarters, discarding the backbone. Add any juices that have accumulated on the platter to the roasting pan, then pour the contents of the pan into a warmed bowl. Serve the duck with the parsnips and sauce.

SAUTÉED CHICKEN BREASTS WITH GINGER-ORANGE GLAZE

SERVES 4

Light and low in fat, this easily prepared main course makes an excellent weekend lunch or weekday supper when accompanied with a simple salad. Although the sautéing of the chicken is best done just before serving, you can do all the preliminary preparation—as well as that of accompanying dishes—ahead of time.

 Freshly grated ginger sparks the flavor of this dish. Ginger has a natural affinity with many foods and seasonings, such as the orange and mustard that also flavor the chicken here. If you like, substitute lemon for the orange.

4 chicken breast halves, 8–9 oz (250–280 g) each, skinned and boned (5–6 oz/155–185 g when boned) (see page 286)

½ cup (2½ oz/75 g) all-purpose (plain) flour

salt and freshly ground pepper

2 tablespoons unsalted butter

1 tablespoon extra-virgin olive oil

1 tablespoon minced green (spring) onion, including some tender green tops

1 cup (8 fl oz/250 ml) fresh orange juice

1 tablespoon light brown sugar

½ teaspoon peeled and grated fresh ginger, or more for stronger flavor

2 teaspoons Dijon mustard

1 orange

Remove all excess fat from the chicken breasts. Rinse and pat dry with paper towels. Place each breast between 2 sheets of plastic wrap and, using a rolling pin, flatten to an even thickness. Put the flour on a plate or on a piece of waxed paper. Lightly salt and pepper each breast and then lightly coat with flour, shaking off any excess.

 In a large sauté pan or frying pan (preferably nonstick) over medium heat, melt the butter with the olive oil. When hot, add the chicken and sauté, turning once, until lightly browned and opaque throughout when pierced with a knife, about 5 minutes on each side. Transfer to a plate and keep warm.

 Pour off any excess fat from the pan and place the pan over medium-high heat. Add the green onion, orange juice, brown sugar, ginger, and mustard and mix well, scraping up any browned bits from the bottom. Cook, stirring, until thickened and reduced, about 5 minutes. Taste and adjust the seasoning.

 Return the chicken to the pan and turn the breasts over several times to coat them well with the sauce. Transfer to a warmed serving platter or individual plates and spoon the remaining sauce over the breasts.

 Remove the zest from the orange (see page 287): Using a zester or a fine-holed shredder, and holding the orange directly over the chicken, shred the zest (orange part only) from the skin directly onto each breast. Serve immediately.

A

SAUTÉED CHICKEN BREASTS WITH PARMESAN CHEESE

SERVES 4

Thin, golden crusts of Parmesan cheese seal in the juices of these pan-cooked chicken breasts. Good-quality Parmesan will produce the finest dish.

❧ Dry white vermouth adds a hint of intriguing flavor to the sauce, but any dry white wine can be substituted. Be sure to let the sauce boil for a few seconds to evaporate the alcohol.

❧ Serve this simple main course alongside your favorite vegetable. Baked Stuffed Tomatoes with Basil (recipe on page 225) or Italian Green Beans with Mint (page 222) are good choices.

4 chicken breast halves, about 10 oz (315 g) each, skinned and boned (about 6 oz/185 g each, if buying boneless breasts)

¼ cup (1 oz/30 g) freshly grated Italian Parmesan cheese, preferably Parmigiano-Reggiano

2 tablespoons all-purpose (plain) flour

salt and freshly ground pepper

2 tablespoons unsalted butter

2 tablespoons olive oil

⅓ cup (3 fl oz/80 ml) dry white vermouth

2–3 tablespoons capers, rinsed and drained

Remove any excess fat from the chicken breasts. Rinse and pat dry with paper towels. Place each breast between 2 sheets of waxed paper and, using a rolling pin, flatten the breasts to an even thickness. On a plate, combine the Parmesan cheese, flour, and a little salt and pepper. Stir until well mixed. Coat each breast evenly with the cheese mixture. Set aside.

❧ In a large sauté pan or frying pan over medium-high heat, melt the butter with the olive oil. When hot, add the chicken breasts to the pan, in 2 batches if necessary to avoid crowding, and sauté, turning once, until golden and cooked through, 4–5 minutes on each side. To test, pierce the breasts with the tip of a sharp knife; the juices should run clear. Transfer to a warmed serving platter or to individual warmed plates.

❧ Pour off any excess fat from the pan and return to medium heat. Add the vermouth, stirring to dislodge any browned bits from the pan bottom. Add the capers and boil for a few seconds.

❧ Spoon the caper sauce over the chicken breasts and serve immediately.

"Poultry is for the cook what canvas is for the painter."

–Jean-Anthelme Brillat-Savarin

BASQUE CHICKEN STEW

SERVES 4

You'll find chicken stews like this in the Basque region of France, located near the border with Spain. The combination of tomatoes, peppers, and bacon gives the dish a robust flavor. Serve it with crusty country bread to sop up the juices.

Shop for a good lean smoked bacon. The kind sliced to order from a slab by your butcher is likely to have the best flavor.

1 red and 1 green bell pepper (capsicum), about 6 oz (185 g) each

2 chicken breast halves, 2 legs, and 2 thighs, 2½–3 lb (1.25–1.5 kg) total weight

¼ lb (125 g) thickly sliced bacon, cut into pieces ½ inch (12 mm) wide

3 cloves garlic, chopped

1 yellow onion, about ½ lb (250 g), cut into thin wedges

1 lb (500 g) small white boiling potatoes such as Yukon gold or white rose, peeled and cut into halves or quarters, depending upon size

1 lb (500 g) ripe tomatoes, peeled, seeded, and chopped (see page 289)

2 or 3 fresh parsley sprigs

3 fresh thyme sprigs

1 bay leaf

1 celery stalk, cut crosswise into 4 equal pieces

1½ tablespoons all-purpose (plain) flour

½ cup (4 fl oz/125 ml) each dry white wine and chicken stock, heated

salt, freshly ground black pepper, and cayenne pepper

Roast and peel the bell peppers (see page 290). Cut into long strips ½ inch (12 mm) wide. Set aside. Remove the skin and fat from the chicken pieces; cut the breasts in half crosswise.

In a large sauté pan over medium heat, cook the bacon until golden, about 10 minutes. Using a slotted spoon, transfer to a stew pot. Reduce the heat to medium-low, add the garlic and onion and sauté until soft, 6–7 minutes. Using the slotted spoon, transfer to the stew pot. Set the pan aside. Add the potatoes, tomatoes, and pepper strips to the stew pot. Place the parsley and thyme sprigs and the bay leaf inside the celery pieces and tie with kitchen string; add to the pot.

Return the sauté pan to medium-high heat. Add the chicken and sauté in the bacon fat until lightly browned, 5–6 minutes on each side. Transfer to the stew pot. Pour off all but 1 tablespoon of the fat from the pan. Add the flour and stir over medium heat until blended. Cook, stirring, for 1 minute, then add the wine and stock. Continue to stir, scraping up any browned bits. Cook until thickened, 2–3 minutes. Pour over the chicken; add salt, black pepper, and cayenne to taste. Cover and bring to a simmer, reduce the heat, and simmer until the juices have increased, about 25 minutes. Rearrange the chicken and vegetables, re-cover, and simmer until the chicken is tender, 20–25 minutes longer. The meat should be opaque throughout.

Adjust the seasoning. Discard the herb bouquet. Transfer the chicken, vegetables, and sauce to a warmed serving dish and serve at once.

ROAST CHICKEN WITH APPLE AND SAGE

SERVES 4–6

Roasting a chicken takes little more effort than the preparation of a first-course salad and the cooking of a vegetable side dish, yet you produce a main course that makes an everyday meal seem like a special occasion.
❧ *I start roasting the chicken with the breast side down for the first 25 minutes. This enables the thighs and back to cook faster while slowing down the cooking of the breast, so that the chicken cooks more evenly; it also keeps the breast more moist. Olive oil brushed over the chicken before roasting adds a nice flavor and promotes a golden color. If you like, substitute a vegetable oil or unsalted butter.*

1 roasting chicken, 4–4½ lb (2–2.25 kg),
   preferably free-range
1 lemon, cut in half
salt
½ yellow onion, cut into pieces
1 celery stalk with leaves, cut into pieces
1 small apple, cut into quarters
4 fresh sage sprigs
crushed whole peppercorns or freshly
   ground pepper
2–3 tablespoons extra-virgin olive oil
1 cup (8 fl oz/250 ml) water

Position a rack in the lower part of an oven and preheat the oven to 425°F (220°C). Grease a rack in an open roasting pan, preferably a nonstick roasting pan with a V-shaped rack.
❧ Remove giblets, if any, from the chicken cavity and put aside for another purpose. Remove all the excess fat from around the cavity opening and rinse the chicken inside and out. Dry thoroughly with paper towels. Rub the inside of the cavity with one of the lemon halves, squeezing out some of the juice as you

do. Sprinkle the cavity lightly with salt and slip in the onion, celery, apple, 2 of the sage sprigs, both lemon halves, and a few crushed peppercorns or ground pepper. Close the cavity and secure with a short metal skewer or a sturdy toothpick. To truss the chicken, use kitchen string to tie the legs together and then tie the legs and wings close to the body (see page 292). Brush the outside of the chicken with some of the oil and sprinkle with salt and pepper.
❧ Place the chicken in the rack, breast side down. Add the water to the pan. Place in the oven and roast for 25 minutes. Turn the chicken breast side up and brush with more oil. Tear the remaining 2 sage sprigs into small pieces and scatter over the breast. Reduce the heat to 400°F (200°C) and continue to roast, basting with the pan juices every 7–8 minutes, until golden brown, 30–40 minutes longer. To test for doneness, insert an instant-read thermometer in the thickest part of the breast or the thigh away from the bone; it should read 165°F (74°C) in the breast or 180°F (82°C) in the thigh.
❧ Transfer to a warmed serving platter, cover loosely with aluminum foil, and let rest for 5–10 minutes before carving. Meanwhile, place the roasting pan on the stove top and, using a spoon, skim off the fat from the pan juices. Reheat the juices over medium heat, adding a little more water to the pan if only 1–2 tablespoons pan juices remain; scrape any browned bits from the pan bottom. Season to taste. Pass the pan juices in a bowl at the table. A ❧

"A handsomely contrived, and well furnished Fruit Garden is an Epitome of Paradise, which was a most glorious place without a palace."

–John Evelyn

POT-ROASTED CHICKEN WITH ONIONS AND POTATOES

SERVES 4

Pot roasting dates back to the early days when ovens took constant watching and refueling; roasting in a covered heavy pot on top of the stove was much easier and more economical and reliable. Still a practical method today, pot roasting yields delicious results—either on top of the stove or in the oven. Its popularity over the last 20 years can be measured by the steady interest in clay-pot cooking—essentially pot roasting in the oven.

Beef may come to mind first when pot roasting is mentioned, but chicken makes an equally good candidate. The poultry gains excellent flavor from the surrounding herbs and vegetables—an exchange of flavors and aromas that doesn't take place in an uncovered roasting pan. If you like, add other favorite vegetables such as sliced red bell pepper (capsicum), green beans, or tomatoes to the pot.

1 roasting chicken, 3½–4 lb (1.75–2 kg), preferably free-range
2 lemons, cut into quarters
1 celery stalk, cut into pieces
4 or 5 fresh oregano sprigs
salt and freshly ground pepper
2 lb (1 kg) small white boiling onions (about 48), 1 inch (2.5 cm) in diameter
2 lb (1 kg) small red new potatoes, unpeeled, halved or quartered
4 tablespoons (2 oz/60 g) unsalted butter, melted

Position a rack in the lower part of an oven and preheat to 425°F (220°C).
Remove the giblets, if any, from the chicken cavity and put aside for another purpose. Remove all excess fat from around the cavity opening and rinse the chicken inside and out. Dry thoroughly with paper towels. Slip 2 lemon quarters, the celery, and 2 or 3 oregano sprigs into the cavity. Sprinkle with a little salt and pepper. Close the opening with a small skewer or a sturdy wooden toothpick. To truss the chicken, use kitchen string to tie the legs together and then tie the legs and wings close to the body. Place in an ovenproof casserole or dutch oven large and deep enough to accommodate it comfortably.
Trim and cut an X in the root end of each onion, then peel the onions. Arrange the onions and potatoes around the chicken. Add 2 more lemon quarters and the remaining 2 or 3 oregano sprigs to the pot. Generously brush the chicken, onions, and potatoes with 2 tablespoons of the butter. Sprinkle to taste with salt and pepper.
Cover, place in the oven, and roast for 20 minutes. Reduce the heat to 325°F (165°C) and continue to roast, brushing with the remaining 2 tablespoons butter and then basting every 10 minutes with the pot juices, until the chicken is tender, about 1 hour longer. To check for doneness, insert an instant-read thermometer in the thickest part of the breast or thigh away from the bone; it should read 165°F (74°C) in the breast or 180°F (82°C) in the thigh.
Transfer the chicken to a warmed serving platter, cover loosely with aluminum foil and let rest for 5–10 minutes before carving. Remove the oregano

sprigs and lemon quarters from the pot and discard. Using a slotted spoon, remove the onions and potatoes from the pot and arrange around the perimeter of the platter. Garnish with the remaining 4 lemon quarters. Skim off the fat from the pot juices and discard. Reheat the juices to serving temperature and taste and adjust the seasoning. Pass the juices in a bowl at the table. [A] ∾

CHICKEN WITH FENNEL

SERVES 4

Fennel, I have found, is one of the best vegetables to cook with chicken. This is especially so when you slowly roast the bird in a pot, as the extended cooking allows the vegetable's mild anise flavor to be absorbed by the meat.

2 fennel bulbs, about 2 lb (1 kg)
   total weight
1 chicken, 3½–4 lb (1.75–2 kg),
   preferably free-range
½ yellow onion, cut into 4 wedges
2 bay leaves
salt and freshly ground pepper
2 tablespoons unsalted butter
2 tablespoons olive oil
4 carrots, peeled and cut crosswise into
   slices ¼ inch (6 mm) thick
¼ cup (2 fl oz/60 ml) dry white wine

Position a rack in the lower third of an oven and preheat to 400°F (200°C).
∾ Trim the root end and the stalks from the fennel bulbs and remove any old or bruised outer leaves. Holding the bulbs root end down and starting on the narrow side, cut vertically into slices ¼ inch (6 mm) thick. Set aside.
∾ Remove the giblets, if any, from the chicken cavity and put aside for another use. Remove the fat from around the cavity openings. Rinse the chicken inside and out and pat dry with paper towels.
∾ Place the onion wedges and 1 of the bay leaves in the cavity and sprinkle the cavity with salt and pepper to taste. Secure the cavity closed with a short metal skewer, trussing pin or sturdy toothpick. Using kitchen string, truss the chicken (see page 292). Select a heavy ovenproof stew pot that will accommodate the chicken comfortably and place it over medium-high heat. Add the butter and olive oil. When foaming, add the chicken and lightly brown on all sides, 10–12 minutes. Transfer to a plate.
∾ Pour off the fat and wipe out the pot with paper towels. Place the remaining bay leaf, fennel, and carrots in a layer on the pot bottom. Place the chicken, breast side down, on the vegetables. Sprinkle with salt and pepper and pour in the wine. Cover and roast for 30 minutes. Turn the chicken breast side up, cover, and continue to roast until tender, 20–30 minutes longer. To test for doneness, insert an instant-read thermometer in the thickest part of the breast or the thigh without touching the bone; it should register 165°F (74°C) in the breast or 180°F (82°C) in the thigh. Or pierce the thigh joint with the tip of a knife; the juices should run clear. Set aside with the cover ajar for 5–10 minutes.
∾ Transfer the chicken to a warmed deep serving platter and carve. Using a slotted spoon, transfer the vegetables to the platter, arranging them around the chicken. Using a large spoon, skim off any fat from the pot juices. Taste the juices and adjust the seasoning. Spoon over the chicken and serve. [I] ∾

BAKED CHICKEN WITH ARTICHOKES

SERVES 4

A dish you are apt to encounter in a country restaurant in Tuscany, this hearty main course would be a good choice for a weekend dinner. The combination of lemon and sage is quintessentially Mediterranean.

Fresh baby artichokes, especially available in spring, are well worth the little time their preparation takes. Choose ones that are small, solid, and compact—certain signs that they are young and tender. If fresh are unavailable, the dish will work with frozen artichokes.

If you've never used fresh sage before, you'll find it a great improvement over its dried counterpart—and nothing at all like the flavor of typical poultry-seasoning mixes. You might even try growing the herb in your garden.

For the best flavor, get a fresh free-range chicken from your poultry market.

3 lemons
10 baby artichokes, about 1 lb (500 g) total weight
1 chicken, 3–3½ lb (1.5–1.75 kg), preferably free-range, cut into serving pieces
1 tablespoon unsalted butter
1 tablespoon olive oil
8 fresh sage leaves
2 large shallots, chopped
¼ cup (2 fl oz/60 ml) dry white wine or water
salt and freshly ground pepper

Position a rack in the center of an oven and preheat to 425°F (220°C).

Squeeze the juice from 1 of the lemons into a medium-sized bowl. Trim the artichokes (see page 291). Cut in half lengthwise and immediately put into the bowl of lemon juice. Toss to coat the cut surfaces with the juice.

Fill a large saucepan half full of water and bring to a boil. Add the artichokes and lemon juice, reduce the heat to medium-high and cook, uncovered, until almost tender when pierced with a knife tip, 5–6 minutes. Drain and set aside.

Trim any excess fat from the chicken pieces. Cut each breast half crosswise into 2 pieces. Discard the chicken back, neck, and giblets (if any) or save for another use. Cut off the wing tips and discard.

In a large sauté pan over medium-high heat, melt the butter with the olive oil. When hot, add the chicken pieces, in 2 batches if necessary to avoid crowding, and brown lightly on both sides, turning once, 4–5 minutes on each side. Using tongs, transfer to a baking dish or pan, skin side down. Tuck 4 of the sage leaves under the chicken pieces.

Reduce the heat under the sauté pan to medium-low and add the shallots. Sauté gently until translucent, 2–3 minutes. Add the wine or water, stirring to dislodge any browned bits. Bring to a boil, raising the heat if necessary, and pour over the chicken. Cut another lemon in half and squeeze the juice from 1 of the lemon halves over the chicken. Season to taste with salt and pepper.

Bake for 20 minutes, basting several times. Turn the chicken over, skin side up, add the artichoke halves, and continue to bake, basting occasionally, until the chicken and artichokes are tender, 20–30 minutes longer. To test, cut into the chicken; it should be opaque throughout and the juices should run clear.

Using tongs, transfer the chicken and artichokes to a warmed serving dish. If necessary, place the pan over high heat to thicken the juices. Season to taste with lemon juice from the remaining cut half and salt and pepper. Pour the juices over the chicken. Using a zester or fine-holed shredder, shred the zest (yellow part only) from the remaining lemon directly onto the chicken pieces (see page 287). Garnish with the remaining 4 sage leaves. Serve immediately.

ROAST TARRAGON CHICKEN

SERVES 4

To roast the chicken to the ideal degree of doneness, I suggest you use an instant-read thermometer to check the temperature (see page 292). Because the thighs need to reach a higher internal temperature than the breast, the recipe calls for placing the chicken on its side for part of the roasting time. During roasting, add chicken stock to the pan as needed for basting.

Champagne grapes and tarragon sprigs make a festive garnish.

1 roasting chicken, 4–4½ lb (2–2.25 kg), preferably free-range

½ lemon

8 large fresh tarragon sprigs, plus 1 tablespoon chopped fresh tarragon

1 large green (spring) onion, trimmed and cut in half crosswise, plus 2 teaspoons chopped green (spring) onion

salt

3 tablespoons unsalted butter, at room temperature

freshly ground pepper

1 cup (8 fl oz/250 ml) chicken stock, plus additional stock as needed

2 teaspoons all-purpose (plain) flour

Position a rack in the lower part of an oven and preheat the oven to 425°F (220°C). Grease a rack, preferably V-shaped, and place in a roasting pan.

Remove the fat from around the chicken cavity openings. Rinse the chicken inside and out and pat dry with paper towels. Firmly rub the cavity of the chicken with the lemon half, squeezing out a little of the juice as you do so. Place 6 of the tarragon sprigs in the cavity together with the halved green onion and a sprinkling of salt.

Secure the cavity closed with a short metal skewer, trussing pin, or sturdy toothpick. Using kitchen string, truss the chicken (see page 292). Tuck 1 tarragon sprig between each leg and the body of the chicken.

Using 2 tablespoons of the butter, butter the outside of the chicken and sprinkle with salt and pepper. Place it on its side on the greased rack. Add the 1 cup (8 fl oz/250 ml) chicken stock to the pan and roast for 20 minutes, basting occasionally. Turn the chicken onto its opposite side and roast for another 20 minutes, adding more stock if needed. Turn the chicken breast side up, reduce the heat to 375°F (190°C), and continue to roast, basting with the pan juices every 10 minutes, until it is golden brown and tests done, 30–40 minutes longer; test for doneness as shown on page 292.

Transfer the chicken to a warmed serving platter and cover with aluminum foil. Let rest for 10–15 minutes before carving. Remove the rack and skim off the fat from the pan juices. Pour the pan juices into a glass measuring cup and add stock as needed to make 1½ cups (12 fl oz/375 ml). In a small saucepan over medium-low heat, melt the remaining 1 tablespoon butter. Add the chopped green onion and sauté for 1 minute. Add the flour and cook, stirring, until bubbly, 1–2 minutes. Raise the heat to medium and gradually add the pan juices, stirring constantly. Stir until the mixture thickens and comes to a boil, 3–4 minutes. Add the chopped tarragon and season to taste with salt and pepper.

Carve the chicken and serve with a little sauce spooned on top.

POACHED CHICKEN BREASTS WITH TARRAGON

SERVES 4

Subtly flavored, tender, low in fat and calories, and easily prepared, poached chicken should be a regular item on everyone's home menu. If you want to make this particular recipe even lighter, substitute milk for the cream.

Although fresh tarragon imparts the best flavor to the poaching liquid, dried tarragon can be used if fresh is unavailable. Be sure the dried herb has a good green color and has not been sitting on your shelf for a long time. Use 2–3 teaspoons, and crush it in the palm of your hand with your thumb to develop its flavor before adding to the liquid.

2 cups (16 fl oz/500 ml) chicken stock, or as needed

2 cups (16 fl oz/500 ml) dry white wine or water, or as needed

6 or 7 fresh tarragon sprigs, plus fresh tarragon leaves for garnish

½ yellow onion, cut in half

1 celery stalk, cut crosswise into quarters

1 teaspoon salt

4 or 5 peppercorns

2 or 3 lemon slices

4 chicken breast halves, 8–9 oz (250–280 g) each, skinned and boned (5–6 oz/155–185 g when boned) (see page 286)

2 tablespoons unsalted butter

2 tablespoons all-purpose (plain) flour

½ cup (4 fl oz/125 ml) heavy (double) cream

In a large sauté pan or wide saucepan that will accommodate the 4 chicken breasts without crowding, combine the chicken stock and wine or water. Add the tarragon sprigs, onion, celery, salt, peppercorns, and lemon slices. Bring to a boil, reduce the heat to low, cover, and simmer gently for 15–20 minutes to extract the flavor from the vegetables.

Remove all excess fat from the chicken breasts. Rinse the breasts, then place them in the stock, adding more stock or water if the breasts are not completely covered. Bring back just to a bare simmer (do not allow it to boil), cover (or cover partially), and poach gently until the breasts are tender and the flesh is opaque throughout when pierced with a sharp knife, 20–25 minutes. Alternatively, test the chicken with an instant-read thermometer; it should register 165°F (74°C) at its center. Transfer the breasts to a plate and keep warm. Strain the poaching liquid and reserve.

In a heavy saucepan (preferably nonstick) over medium-low heat, warm the butter until bubbling. Stir in the flour and cook, stirring, for a few seconds. While continuously stirring to avoid lumps, quickly add 1 cup (8 fl oz/ 250 ml) of the poaching liquid. Cook, stirring, until the mixture thickens and comes to a boil. Reduce the heat to low and cook for 1 minute longer, stirring a couple of times. Add the cream and stir until well blended. You should have a very smooth white sauce. Do not allow it to burn or stick.

Arrange the chicken breasts on individual plates and spoon the sauce evenly over the top to cover completely. Garnish with tarragon leaves. A

BAKED CHICKEN WITH HONEY-LEMON GLAZE

SERVES 4

Seek out a fresh free-range chicken. They are not hard to find, and the flavor is so much better than factory-raised birds. (The term, by the way, doesn't mean that the chickens are free to roam; they're just raised in open areas and fed well.) A good poultry market will cut up the chicken just the way you want it. Have them trim off the excess fat from the breasts and thighs, and cut the breasts into halves. Reserve the back, neck, and giblets for another use or discard.

&» For good, juicy results, take care not to overbake the chicken. Start testing for doneness toward the end of the cooking time by piercing a breast at its thickest part with a sharp knife: the flesh should look opaque and the juices should run clear.

&» I find the lighter-colored honeys taste milder than the dark and are preferable in this recipe. Fresh thyme will contribute the best flavor, too; but if you can't find it, feel free to substitute 1–1½ teaspoons of the dried herb.

1 lb (500 g) white boiling onions (about 24), 1 inch (2.5 cm) in diameter
1 lemon
¼ cup (3 oz/90 g) light honey
3 teaspoons chopped fresh thyme
1 chicken, 3½–4 lb (1.75–2 kg), preferably free-range, cut into serving pieces
3 tablespoons unsalted butter
2 tablespoons minced shallot
salt and freshly ground pepper
½ cup (3 oz/90 g) golden raisins (sultanas)

Position a rack in the middle of an oven and preheat to 375°F (190°C).

&» Trim and cut an X in the root end of each onion. Peel the onions and put

into a saucepan. Add water to cover and bring to a boil. Reduce the heat to medium-low and simmer, uncovered, for 5 minutes. Drain and set aside.

&» Using a zester or a fine-holed shredder, and holding the lemon over a bowl, shred the zest from the lemon as directed on page 287. Then squeeze the juice into another bowl. Measure 2 tablespoons of the juice and add to the zest. Stir in the honey and 2 teaspoons of the thyme. Set aside.

&» Remove any excess fat from the chicken pieces. Cut each breast in half crosswise. Be sure the drumsticks and thighs are separated. Remove the wing tips and discard. Rinse the chicken pieces and pat dry with paper towels.

&» Select a 2½- to 3-qt (2.5- to 3-l) baking pan that holds the chicken comfortably in one layer. Combine the butter and shallot in the pan; place in the oven for 1–2 minutes to melt the butter. Add the chicken pieces and turn to coat well; leave the pieces skin side

down. Sprinkle with salt and pepper and the remaining 1 teaspoon thyme. Bake uncovered, basting a couple of times with the pan juices, for 15 minutes.

&» Turn the chicken skin side up and add the onions and raisins to the pan. Baste the chicken and onions with half of the honey-lemon mixture. Return to the oven for another 10 minutes. Baste with the remaining honey-lemon mixture, reduce the heat to 350°F (180°C), and continue to bake, basting every 7–8 minutes with the pan juices, until the chicken and onions are fork-tender and golden and the pan juices have thickened to a glaze, another 25–30 minutes. If the juices have not thickened sufficiently, transfer the chicken pieces to a plate and boil the juices on the stove top until reduced to a glaze, 2–3 minutes. Return the chicken to the pan and turn several times in the glaze.

&» Arrange the chicken and onions on a serving platter. Spoon the glaze over the top and serve. A &»

"I wish the Bald Eagle had not been chosen as the representation of our country. The turkey is a much more respectable bird, and withal a true original native of America."

—Benjamin Franklin

ROAST WHOLE TURKEY BREAST WITH FENNEL AND BAY LEAVES

SERVES 6–8

Seek out a market that sell fresh turkeys. Be sure the neck and backbones have been removed, so the breast lays flat, and remember to remove the breast from the refrigerator about 45 minutes before roasting. If you can find dried fennel stalks, use 3 or 4 pieces, each about 6 inches (15 cm) long, instead of the fresh bulb.

1 small fennel bulb, preferably with stalks intact

1 whole turkey breast with breast-bone in, 6–7 lb (3–3.5 kg), at room temperature

1 yellow onion, cut into large cubes

1 lemon, cut into quarters

2 or 3 bay leaves

salt and freshly ground pepper

¼ cup (2 oz/60 g) unsalted butter, melted

¼ cup (2 fl oz/60 ml) dry white wine

¼ cup (2 fl oz/60 ml) water

5 tablespoons all-purpose (plain) flour

4 cups (32 fl oz/1 l) chicken stock, heated

🐌 Position a rack in the lower third of an oven and preheat to 350°F (180°C). Lightly oil a flat rack in a roasting pan.

🐌 Trim off any bruised stalks from the fennel, then slice. Rinse the turkey breast and pat dry with paper towels. Place the breast, skin side down, on a work surface. Place the fennel, onion, lemon, and bay leaves in the breast cavity. Sprinkle with salt and pepper. Place the oiled rack, upside side down, over the turkey cavity and, holding the rack tightly against the cavity, turn the breast over and place in the roasting pan, skin side up. Brush with some of the melted butter and cover loosely with aluminum foil.

🐌 Roast for 50 minutes, basting a couple of times with the butter. Remove the foil and reserve it. Continue to roast, basting several times with the pan juices, until is golden and cooked through, 50–60 minutes longer. To test for doneness, insert an instant-read thermometer into the thickest part of the breast away from the bone. It should read 165°–170°F (74°–76°C). Do not overcook, or the meat will be dry. Transfer the breast to a warmed platter, cover loosely with the foil, and let rest for 20 minutes before carving.

🐌 Meanwhile, make the gravy: Using a spoon, skim the fat from the pan juices and reserve 3–4 tablespoons of the fat. To the remaining pan juices, add the wine and water and place over medium heat. Bring to a boil and boil for 2–3 minutes, stirring to dislodge any browned bits from the pan bottom. Strain into a bowl and set aside. In a saucepan over medium heat, warm the reserved fat until it is bubbly. Add the flour and stir rapidly for a few seconds to cook the flour. Add the strained pan juices and 3½ cups (28 fl oz/875 ml) of the stock. Cook, while rapidly stirring, until smooth and thickened, 1–2 minutes. Add the remaining stock as needed to achieve the desired gravy consistency. Season with salt and pepper. Keep warm.

🐌 Carve the turkey breast and arrange on the platter. Pour the gravy into a warmed bowl and pass at the table.

A

BRAISED CHICKEN WITH EGGPLANT AND ORANGE

SERVES 4

The aromatic, sweet flavors of this southern Italian dish reflect the exotic influence of North Africa. It goes very well with mashed potatoes or egg noodles.

Trim off any excess fat from the chicken pieces before cooking them. When I cut up a chicken, I always make a little stock by combining the back, neck, giblets (not the liver), and wing tips in a saucepan with water to cover, a piece of yellow onion and celery, a bay leaf, 2 fresh thyme sprigs, and salt and freshly ground pepper to taste. I simmer the stock for about 45 minutes, then strain it and use it for soups and sauces.

Gaeta, Kalamata, or Spanish olives will impart a distinctive flavor to the dish. As these olives are preserved in brine, you may find them too salty, in which case you should rinse and drain them. Or soak them in water for 30 minutes, then drain.

If fresh marjoram is unavailable, substitute fresh oregano, mint, basil, or dill, or 1 teaspoon dried marjoram.

1 globe eggplant (aubergine), about
   1 lb (500 g), unpeeled
salt
1½ lb (750 g) ripe plum (Roma)
   tomatoes
1 chicken, 3½–4 lb (1.75–2 kg), preferably free-range, cut into serving pieces
3 tablespoons olive oil
2 large cloves garlic, thinly sliced (about
   2 tablespoons)
2 teaspoons chopped fresh marjoram
1 orange
freshly ground pepper
½ cup (2½ oz/75 g) European black
   olives (see note)
coarsely chopped fresh flat-leaf (Italian)
   parsley for garnish

Cut the eggplant into 1-inch (2.5-cm) cubes and place in a colander. Sprinkle with salt, tossing them to mix evenly. Place the colander over a bowl for about 1 hour to drain the bitter juices. Rinse and drain. Set aside.

Meanwhile, core and peel the tomatoes (see page 289). Cut in half crosswise and squeeze out the seeds. Chop the tomatoes coarsely; you should have about 3 cups (18 oz/ 560 g). Set aside.

Trim any excess fat from the chicken pieces. Cut each breast half crosswise into 2 pieces. Cut off the wing tips and discard, along with the back, neck, and giblets (if any), or save for another use (see note).

In a large sauté pan over medium-high heat, warm the olive oil. When hot, add the chicken pieces, in 2 batches if necessary to avoid crowding, and lightly brown on both sides, 4–5 minutes on each side. Transfer to a plate. Reduce the heat to medium-low, add the garlic, and sauté gently, stirring, until it just starts to change color, 1–2 minutes. Add the tomatoes and marjoram and cook, stirring occasionally, for 2–3 minutes. Return the chicken to the pan.

Using a zester or fine-holed shredder, shred the zest (orange part only) from the orange directly onto the chicken (see page 287). Then squeeze enough juice to measure ½ cup (4 fl oz/ 125 ml). Pour over the chicken and season with salt and pepper. Arrange the eggplant cubes and the olives over the chicken.

Cover and simmer over low heat for 30 minutes. Using tongs, rearrange the chicken to mix in the eggplant and olives. Cover partially and simmer until tender, about 30 minutes longer. To test, cut into the chicken; it should be opaque throughout and the juices should run clear. Adjust the seasoning.

To serve, arrange the chicken pieces on a warmed platter and spoon the tomato mixture over the top. Garnish with chopped parsley and serve at once.

"*A Chicken is just a barnyard fowl, and it may be rightly called the best of all birds covered by the name of Poultry.*"

—André Simon

Chicken and Sweet Potato

SERVES 4

This is a dish you are apt to find in a small country hotel in the northwestern province of Normandy. They would probably use the region's familiar apple brandy, calvados, rather than the apple juice I call for in this recipe. If you like, you can add 1 or 2 tablespoons calvados to the dish. Look for apple juice labeled "pure"; avoid those made from apple concentrate.

Do not use dried sage. The fresh leaves have a much better flavor and are worth seeking out in a well-stocked market.

1 chicken, 3½–4 lb (1.75–2 kg), cut into
 serving pieces
3 tablespoons unsalted butter
2 tablespoons vegetable oil
2 or 3 sweet potatoes, 1½–2 lb
 (750 g–1 kg) total weight, peeled
 and cut crosswise into slices
 ½ inch (12 mm) thick
8–10 shallots, cut crosswise into slices
 ⅛ inch (3 mm) thick
½ cup (4 fl oz/125 ml) pure apple juice,
 plus additional juice as needed
½ cup (4 fl oz/125 ml) chicken stock,
 plus additional stock as needed
6–8 fresh sage leaves, plus 2 or 3 fresh
 sage sprigs for garnish
salt and freshly ground pepper
1 tablespoon all-purpose (plain) flour
¼ cup (2 fl oz/60 ml) heavy
 (double) cream

Position a rack in the middle of an oven and preheat to 375°F (190°C). Butter a large baking dish or pan that will hold the chicken and potatoes in a single layer.

Cut the 2 chicken breast halves in half crosswise. Cut the thighs and legs apart. Remove the wing tips and save along with the back for another use. You should have 10 pieces. Remove any fat from them. Rinse and pat dry with paper towels.

In a sauté pan over medium-high heat, melt 2 tablespoons of the butter with the oil. When foaming, add half of the chicken and quickly sear until golden, 4–5 minutes on each side. Transfer to the prepared dish. Repeat with the remaining chicken. Arrange the potato slices among the meat.

Reduce the heat to medium-low and add the shallots. Sauté until translucent, 2–3 minutes. Add half each of the apple juice and stock and stir, scraping up any browned bits. Bring to a boil and pour over the chicken and potatoes. Tuck the 6–8 sage leaves around the chicken. Sprinkle with salt and pepper.

Bake until the potatoes and chicken are tender, 45–50 minutes. The meat should be opaque throughout. Using a slotted spoon, transfer the chicken and potatoes to a warmed serving dish and cover to keep warm. Using a large spoon, skim off the fat from the juices and pour the juices into a pitcher.

In a small saucepan over medium-low heat, melt the remaining 1 tablespoon butter. Add the flour and cook, stirring, until bubbly, 1–2 minutes. Raise the heat to medium. Stirring constantly, gradually add the remaining ¼ cup (2 fl oz/60 ml) each apple juice and stock and the pan juices. Stir until the mixture thickens and comes to a boil, 3–4 minutes. Add the cream and cook for a few seconds. Thin, if desired, with apple juice or stock; adjust the seasoning. Pour the sauce over the chicken and potatoes. Garnish with sage sprigs and serve. F

Trim any fat from the chicken breasts. Rinse and pat dry with paper towels. One at a time, place each chicken breast between 2 sheets of waxed paper or plastic wrap and, using a rolling pin, roll across the thickest part of the breast to flatten to an even thickness of about ½ inch (12 mm).

❧ In a large, preferably nonstick, sauté pan or frying pan over medium-high heat, melt the butter with the oil. When foaming, add the chicken breasts and sprinkle with salt and pepper to taste. Sauté, adjusting the heat as needed to keep the breasts from releasing their juices, until golden and just tender, about 5 minutes on each side. To test for doneness, insert the tip of a sharp knife into the center of a breast; the juices should run clear and the meat should no longer be pink at the center. Transfer to a warmed plate and keep warm.

❧ Pour off any excess fat from the pan and return the pan to medium-low heat. Add the shallots and sauté, stirring, until translucent, 1–2 minutes. Add the mustard and cream, raise the heat to medium, and stir with a wooden spoon, scraping up any browned bits stuck to the pan bottom. Cook, stirring, until thickened and blended, 2–3 minutes. Taste and adjust the seasoning.

❧ Return the chicken breasts to the pan and turn the breasts over several times to coat them well with the sauce and to heat them through. Transfer to a warmed platter or individual plates and spoon the sauce over the breasts. Sprinkle with chopped parsley and serve at once.

CHICKEN BREASTS WITH MUSTARD SAUCE

SERVES 4

I recommend serving this simple chicken sauté with freshly cooked asparagus or peas. To begin the meal, serve Asparagus with Orange Hollandaise Sauce (page 29) or the Mango and Melon Salad (page 83) and perhaps finish with a fruit tart.

❧ *The key to this recipe's success comes in flattening the chicken breasts to an even thickness before cooking them. They will cook evenly and stay perfectly moist throughout.*

4 chicken breast halves, 8–9 oz (250–280 g) each, skinned and boned (5–6 oz/155–185 g when boned)
1 tablespoon unsalted butter
1 tablespoon vegetable oil
salt and freshly ground pepper
3 tablespoons chopped shallots (2 or 3 shallots)
2 tablespoons Dijon mustard
½ cup (4 fl oz/125 ml) heavy (double) cream
chopped fresh parsley

BOILED CHICKEN AND HAM

SERVES 4–6

Italy's bollito misto—*a mixed boiled dinner that might include chicken, ham, sausages, and other meats—is one of the country's most satisfying rustic dishes. This short version offers all the satisfaction with considerably less effort.*

⁂ *The chunk of ham contributes a delicious accent to the chicken; the two meats go together particularly well. Cook them at a bare simmer (with just a few bubbles rising to the surface) until just tender; any faster and longer and they will dry out. Technically, the recipe should be called "poached" rather than "boiled."*

⁂ *Be sure to seek out a free-range chicken for this dish. They are available at most poultry shops and better food stores.*

⁂ *I like to serve the meat in a deep dish with some of the cooking stock, accompanied by steamed vegetables.*

3 cups (24 fl oz/750 ml) chicken stock
2 cups (16 fl oz/500 ml) dry white wine
1 chicken, 3½–4 lb (1.75–2 kg),
    preferably free-range
1 yellow onion, quartered
1 carrot, peeled and cut into 2-inch
    (5-cm) lengths
1 celery stalk, cut into 2-inch
    (5-cm) lengths
1 or 2 cloves garlic
1 piece boneless lean smoked ham,
    1–1½ lb (500–750 g), about 2½ inches
    (6 cm) thick (or 1½–2 lb/750 g–1 kg
    with bone), trimmed of fat
boiling water, as needed
1 bay leaf

2 or 3 fresh marjoram sprigs or
    1 teaspoon dried marjoram
3 or 4 whole peppercorns
2 tablespoons unsalted butter
2 tablespoons all-purpose (plain) flour
½ cup (4 fl oz/125 ml) heavy (double)
    cream, or as needed
1–2 teaspoons fresh lemon juice
salt and freshly ground pepper

Combine the stock and wine in a saucepan and heat almost to a boil. Remove any fat from the chicken cavity, rinse inside and out, and pat dry. Place the onion, carrot, celery, and garlic in the cavity and secure closed with a small skewer. Truss the chicken: using kitchen string, tie the legs and wings close to the body (see page 292).

⁂ In a deep pot just large enough to accommodate them, place the chicken, breast side up, and the ham. Add the stock mixture and enough of the boiling water just to cover the chicken. Place the bay leaf, marjoram, and peppercorns on a small square of cheesecloth (muslin). Tie the edges together with kitchen string and add to the pot. Bring to a boil, skimming off any froth. Reduce the heat to low, cover tightly, and barely simmer, skimming

occasionally, until the chicken is tender, about 1 hour. To test, cut into the thigh or breast; it should be opaque throughout and the juices should run clear. Remove from the heat, skim off any fat from the liquid, and set aside, partially covered.

⁂ In a small saucepan over medium heat, melt the butter. Add the flour and stir and cook until the mixture begins to color, 1–2 minutes. Slowly whisk in 1 cup (8 fl oz/250 ml) of the liquid from the chicken pot. Whisk until thickened and smooth, about 2 minutes. Whisk in the ½ cup (4 fl oz/125 ml) cream and 1 teaspoon of the lemon juice, adding more cream or stock if needed to thin slightly. Season to taste with salt, pepper, and more lemon juice, if necessary.

⁂ To serve, transfer the chicken and ham to a warmed platter. Carve the chicken and slice the ham. Serve the lemon sauce alongside. ⁂

"It is not really an exaggeration
to say that peace and happiness begin,
geographically, where garlic is
used in cooking."

−X. Marcel Boulestin

CHICKEN WITH BASIL AIOLI

SERVES 4

Basil aioli is an herbed variation on the French garlic mayonnaise known as aioli, made here with fresh basil and less garlic. It is a lovely accompaniment to the mild, tender poultry.

Although you might not think so at first, it is just as important to guard against overcooking a chicken when poaching as when roasting or sautéing it. Be careful not to let the liquid boil; maintain a very gentle simmer with only a few bubbles rising to the surface. As the poaching progresses, I usually find it necessary to reduce the heat slightly.

Save the cooking stock for another meal. Serve it as a clear soup, or add vegetables and chicken pieces for a more hearty soup. The stock can be refrigerated for several days.

1 chicken, 3½–4 lb (1.75–2 kg), preferably free-range
1 small yellow onion, quartered
1 celery stalk, cut into 2-inch (5-cm) lengths
3 fresh thyme sprigs
3 fresh parsley sprigs, plus chopped parsley for garnish
1 bay leaf
1 large lemon wedge
8 cups (64 fl oz/2 l) chicken stock, heated almost to boiling
basil aioli (recipe on page 282)
1½ lb (750 g) leeks (about 4 leeks), trimmed and cleaned (see page 291)
6 carrots, peeled, cut in half crosswise and top section cut in half lengthwise
salt and freshly ground pepper

Remove the neck and giblets, if any, from the chicken cavity; set aside. Remove the fat from around the cavity openings. Rinse inside and out and pat dry with paper towels. Place the onion, celery, thyme and parsley sprigs, bay leaf, and lemon wedge in the cavity. Close the cavity with a short metal skewer, trussing pin, or sturdy toothpick. Using kitchen string, truss the chicken (see page 292). Place breast side up in a deep pot in which it just fits. Add the neck and giblets as well, if included. Pour in the stock. If the liquid does not reach three-fourths of the way up the sides of the chicken, add hot water as needed. Place over high heat and bring just under a boil. Using a skimmer, remove any scum as it rises to the surface. Reduce the heat to medium-low or low, cover, and cook at a bare simmer for 30 minutes. Meanwhile, make the basil aioli.

Turn the chicken breast side down and add the leeks, carrots, and salt and pepper to taste. Continue to simmer until tender, another 35–50 minutes. To test for doneness, insert an instant-read thermometer in the thickest part of the thigh without touching the bone; it should register 180°F (82°C). Or turn breast side up and test the breast; it should register 165°F (74°C). Alternatively, pierce the thigh joint with a knife tip; the juices should run clear.

Transfer the chicken to a warmed platter and cover loosely with aluminum foil. Let rest for 10 minutes. Continue to cook the vegetables until tender, if necessary. Then, using a slotted spoon, transfer the vegetables to the platter.

Carve the chicken and serve on warmed plates with the vegetables. Make sure that the chicken and vegetables are thoroughly moistened with the cooking liquid. Garnish with chopped parsley. Spoon the aioli over the chicken or pass it in a bowl.

CHICKEN WITH COUSCOUS

SERVES 4

A holdover from France's colonial years in North Africa, couscous rivals rice in popularity. I find that this tiny form of pasta makes a great accompaniment to stews, braises, and other dishes that have an abundance of sauce.

❧ *Quick-cooking varieties of packaged couscous produce satisfactory results and are far more convenient to cook than rice. Take care to read the cooking instructions on the package, as products can vary from one manufacturer to another.*

❧ *This recipe is easy to put together, and much of the preparation can be done in advance. For a weekend dinner, accompany it with a salad and a fruit dessert.*

2 red bell peppers (capsicums)
1 bunch leeks, 1–1½ lb (500–750 g)
1 chicken, 3½–4 lb (1.75–2 kg), preferably free-range, cut into serving pieces
3 tablespoons unsalted butter
2 tablespoons olive oil
2 large cloves garlic, thinly sliced
½ cup (4 fl oz/125 ml) chicken stock, plus additional stock as needed
1 bay leaf
3 fresh thyme sprigs
salt and freshly ground pepper
1 tablespoon all-purpose (plain) flour
couscous (recipe on page 283)
chopped fresh parsley

Roast and peel the peppers (see page 290). Cut into long strips ¼ inch (6 mm) wide. Trim and rinse the leeks, leaving 1 inch (2.5 cm) of the greens (see page 291). Slice crosswise ½ inch (12 mm) thick. Set aside.

❧ Cut the 2 chicken breast halves in half crosswise. Cut the thighs and legs apart. Remove the wing tips and save along with the back for another use. You should have 10 pieces. Remove any fat. Rinse and pat dry with paper towels.

❧ In a dutch oven over medium-high heat, melt 2 tablespoons of the butter with the olive oil. Add half of the chicken and brown lightly, 4–5 minutes on each side. Transfer to a plate. Repeat with the remaining chicken.

❧ Pour off most of the fat from the pot and place over low heat. Add the garlic and sauté until it begins to change color, 30–40 seconds. Add the leeks and sauté until they begin to wilt, 3–4 minutes. Add the ½ cup (4 fl oz/125 ml) stock and stir, scraping up any browned bits. Return the chicken pieces to the pot, in a single layer, over the leeks. Tuck the bay leaf and thyme sprigs under the chicken. Cover and barely simmer for 40 minutes. Add the pepper strips and salt and pepper to taste and simmer until the chicken is opaque throughout when pierced with a knife, another 30–45 minutes.

❧ Transfer the chicken and leeks to a plate. Skim off the fat from the pot juices. Transfer the juices to a measuring pitcher and add chicken stock to make 1½ cups (12 fl oz/375 ml). Add the remaining 1 tablespoon butter to the pot and return to medium heat. When foaming, add the flour and cook, stirring, until bubbly, 2–3 minutes. Gradually add the pot juices, stirring constantly until thickened and boiling, 3–4 minutes. Return the chicken and leeks to the pot; keep warm.

❧ Make the couscous and spoon onto a warmed platter. Surround with the chicken and leeks, sprinkle with chopped parsley and serve. F ❧

FRESH CHICKEN SAUSAGES WITH SWEET ONIONS AND GRAPES

SERVES 4

Most good food stores now offer a selection of delicious fresh chicken and turkey sausages, many of which are the creations of talented young chefs who have launched their own small sausage businesses. The sausages are generally low in fat and calories and full of flavor, not to mention quick and easy to prepare. If you have not tried these quality products, I recommend them highly.

≫ In this recipe, the tartness and lightness of the grapes nicely complements the sausages and adds a touch of elegance that makes the dish suitable for serving at a small dinner party. Do not cook the grapes too long or they will begin to break down; they should just color slightly.

≫ Accompany this dish with Spoon Corn Bread (recipe on page 241), a tossed green salad, and fruit for dessert.

2 tablespoons extra-virgin olive oil or vegetable oil

8 fresh chicken sausages such as chicken with apple, herbs, curry, or lemon, about 2 lb (1 kg)

¼ cup (2 fl oz/60 ml) dry white wine or apple juice

1 sweet red (Spanish) onion or other sweet onion, cut into chunks

2 cups (12 oz/375 g) ripe seedless white grapes

In a large sauté pan or frying pan over medium-high heat, warm the oil. When hot, add the sausages in a single layer, being careful not to crowd them. Cover partially (to help control splatter) and fry until nicely browned, 6–8 minutes on each side. Transfer to a warmed serving plate and keep warm.

≫ Drain off the fat from the pan and add the wine or apple juice. Heat to bubbling over medium-high heat. Add the onion and sauté, stirring, for 1–2 minutes. Add the grapes and sauté, stirring often or shaking the pan to keep the grapes moving so they cook evenly, until they have colored a little, the onion has softened, and the liquid has evaporated, another 5–7 minutes.

≫ Spoon the onion chunks and grapes over the sausages. Serve at once. A ≫

CURRIED CHICKEN BREASTS WITH BASMATI RICE

SERVES 4

Many people think of a curry sauce as a great way to mask leftovers. But I find that curried chicken tastes so much better when made with freshly sautéed chicken that the dish merits the extra effort.

A number of small details will make a big difference in the quality of your curry. Start with a good, fresh curry powder, purchased in a small container from a food store that has a regular turnover in its stock; curry powder's flavor dissipates quickly, so it won't keep long on your shelf. Also, use basmati rice, available in good food stores, specialty shops, and ethnic markets; it has a delicately perfumed flavor and fluffy texture. If you can't find basmati, substitute a medium-grain white rice.

Finally, I find that curry gains a wonderful richness from coconut milk. This is not the watery liquid found inside coconuts, but rather a commercial product made by combining chopped coconut flesh with hot water and then straining the resulting thick, milky liquid through cheesecloth (muslin). You can find canned coconut milk in specialty-food shops, Asian markets, and well-stocked food stores.

4 chicken breast halves, 8–9 oz
   (250–280 g) each, skinned and boned
   (5–6 oz/155–185 g when boned)
   (see page 286)
2 tablespoons plus 1 teaspoon fresh
   lime juice, or as needed
1¾ cups (14 fl oz/430 ml) water
½ teaspoon salt, plus salt to taste
1 cup (7 oz/220 g) basmati rice, rinsed
   and drained
2 tablespoons unsalted butter
2 tablespoons extra-virgin olive oil
freshly ground pepper

1 yellow onion, diced
   (1 cup/4 oz/125 g)
2–3 tablespoons curry powder, to taste
½ cup (4 fl oz/125 ml) chicken stock
1 cup (8 fl oz/250 ml) coconut milk
   or heavy (double) cream
1 tablespoon chopped fresh parsley

Remove any excess fat from the chicken breasts. Rinse and pat dry with paper towels. Slice crosswise into strips 1 inch (2.5 cm) wide. Place in a bowl, add the 2 tablespoons lime juice, and toss to coat. Set aside for about 15 minutes.

In a saucepan (preferably nonstick), combine the water and the ½ teaspoon salt. Bring to a rapid boil and gradually add the rice. Reduce the heat to low, cover and barely simmer just until tender and the water is absorbed, 15–20 minutes. Remove from the heat and let stand, covered, for 5 minutes. Uncover, fluff with a fork, and re-cover until serving.

Dry the chicken pieces with paper towels. In a large sauté pan or frying pan (preferably nonstick) over medium-high heat, warm 1 tablespoon each of the butter and olive oil. When hot, add half of the chicken, sprinkle with salt and pepper, and sauté until golden, 2–3 minutes on each side. Transfer to a warm plate. Add the remaining 1 tablespoon each butter and oil to the pan and cook the remaining chicken. Transfer to the plate.

Pour off most of the fat and place the pan over low heat. Add the onion and sauté for 1 minute. Stir in the curry powder and sauté for 2 minutes longer. Stir in the chicken stock, scraping up any browned bits stuck to the bottom; cover and simmer over low heat for 5–6 minutes. Stir in the coconut milk or cream and continue to cook, uncovered, stirring occasionally, until slightly thickened, 1–2 minutes. Stir in the remaining 1 teaspoon lime juice and salt and pepper to taste. Return the chicken to the pan, stir to coat well, and heat through. Adjust the seasoning with more lime juice or salt and pepper.

Toss the rice with the parsley. Arrange the rice in a ring around the edge of a warmed platter. Spoon the chicken and sauce into the center and serve. A

*M*EAT

When most people think of robust dining, their thoughts turn to main courses of meat. Whether the featured ingredient is beef, veal, lamb, or pork, the dish is guaranteed to be hearty.

Regardless of their country of origin, the recipes that follow offer excellent flavor and texture. A French Roast Fillet of Beef with Madeira Sauce (page 158) and an American Braised Brisket of Beef with Port Wine (page 164) yield meals that are both elegant and hearty. Sautéed Pork Tenderloin with Gingered Apples (page 161), a recipe straight out of America's Corn Belt, seems a close cousin to Italian Braised Pork Loin with Sage (page 154). French Country Veal Stew (page 170), Italian Lamb Stew with Polenta (page 169), and American Lamb Stew with Raisins (page 172) promise equal servings of comfort on a chilly winter evening.

VEAL SCALOPPINE WITH MARSALA

SERVES 4

Thin scallops of veal are one of the most popular and typical main courses of Italy—and one of the best, especially when accented with fresh sage. The only veal that works well for this purpose comes from a truly young animal; otherwise, the meat is likely to be tough. Seek out a good butcher who stocks the best-quality veal and who knows how to prepare scallops the right way: each scallop should be no more than 4–6 inches (10–15 cm) square, weighing 1½–2 ounces (45–60 g) and pounded to a thickness of ¼ inch (6 mm) or less.

Cooking the scaloppine successfully depends upon having hot oil in a large pan and searing the meat quickly. Longer cooking will toughen the veal. The sauce is then prepared very quickly, so the veal has no time to cool.

This timing requires a little practice, but once it is achieved you will have mastered a quick and elegant dish.

12–16 thin veal scallops, 1½–2 oz (45–60 g) each
½ cup (2½ oz/75 g) all-purpose (plain) flour
3–4 tablespoons vegetable oil
12 fresh sage leaves, plus extra for garnish
⅓ cup (3 fl oz/80 ml) dry Marsala, preferably Italian
2 tablespoons unsalted butter
salt and freshly ground pepper
lemon slices for garnish

Trim off any excess fat or any thin white skin remaining on the edges of the veal scallops. Using a sharp knife, make 3 or 4 small cuts around the edge of each scallop, to help keep them flat while cooking. Place each scallop between 2 sheets of waxed paper or plastic wrap and, using a meat pounder or the side of a heavy cleaver blade, pound to flatten to an even thickness of ⅛–¼ inch (3–6 mm). (Or ask your butcher to do this step.) Pat dry with paper towels.

Spread out the flour on a large plate. Dip half of the veal scallops in the flour, coating them evenly and shaking off any excess. In a large sauté pan or frying pan over high heat, warm 3 tablespoons of the oil. When hot but not smoking, add the flour-coated slices to the pan, along with half of the sage leaves. Sear the meat quickly, turning once, until lightly browned, 40–50 seconds on each side. Transfer the veal to a warmed plate, along with the sage leaves. Repeat with the remaining veal scallops and sage leaves, adding more oil to the pan if necessary.

Pour off the oil in the pan. Place the pan over high heat and add the Marsala. Cook, stirring to dislodge any browned bits, until reduced and thickened, 2–3 minutes. Add the butter and stir until blended. Season to taste with salt and pepper.

Return the meat, with any juices, and the sage leaves to the pan and turn the meat over twice to coat well with the sauce. Transfer the veal and sage leaves to a warmed serving platter or warmed individual plates and spoon the sauce on top. Garnish with fresh sage leaves and lemon slices. Serve immediately.

RACK OF LAMB WITH FLAGEOLET BEANS

SERVES 4

Sweet-tasting lamb and earthy flageolet beans seem a perfect pairing, and the combination is even more appealing for the ease with which it is prepared. Instead of the usual leg of lamb, I have substituted racks of lamb, which make the dish easier still. All you need to complete the meal is a salad and a simple dessert.

The best choice of meat is the center section of the rack, which usually consists of six chops. You will need two such racks.

Dried flageolet beans may be found in specialty-food shops and in the international section of some large food stores. Now being grown in America, they are becoming more widely available. Be sure to look for small, young beans without shriveled skins. Those from a new harvest cook quickly, while older beans take longer to cook. The beans can be prepared in advance.

1 cup (7 oz/220 g) dried flageolet beans
½ yellow onion, diced
 (½ cup/2 oz/60 g)
1 carrot, peeled and diced
 (½ cup/2½ oz/75 g)
salt
2 fresh parsley sprigs
2 fresh thyme sprigs
1 bay leaf
1 celery stalk, cut into 2-inch
 (5-cm) lengths
2 racks of lamb, 6 ribs each, trimmed
 of any fat
1 clove garlic, cut in half
2 tablespoons chopped fresh rosemary
freshly ground pepper
2 tablespoons chopped fresh mint

Sort through the beans, discarding any damaged beans or small stones. Rinse and drain. Place in a saucepan and add water to cover by 2 inches (5 cm). Bring to a boil, remove from the heat, cover and let soak for 1 hour.

Drain, rinse, and return the beans to the pan with water to cover by 1 inch (2.5 cm). Add the onion, carrot, and 1 teaspoon salt. Gather the parsley and thyme sprigs and bay leaf together, enclose inside the celery pieces and tie securely with kitchen string to form a bouquet garni. Add to the pan, pushing it down into the beans. Bring to a boil, reduce the heat to medium-low, cover partially, and simmer until the beans are tender, 30–45 minutes. Remove and discard the bouquet garni and set the pan aside.

Position an oven rack in the center of an oven and preheat to 450°F (230°C). Rub the lamb racks with the garlic halves and coat with the rosemary. Sprinkle with salt and pepper. Place on a flat baking rack, fat side down, in a roasting pan. Roast for 15 minutes. Turn fat side up, reduce the heat to 400°F (200°C) and roast until the meat springs back to the touch, 20–30 minutes. To test, insert an instant-read thermometer into the thickest part of the meat without touching the bone; it should register 125°F (52°C) and be medium pink inside.

Meanwhile, pour off all but about ¼ cup (2 fl oz/60 ml) liquid from the beans. Return the pan to medium heat; add the mint and salt and pepper to taste. Mix gently, then simmer for a few minutes to blend the flavor. Adjust the seasoning.

Transfer the lamb to a warmed platter and cut into chops. Divide the beans among 4 warmed plates and place 3 chops on each plate. Spoon the juices from the platter over the beans. Serve at once. F

"Everything in France is a pretext for a good dinner."
—Jean Anouilh

151

VEAL PAPRIKA

SERVES 4

This simple stew relies on the complementary flavors of tomatoes, onions, green bell peppers (capsicums), and paprika to enrobe cubes of delicate veal. No wonder veal paprika remains a classic. Serve it with egg noodles or rice.

The sweet pepper known as paprika was one of the vegetables transported by Columbus from the New World to Spain. It flourished there and eventually made its way to Hungary, where it became a cornerstone of the cuisine. Early Eastern European settlers in North America brought the pepper back to its home hemisphere, where paprika has become a favorite spice. I prefer the Hungarian Rose brand of sweet paprika; whatever paprika you use, however, must be absolutely fresh, since the flavor of the powdered spice diminishes quickly. If you like paprika, don't be timid with its use.

Be sure to sear the veal without browning it. The ultimate success of the dish lies in the slow cooking and natural thickening of its sauce, so care should be taken that the heat stays low and that you stir regularly to prevent sticking or burning.

1 lb (500 g) ripe plum (Roma) tomatoes

2 lb (1 kg) boneless veal shoulder, cut into 1-inch (2.5-cm) cubes

2 tablespoons extra-virgin olive oil or vegetable oil, or as needed

1 yellow onion, diced (1 cup/4 oz/125 g)

1 green bell pepper (capsicum), seeded, deribbed, and diced (1 cup/5 oz/155 g)

1–2 tablespoons paprika, depending on your taste

½ teaspoon salt, or to taste

freshly ground pepper (optional)

chopped fresh parsley

Core and peel the tomatoes (see page 289): Bring a saucepan three-fourths full of water to a boil. Core the tomatoes and then cut an X in the opposite end. Put them in the boiling water for 20–30 seconds to loosen the skins. Using a slotted spoon, transfer the tomatoes to a bowl of cold water. Using your fingers or a paring knife, immediately remove the skins. Cut in half crosswise and carefully squeeze out the seeds. Chop coarsely; you should have 2–2½ cups (12–15 oz/375–470 g). Set aside.

Trim any excess fat from the veal cubes. In a large, heavy sauté pan or saucepan (preferably nonstick) over medium heat, warm the 2 tablespoons oil. When hot, add the veal pieces in batches and sauté gently until lightly seared on all sides, 3–4 minutes; do not allow to brown. Transfer to a plate and set aside.

Add the onion to the same pan over medium-low heat, adding more oil if needed to prevent scorching, and sauté gently, stirring, until translucent, about 3 minutes. Add the tomatoes, bell pepper, paprika, and salt and cook, stirring occasionally, for another few minutes.

Return the veal to the pan and let cook, uncovered, over medium-low heat until the veal is tender and the sauce thickens, 50–60 minutes or longer. Stir gently every now and again to prevent sticking; add a little water, if needed, to keep the meat from burning.

Season to taste with pepper, if desired, then taste and adjust the seasoning. Serve garnished with parsley.

SAUSAGE WITH SAUTÉED CABBAGE

SERVES 4

Although this dish resembles France's famous choucroute garnie, *it is made with fresh cabbage instead of sauerkraut, a variation I have enjoyed there as well.* Go to a good butcher for a slice of ham cut from a properly smoked whole ham, which is usually only partially cooked. Seek out some of the excellent fresh sausages that are being made by creative food entrepreneurs and sold in specialty-food shops and some large food markets.

1 head green cabbage, about 2 lb (1 kg), damaged leaves removed

1 slice smoked ham, about 1 lb (500 g) and ¼ inch (6 mm) thick

¼ lb (125 g) thickly sliced lean smoked bacon, cut into pieces ½ inch (12 mm) wide

1 yellow onion, diced (1 cup/4 oz/125 g)

1 tablespoon minced garlic (2 or 3 cloves)

2 carrots, peeled and thinly sliced

8–10 juniper berries, crushed with the flat side of a knife blade

1 bay leaf

½ cup (4 fl oz/125 ml) chicken stock

2 teaspoons white wine vinegar

salt and freshly ground pepper

1 tablespoon olive oil or vegetable oil

4–6 well-seasoned fresh pork, chicken, or veal sausages, 1–1½ lb (500–750 g) total weight

½ cup (3 oz/90 g) seedless sweet red grapes

Using a sharp knife, cut the cabbage in half through the core. Slice each half into ½-inch (12-mm) wedges. Set aside.

Trim the ham slice of any fat and cut into 4 pieces. Place in a frying pan and add water to cover, bring to a boil over medium-high heat, and cook for 1 minute. Remove from the heat and set aside to reduce the saltiness of the ham, 10–15 minutes. Drain, pat dry with paper towels, and set aside.

In a large sauté pan or deep frying pan over medium heat, sauté the bacon, stirring, until golden, beginning to crisp, and the fat has been rendered, 3–4 minutes. Drain off most of the fat and discard, leaving the bacon in the pan.

Return the pan to medium-low heat and add the onion and garlic. Sauté, stirring, until the onion is translucent, 6–7 minutes. Add the carrots, juniper berries, and bay leaf and sauté until the carrots begin to soften, 4–5 minutes. Add the stock, vinegar, and cabbage. Season to taste with salt and pepper, cover, and simmer until the cabbage is tender, 15–20 minutes; turn the cabbage and carrots once or twice during cooking. Taste and adjust the seasoning.

Meanwhile, in another frying pan over medium heat, warm the oil. When hot but not smoking, add the sausages, cover, and cook, turning once, for 5 minutes. Add the ham, cover partially, and continue to cook, turning, for 10 minutes. Add the grapes and cook until the sausages and ham are cooked through and browned, another 10 minutes. Place the cabbage on a warmed platter. Arrange the meats and grapes on top of the cabbage. Serve at once.

BRAISED PORK LOIN WITH SAGE

SERVES 4

Some of the best pork dishes I've ever eaten have been in Italy, and pork loin flavored with fresh sage is among the most memorable. Today, pork is the product of new diets and more selective breeding than in the past, so the meat can be very low in fat, especially if you trim off any excess fat before cooking.

The pork loin may be a single piece of meat about 9 inches (23 cm) long, or it can be two shorter pieces tied together by the butcher. Joined with the fresh sage and garlic, balsamic vinegar contributes a slightly tart-sweet flavor that complements the meat. Any leftover pork can be thinly sliced and served cold.

2½–3 lb (1.25–1.5 kg) boneless center-cut pork loin (see note)

8 fresh sage leaves, plus sage leaves and sage blossoms for garnish (optional)

salt and freshly ground pepper

3 tablespoons unsalted butter

1 tablespoon olive oil

2 cloves garlic, left whole

1 bay leaf

½ cup (4 fl oz/125 ml) dry white wine, or as needed

2 tablespoons balsamic vinegar

2 tablespoons all-purpose (plain) flour

Trim any excess fat from the pork loin. If the loin has not been tied by the butcher, tie it with kitchen string in 3 or 4 places. Place 6 of the sage leaves under the string, positioning 3 leaves evenly spaced on top and 3 on the bottom of the meat. Rub the meat all over with salt and pepper.

Select a deep, heavy pot in which the pork loin will just fit comfortably. Place it over medium-high heat and add 2 tablespoons of the butter and the olive oil. When hot, add the pork loin and sear quickly to brown lightly on all sides, 5–6 minutes total. Reduce the heat to medium-low, add the garlic, and sauté gently, stirring, until it just begins to change color, 1–2 minutes. Transfer the meat and garlic cloves to a plate. Pour off the fat from the pot.

Return the meat to the pot. Tuck the garlic cloves under the meat, along with the bay leaf. Add the ½ cup (4 fl oz/125 ml) wine, the balsamic vinegar, and the remaining 2 sage leaves. Cover tightly, reduce the heat to low, and simmer gently until tender when pierced with a fork, 1½–2 hours; turn the roast over halfway through cooking. Add more wine, if needed, to maintain the level of liquid in the pot.

Transfer the meat to a serving platter and cover with aluminum foil to keep warm. Remove the garlic cloves, bay leaf, and sage from the pan juices and discard. Using a spoon, skim off any fat from the surface of the pan juices. Reserve the juices. You should have at least 1 cup (8 fl oz/250 ml); if you have less, add water as needed.

To make the sauce, in a small saucepan over medium heat, melt the remaining 1 tablespoon butter. Add the flour and cook, stirring, for 1–2 minutes. Add the reserved pan juices, whisking constantly. Continue to whisk until thickened and smooth, 2–3 minutes. If the sauce is too thick, add water to achieve the desired consistency. Season with salt and pepper.

To serve, slice the meat and arrange it on the platter. Spoon the sauce over the slices and garnish with sage leaves and sage blossoms, if desired.

"In agricultural areas where communications are spasmodic, the pig figures as the winter saviour of mankind."

—Patience Gray

BAKED PEPPERS STUFFED WITH ITALIAN SAUSAGE

SERVES 4

Splendidly rustic, this dish can be assembled several hours ahead of time, refrigerated, and then baked just before serving.

◑ *Some excellent fresh sausages are being made today by chefs who have rediscovered the art of sausage making. Flavorful chicken or turkey sausages, for example, would be delectable in this colorful dish.*

◑ *Serve the stuffed peppers for supper or a weekend lunch, accompanied by fried polenta (see page 226).*

4 red bell peppers (capsicums), about
   1 lb (500 g) total weight
4 ripe plum (Roma) tomatoes
2 tablespoons unsalted butter or
   olive oil
1 small yellow onion, diced (about
   ½ cup/2 oz/60 g)
1 celery stalk, trimmed and diced
4 fresh mild Italian sausages, about 1 lb
   (500 g) total weight, casings removed
   and meat crumbled into small chunks
8 European black olives, such as
   Gaeta, Kalamata, or Spanish, pitted
   and chopped
salt and freshly ground pepper
1 cup (2 oz/60 g) fresh bread crumbs
1 cup (8 fl oz/250 ml) hot tap water

Position a rack in the center of an oven and preheat to 375°F (190°C).

◑ Carefully cut each bell pepper in half lengthwise. Remove the stem, being careful not to cut into the flesh. Remove the seeds and ribs. Fill a large saucepan three-fourths full of water and bring to a boil over medium-high heat. Add the pepper halves, bring the water back to a boil and parboil for 4–5 minutes. Using a slotted spoon, transfer the pepper halves to a colander to drain. Keep the water at a boil to peel the tomatoes.

◑ Core and peel the tomatoes (see page 289). Cut in half crosswise and carefully squeeze out the seeds. Chop the tomatoes coarsely and set aside.

◑ In a large sauté pan or frying pan over medium-low heat, warm the butter or olive oil. Add the onion and sauté, stirring, until translucent, 4–5 minutes. Add the celery and sauté until starting to soften, another 2–3 minutes. Using a slotted spoon, transfer the onion and celery to a plate. Set aside.

◑ Add the crumbled sausage to the pan and sauté over medium heat, turning several times, until lightly browned, 8–10 minutes. Return the onion mixture to the pan along with the tomatoes. Mix together and continue to cook over medium heat for 3–4 minutes to blend the flavors. Stir in the olives and season to taste with salt and pepper.

◑ Arrange the pepper halves, cut side up, in a baking dish in which they just fit comfortably in a single layer. Spoon the sausage mixture into the peppers, dividing it evenly. Top evenly with the bread crumbs. Add the hot water to the dish.

◑ Bake, uncovered, until the crumbs are golden and the mixture is bubbly, about 40 minutes. Using a slotted spatula, transfer to warmed plates and serve immediately. ◑

MEAT LOAF WITH RED PEPPER SAUCE

SERVES 4–6

Too many of us forget about meat loaf when thinking of cooking dinner for family or friends. But it's easily prepared and can be quite special when you combine different meats and seasonings and serve it with a sauce. Excellent served hot, the meat loaf can yield leftovers; serve them cold with salad as a main course, in sandwiches, or even chopped and added to a tomato sauce for pasta.

❧ Once you mix the meats together, let the mixture come to room temperature. The meat is seasoned with fresh oregano, but you can substitute ½ teaspoon dried oregano if fresh is unavailable. Crush it in the palm of your hand with your thumb before using.

1 lb (500 g) ground (minced) lean beef
  (top or bottom round or sirloin)
½ lb (250 g) ground (minced) veal
½ lb (250 g) ground (minced) pork
2 tablespoons extra-virgin olive oil
  or vegetable oil
1 yellow onion, chopped
  (1 cup/4 oz/125 g)
1 celery stalk, chopped
  (½ cup/2½ oz/75 g)
½ red bell pepper (capsicum), seeded,
  deribbed, and chopped
  (½ cup/2½ oz/75 g)
1 teaspoon minced fresh oregano
3 or 4 slices French or Italian bread,
  preferably day-old
⅓ cup (3 fl oz/80 ml) milk
1 egg, lightly beaten
2 teaspoons salt
freshly ground pepper
¼ cup (2 fl oz/60 ml) dry red wine,
  or as needed
roasted red pepper sauce (recipe
  on page 285)

Position a rack in the middle of an oven and preheat the oven to 375°F (190°C). Grease a 1½- or 2-qt (1.5- or 2-l) baking dish or baking pan. In a large bowl, combine the beef, veal, and pork. Mix lightly. Set aside.

❧ In a sauté pan over medium-low heat, warm the oil. Add the onion and sauté for 1 minute. Stir in the celery, bell pepper, and oregano. Cover and cook over low heat, stirring a couple of times, until tender, 4–5 minutes; do not brown.

❧ Remove the crusts from the bread. Cut or tear the bread into small pieces and put into a food processor fitted with the metal blade or into a blender. Pulse to make coarse crumbs (2 cups/4 oz/125 g). Transfer to a small bowl. Stirring with a fork, dribble the milk onto the crumbs. Let stand for a few minutes.

❧ To the bowl holding the meat add the onion mixture, bread crumbs, egg, the salt, and pepper to taste. Using your hands, mix well. Form into a loaf (do not to pack too solidly) and place in the baking dish or pan. Pour the wine over the meat.

❧ Bake uncovered, basting every 15 minutes with the pan juices, until cooked through, about 1½ hours; add more wine to the dish if it begins to dry out. To test for doneness, insert an instant-read thermometer into the center of the loaf; it should read 165°F (74°C). Remove from the oven and cover loosely with foil; let rest for 5–10 minutes.

❧ Slice thinly and spoon a little of the roasted red pepper sauce over the slices.

ROAST FILLET OF BEEF WITH MADEIRA SAUCE

SERVES 4

As this recipe illustrates, the French are expert at roasting good-quality cuts of beef. The center cut of the fillet (sometimes called the tenderloin) is the best choice here, as its even thickness ensures uniform roasting. The fillet should be well trimmed of any fat. Because the fillet has no internal layer of fat, it needs a strip of pork fatback tied to it so the meat loses none of its moisture during roasting. Ask your butcher to do this for you.

Before you put the roast in the oven, make sure it is at room temperature; to do so, remove it from the refrigerator 30–40 minutes in advance.

1 center-cut beef fillet, 2 lb (1 kg), trimmed of any fat, with a thin piece of pork fatback tied on top in several places (see note)
unsalted butter
salt and freshly ground pepper
⅓ cup (2 oz/60 g) finely chopped shallots (about 5 shallots)
¼ cup (2 fl oz/60 ml) water
½ cup (4 fl oz/125 ml) Madeira wine
1 teaspoon cornstarch mixed with 1 tablespoon water
¾ cup (6 fl oz/180 ml) heavy (double) cream
chopped fresh parsley

Position a rack in the bottom third of an oven and preheat to 425°F (220°C).

Butter the ends and bottom of the beef fillet and place in a small, heavy roasting pan (without a rack) in which it fits comfortably. Sprinkle the meat with salt and pepper. Place in the oven and roast until an instant-read thermometer inserted in the center of the meat registers 120°F (49°C) for rare or 130°F (54°C) for medium-rare, 20–30 minutes. Transfer to a warmed serving plate and cover loosely with a piece of aluminum foil to keep it warm. It will continue to cook a little.

Using a large spoon, skim off the fat from the pan juices. Place the pan over medium-low heat and add the shallots. Cook, stirring, until translucent, 3–4 minutes. Add the water, raise the heat to medium and stir, scraping up any browned bits stuck to the pan bottom. Add the Madeira, bring to a boil over medium heat, and boil until reduced by about one-half. Combine the cornstarch mixture and the cream and stir until blended. Add to the pan and quickly stir into the juices. Cook, stirring, until slightly thickened, 1–2 minutes. Season to taste with salt and pepper.

Cut the strings on the fillet, then remove the strip of fat tied to the top of the fillet and discard. Using a very sharp, thin-bladed knife, slice the meat crosswise into 12–14 slices, each about ½ inch (12 mm) thick. Spoon a little of the sauce onto each warmed plate and place 2 or 3 slices of meat on the sauce. Spoon the remaining sauce over the meat, garnish with the chopped parsley, and serve.

"Roast beef, Medium, is not only a food. It is a philosophy. Seated at Life's Dining Table, you know that Roast Beef, Medium, is safe and sane, and sure."

—Edna Ferber

SAUTÉED PORK TENDERLOIN WITH GINGERED APPLES

SERVES 4

Sautéed apples, sparked with a hint of fresh ginger, complement the natural sweetness of pork—a meat that has always been popular in America, especially in the Midwest. The development in recent years of leaner pork has kept its popularity strong. The tenderloin, relatively free of excess fat and quickly cooked, makes a good choice for simple, easy recipes. Buy it from a reliable butcher who can supply you with good-quality meat that will be absolutely tender.

1 lb (500 g) tart apples such as
   Granny Smith
4 tablespoons (2 oz/60 g)
   unsalted butter
2 tablespoons light brown sugar
1 teaspoon peeled and grated
   fresh ginger
2–4 tablespoons water
8 slices pork tenderloin, each
   3–3½ oz (90–105 g) and about
   2 inches (5 cm) thick
salt and freshly ground pepper
1 tablespoon extra-virgin olive oil or
   vegetable oil
small fresh mint sprigs

Peel, quarter, and core the apples, then thinly slice lengthwise. In a heavy sauté pan or frying pan over medium heat, melt 3 tablespoons of the butter. When hot, add the apples and sauté, stirring and tossing, for 5 minutes. Add the brown sugar and ginger and continue to sauté, stirring, for another 5 minutes. Add 2 tablespoons of the water, cover, reduce the heat, and cook until the apples are almost tender, 6–8 minutes; watch carefully so they do not burn. Set aside.

Trim all excess fat from the pork slices. Place each pork slice, cut side up, between 2 sheets of plastic wrap and, using a rolling pin, flatten to about 1 inch (2.5 cm) thickness. Sprinkle both sides with salt and pepper.

In a large sauté pan or frying pan (preferably nonstick) over medium-high heat, melt the remaining 1 tablespoon butter with the oil. When hot, add the pork slices, 4 at a time, and sauté, turning once or twice, until browned and no longer pink at the center, 4–5 minutes on each side. Transfer to a warmed plate; keep warm.

When all the pork slices are cooked, pour off the fat from the pan and return to medium heat. Add the apples and their juices and stir to loosen any browned bits on the bottom. Add the remaining water if there is too little liquid in the pan or the apples are sticking. Sauté the apples until well heated, 2–3 minutes. Return the pork slices and their juices to the pan and heat on each side for a few seconds.

Arrange the pork slices on a warmed serving platter or on individual plates and top with the apple slices. Garnish with the mint. A

"Everything in a pig is good. What ingratitude has permitted his name to become a term of opprobrium?"

—Grimod de la Reynière

BOILED BEEF WITH GREEN SAUCE

SERVES 4

In Italy meat is often served boiled—that is, gently poached—with a tangy green herb sauce. The sauce I include here combines fresh parsley and sage with garlic, balsamic vinegar, and olive oil, a blend that contrasts nicely with the beef. You can also offer the sauce with any cold sliced meats. ⤷ *Simmer the beef very slowly for the most moist, tender results. This is a good meal to prepare on a weekend, when you have a little extra time for the cooking. There may even be leftovers for another meal during the week.*

1 lean beef brisket, 3–3½ lb
    (1.5–1.75 kg), preferably center cut
8 cups (64 fl oz/2 l) water
salt
6 carrots, peeled and trimmed
6 celery stalks, trimmed
1 yellow onion, cut in half
2 cloves garlic, left whole
1 tablespoon balsamic vinegar
4 leeks
1 lemon
8 baby artichokes
green sauce (recipe on page 284)

Trim any excess fat from the meat. Select a large, heavy pot in which the meat fits comfortably. Place it over medium-high heat, add the water, and bring to a boil. Add 2 teaspoons salt and the meat. The water should just cover the meat; add more if necessary. Bring back to a boil and, using a skimmer or spoon, remove any froth that collects on the surface. Cut 1 of the carrots and 1 of the celery stalks into small pieces and add to the pot, along with the onion halves, garlic, and balsamic vinegar. Reduce the heat to low, cover, and barely simmer until the meat is almost tender when pierced with a fork, 2½–3 hours.

⤷ Meanwhile, trim the leeks, cutting off the root end and leaving some of the tender green top intact. Cut all the leeks to the same length. Starting at the top, make a shallow lengthwise slit along each leek to within 2 inches (5 cm) of the root end. Rinse away any dirt lodged between the leaves. Set aside.

⤷ Squeeze the juice from the lemon into a bowl of water large enough to hold the artichokes. Trim the artichokes (see page 291). Immediately put the artichokes into the bowl of lemon water. Set aside.

⤷ When the meat is almost done, remove and discard the onion halves and the carrot and celery pieces. Cut the 5 remaining celery stalks into 4-inch (10-cm) lengths. Drain the artichokes. Add the celery and artichokes to the pot, along with the 5 remaining whole carrots and the trimmed leeks. Season the broth with salt to taste. Raise the heat for a few minutes to bring back to a simmer. Cover and simmer until the vegetables and meat are tender, 20–30 minutes longer. Remove from the heat and let stand for 5–6 minutes.

⤷ Just before the meat and vegetables have finished cooking, make the green sauce and cover to keep warm. Then, to serve, transfer the meat to a serving platter and slice thinly. Remove the vegetables from the cooking liquid and place them around the meat. Spoon the warm green sauce over the meat.

CORNED BEEF HASH WITH POACHED EGGS

SERVES 4

Since the 19th century, corned beef hash has been a staple on the breakfast menus of cafés and restaurants throughout the United States: nothing could be more American. In fact, cafés known for their corned beef hash affectionately became known as hash houses. Use the leftovers from your corned beef dinner (recipe on page 166) for making the hash. Then all you need is a simple green salad to round out the menu for a delightful weekend brunch or supper. Try serving the hash with roasted red pepper sauce (see page 285) with 1 teaspoon of prepared horseradish added to it.

A few insider's secrets and a little practice will ensure perfect poached eggs for serving on top of your hash. Start with very fresh eggs, which have the firmest whites and yolks. A splash of vinegar in the poaching water helps firm up the whites quickly. And swirling the water while gently lowering the egg into the vortex of the swirl will prevent the white from spreading out in the water.

2 baking potatoes, about 1½ lb (750 g) total weight, unpeeled

1½ teaspoons salt, plus salt to taste

5 tablespoons (2½ oz/75 g) unsalted butter

1 yellow onion, diced (1 cup/4 oz/125 g)

1 red or green bell pepper (capsicum), seeded, deribbed, and diced (1 cup/5 oz/155 g)

1 celery stalk, diced (½ cup/2½ oz/75 g)

1 teaspoon chopped fresh oregano or ½ teaspoon dried oregano

3 cups (about 1 lb/500 g) diced, chopped, or shredded cooked corned beef

4 tablespoons chopped fresh parsley, plus extra for garnish

freshly ground pepper

2–3 tablespoons water or chicken stock, if needed

2–3 tablespoons white cider vinegar

4 or 8 very fresh extra-large or jumbo eggs

In a saucepan, combine the potatoes and 1 teaspoon of the salt with water to cover. Bring to a boil, cover partially, and boil until slightly underdone,
15–20 minutes. Drain and set aside until cool enough to handle.

In a large sauté pan or frying pan over medium-low heat, melt 2 tablespoons of the butter. Add the onion and sauté until almost translucent, 2–3 minutes. Add the bell pepper, celery, and oregano; cover and cook over low heat, stirring occasionally, until soft, 8–10 minutes. Set aside.

Peel and cut the potatoes into ½-inch (12-mm) dice. In a large frying pan (preferably nonstick) over medium heat, melt the remaining 3 tablespoons butter. Add the potatoes and sauté for 5–6 minutes. Mix in the onion-pepper mixture, corned beef, the 4 tablespoons parsley, and pepper to taste. Cover and cook until heated through, 2–3 minutes. If the mixture is too dry, add the water or chicken stock. Season with salt and pepper. Cover and keep warm.

To poach the eggs, in a large frying pan or sauté pan, pour in water to a depth of 1½ inches (4 cm). Add the vinegar and the remaining ½ teaspoon salt and bring to a boil. Reduce the heat so that the liquid is just under a boil. Break an egg into a saucer and gently slip the egg into the water. Repeat with the remaining eggs, spacing well apart. Cook in the hot water until the whites are firm and the yolks are glazed over but still liquid, 3–5 minutes. Carefully remove the eggs with a skimmer, a large slotted spoon, or a slotted spatula, allowing them to drain, and place on a flat plate. Trim the edges of the whites if they are ragged.

Arrange the hash on a warmed platter and top with the eggs, or serve the hash and eggs on individual plates. Garnish with chopped parsley. A

BRAISED BRISKET OF BEEF WITH PORT WINE

SERVES 4–6 WITH LEFTOVERS

A classic of American cooking, braised brisket of beef was brought to this country by Jewish and other Eastern European immigrants. Many people today think they don't have the time to cook in this old-fashioned way, but I like to think that the slow, moist braising method can actually save you time: With a little advance planning, you can set aside a bit of time to prepare this dish on the weekend using a larger cut of meat (4½–5 lb/2.25–2.5 kg), yielding enough leftovers for one or two easy meals later in the week. The braised meat reheats successfully, can also be made into a hash or combined with a sauce for pasta, or is delicious cold.

The best choice for braising is the center cut of brisket, but other tough, lean cuts such as chuck or rump roast are also excellent cooked this way. A good butcher will help you make the right choice. Serve the brisket with mashed potatoes, noodles, or rice to soak up the sauce.

1 center-cut beef brisket, 3½–4 lb
   (1.75–2 kg)
3 tablespoons extra-virgin olive oil
   or vegetable oil
2 cloves garlic, chopped
1 yellow onion, chopped
   (1 cup/4 oz/125 g)
¾ cup (4 oz/125 g) chopped celery
1 lb (500 g) ripe plum (Roma)
   tomatoes, cored and chopped
   (3 cups/18 oz/560 g)
3 whole cloves
2 orange zest strips, each 3 inches
   (7.5 cm) long by 1 inch (2.5 cm) wide
   (see page 287)
1 bay leaf
4 fresh thyme sprigs
3 fresh parsley sprigs

½ teaspoon salt, or to taste
freshly ground pepper
1 cup (8 fl oz/250 ml) port wine

Position a rack in the lower part of an oven and preheat to 350°F (180°C).

Trim any excess fat from the beef. Select a large ovenproof pot or dutch oven that will hold the meat comfortably. Add the oil and warm over medium-high heat. When hot, add the beef and brown on all sides, 4–5 minutes. Transfer to a plate and set aside. Reduce the heat to low, add the garlic and onion, and sauté until translucent, 3–4 minutes. Stir in the celery and tomatoes.

To make a bouquet garni, stick the cloves into the orange zest strips, then tie together the strips, bay leaf, thyme, and parsley with kitchen string. Add to the pot along with the salt, pepper to taste, the browned beef and ½ cup (4 fl oz/125 ml) of the port. Cover tightly and place in the oven. Braise, basting frequently with the pan juices, until tender, 2–2½ hours. Transfer the meat to a warmed platter, cover loosely with aluminum foil and keep warm.

Discard the bouquet garni. Rest a sieve over a bowl and pour in the pot contents, capturing the juices in the bowl. Transfer the vegetables in the sieve to a food processor fitted with the metal blade or to a blender. Purée until smooth.

Using a spoon, skim off the fat from the reserved juices. Return the juices and puréed vegetables to the pot, add the remaining ½ cup (4 fl oz/125 ml) port, and bring to a boil. Boil for a few seconds to dispel the alcohol. Adjust the seasoning.

Slice the meat about ¼ inch (6 mm) thick. Spoon the sauce over the slices.

CORNED BEEF AND VEGETABLES

SERVES 4 WITH LEFTOVERS

Of all the long-cooked meats, corned beef is probably the most practical and versatile. It is delicious hot or cold, and the leftovers are excellent cooked in new dishes. Cooking corned beef on a weekend provides a great Sunday family supper, plus other easy meals during the week, including Corned Beef Hash with Poached Eggs (recipe on page 163) or sliced corned beef sandwiches with mustard on a good delicatessen rye bread.

Buy your corned beef from a reliable butcher shop—preferably one that corns its own beef. (The word corn refers to the kernels of coarse salt used in the meat's preserving process.) Kosher butcher shops are often good sources. Select a high-quality cut such as center-cut brisket or top round.

Have a selection of good mustards on hand to offer with the meat, or serve it with roasted red pepper sauce (page 285) with 1 teaspoon mustard or prepared horseradish added to it.

1 corned center-cut brisket or top
   round of beef, 3½–4 lb (1.75–2 kg)
2 celery stalks, cut into pieces
1 large carrot, peeled and cut in half
1 large yellow onion, quartered
3 whole cloves
4 or 5 fresh thyme sprigs
1 large bay leaf
⅛ teaspoon red pepper flakes
3 orange zest strips, each 3 inches
   (7.5 cm) long by 1 inch (2.5 cm)
   wide (see page 287)
4 or 5 large fresh parsley sprigs
6 white potatoes (about 2 lb/1 kg)
6 young turnips or small rutabagas
   (about 2 lb/1 kg)
1 small head cabbage

Rinse the corned beef well, put into a large bowl with water to cover, and let soak for 1 hour to remove some of the brine.

Drain the beef, rinse again, and put into a large, heavy pot or dutch oven in which it fits comfortably. Add water to cover by 1 inch (2.5 cm). Bring to a boil and, using a skimmer or kitchen spoon, skim off the scum from the surface. Reduce the heat so that the water just simmers and add the celery, carrot, onion, cloves, thyme, bay leaf, red pepper flakes, orange zest strips, and parsley. Cover with the lid slightly ajar and simmer over low heat until tender, 2½–3 hours, adding water as needed to maintain the original level. To test for doneness, insert a sharp 2-prong fork in the meat; it should go in easily. Do not overcook, however, or the meat will be dry and stringy.

While the corned beef cooks, peel the potatoes and the turnips or rutabagas and cut in half or into quarters. Put the vegetables into a large bowl and add

water to cover; set aside. Remove any bruised or old leaves from the cabbage and cut the head into 6 or 8 wedges. Put into a plastic bag and set aside.

About 25 minutes before the meat is done, add the potatoes to the pot, let cook for 10 minutes, then add the turnips or rutabagas. Test the meat and vegetables for doneness by piercing with a fork. When tender, transfer to a plate, cover with aluminum foil, and keep warm. Raise the heat to high, add the cabbage, and boil until tender, about 5 minutes. Transfer to the plate holding the other vegetables.

Slice the meat thinly across the grain and arrange on a serving platter. Surround with the vegetables and serve.

PORK LOIN WITH ORANGE

SERVES 4

Food-loving American travelers to Paris raved about this dish during the 1950s and 1960s, a time when anyone with just a few extra dollars could enjoy the pleasures of going to Paris and eating in the best restaurants. I was fortunate to be among those well-fed visitors, and I have long enjoyed re-creating the great combination of flavors in this easy and satisfying recipe.

You can ask your butcher to tie the loin, or you can do it yourself: trim off all but a thin layer of fat from the loin and tie the loin in three or four places with kitchen string to hold its shape.

Be careful to hold the pan of cognac away from the heat when lighting it.

1 tablespoon vegetable oil
1 boneless pork loin, 2–2½ lb
  (1–1.25 kg), tied (see note)
1 sweet white onion, chopped
  (¾–1 cup/4–5 oz/125–155 g)
5 or 6 carrots, 12–14 oz (375–440 g)
  total weight, peeled and cut crosswise
  into slices ¼ inch (6 mm) thick
¼ cup (2 fl oz/60 ml) cognac, warmed
  in a small pan
1 bay leaf
2 fresh thyme sprigs
½ cup (4 fl oz/125 ml) dry white wine
salt and freshly ground pepper
3 oranges
1½–2 teaspoons Dijon mustard
1 teaspoon cornstarch (cornflour)
  mixed with 2 tablespoons water
chopped fresh parsley

Position a rack in the lower third of an oven and preheat to 350°F (180°C).

In an ovenproof pot over medium-high heat, warm the oil. Add the pork, fat side down, and brown on all sides, 8–10 minutes. Transfer to a plate. Add the onion, reduce the heat to medium-low, and sauté until translucent, 6–7 minutes. Add the carrots, sauté for 1–2 minutes and remove from the heat. Return the pork to the pot, fat side up. Light the cognac, pour it flaming over the pork, and let it burn out.

Tuck the bay leaf and thyme under the loin, add the wine, and sprinkle with salt and pepper. Cover and bake until the meat is just tender, 50–60 minutes. Insert an instant-read thermometer into the center; it should read 160°F (71°C).

Meanwhile, shred the zest from 1 of the oranges (see page 287). Place in a small pan, add water to cover, and bring to a boil. Boil for 2–3 minutes, then drain. Squeeze the juice from the same orange plus 1 additional orange. You should have 1 cup (8 fl oz/250 ml). Slice the remaining orange crosswise, then cut each slice in half. Set aside.

Transfer the pork to a warmed platter. Cover loosely with aluminum foil. Skim off the fat from the pot juices. Stir in the mustard, orange juice, and zest. Bring to a boil and boil until reduced by half, then reduce the heat to medium-low. Stir a little of the juices into the cornstarch mixture, then stir into the pot juices. Stir until slightly thickened, 2–3 minutes. Season with salt and pepper.

Spoon a little sauce with vegetables onto each warmed plate. Slice the pork and arrange on top of the vegetables. Garnish with the reserved orange slices and parsley and serve at once.

LAMB STEW WITH POLENTA

SERVES 4

What could be more typically Italian than a simple lamb stew with tomatoes and black olives seasoned with garlic, lemon and rosemary, all served over polenta? I enjoyed just such a dish at a restaurant near Florence in the early 1970s, and I've been making my own version of it ever since.

❧ *For such a stew to be at its very best, the meat must be young lamb—boneless cubes cut from the shoulder, and all fat removed before cooking. The pieces need to be seared quickly to seal in their juices and develop their flavor, then combined with the other ingredients and slowly simmered to tenderness.*

❧ *Take care, as well, to cook the polenta slowly and serve it the instant it is done.*

1½ lb (750 g) ripe plum (Roma) tomatoes

3 tablespoons olive oil

3 cloves garlic, minced (1 tablespoon)

1 small yellow onion, chopped (about ½ cup/2 oz/60 g)

2 lb (1 kg) lean, boneless lamb shoulder, cut into 1-inch (2.5-cm) cubes and trimmed of excess fat

½ cup (4 fl oz/125 ml) chicken stock

1 cup (5 oz/155 g) European black olives, such as Gaeta, Kalamata, or Spanish, pitted if desired

2 lemon zest strips (see page 287), each 2 inches (5 cm) by 1 inch (2.5 cm)

2 whole cloves

2 fresh rosemary sprigs, coarsely chopped, plus extra sprigs for garnish

Polenta with Parmesan Cheese (recipe on page 226)

Salt and freshly ground pepper

1 teaspoon cornstarch (cornflour) mixed with 2 tablespoons water, if needed

Core and peel the tomatoes (see page 289). Cut in half crosswise and squeeze out the seeds. Chop the tomatoes coarsely; set aside.

❧ In a large sauté pan over medium-low heat, warm 1 tablespoon of the oil. Add the garlic and sauté for 30–40 seconds. Add the onion and sauté until translucent, 4–5 minutes. Using a slotted spoon, transfer the onion and garlic to a plate.

❧ Add the remaining 2 tablespoons oil to the pan, raise the heat to medium-high, and add half of the lamb cubes. Sauté, turning, until lightly browned on all sides, 4–6 minutes. Transfer to the plate with the onion. Repeat with the remaining lamb. Pour off any fat left in the pan.

❧ Return the meat and onions to the pan. Add the tomatoes, stock, and olives. Make a bouquet garni: Place the lemon strips, whole cloves, and chopped rosemary in the center of a 6-inch (15-cm) piece of cheesecloth (muslin). Gather the edges together and tie with kitchen string. Add to the pan. Cover and barely simmer over low heat, stirring occasionally, until the meat is tender, about 1½ hours. Begin to cook the polenta about 30 minutes before the stew is ready.

❧ When the stew is done, remove the bouquet garni and discard. Season with salt and pepper. If a thicker stew is desired, stir in the cornstarch-water mixture. Cook over medium heat, stirring, until the sauce thickens a little.

❧ To serve, spoon the polenta onto warmed plates, then spoon the stew partially over it. Garnish each serving with a rosemary sprig. Top the polenta with a little of the Parmesan cheese, passing the remaining cheese in a bowl.

"The olive fruit is the greatest cure for any problem of life."

–Solon

COUNTRY VEAL STEW

SERVES 4

Blanquette de veau is one of the classic dishes of French provincial cuisine. For the most tender results, take special care to sear the veal pieces quickly and lightly, and to maintain the barest simmer during cooking.
If the carrots in your market are large and thick, cut them in half lengthwise before cutting them crosswise. Have your butcher cut the veal into strips as indicated, or do it yourself. Strips of this size will yield better texture and flavor than smaller pieces.
Serve the stew over rice, couscous (recipe on page 283), or noodles.

3 fresh parsley sprigs, plus chopped
   fresh parsley for garnish
2 fresh thyme sprigs
1 bay leaf
1 celery stalk, cut crosswise into
   4 equal pieces
½ cup (2½ oz/75 g) all-purpose
   (plain) flour
salt and freshly ground pepper
2 lb (1 kg) boneless shoulder of veal,
   trimmed of any fat and cut into
   strips 2½ inches (6 cm) long,
   1 inch (2.5 cm) wide and ¾ inch
   (2 cm) thick
2 tablespoons unsalted butter
1 tablespoon vegetable oil
3 cloves garlic, thinly sliced
½ cup (4 fl oz/125 ml) dry white wine
½ cup (4 fl oz/125 ml) water
24 small boiling onions (about
   1 lb/500 g), about 1 inch (2.5 cm)
   in diameter
1 lb (500 g) ripe tomatoes, peeled,
   seeded, and finely diced (see page 289)
1 bunch small carrots, peeled and cut
   on the diagonal into 2-inch (5-cm)
   lengths
1 tablespoon cornstarch (cornflour)
   mixed with 2 tablespoons water
   (optional)

4 fresh sage leaves, coarsely chopped,
   plus chopped fresh sage for garnish
juice of 1 lemon

To make a bouquet garni, place the parsley and thyme sprigs and bay leaf inside the celery pieces and tie with kitchen string. Set aside. Mix the flour, ¾ teaspoon salt, and ⅛ teaspoon pepper on a plate. Lightly coat the veal pieces with the mixture.
In a large sauté pan over medium-high heat, melt the butter with the oil. Add the veal and quickly sear, 3–4 minutes on each side. Transfer to a plate. Pour off any fat and reduce the heat to medium-low. Add the garlic and sauté for 30–40 seconds. Add the wine and water and raise the heat to medium. Simmer, scraping up any browned bits. Return the meat to the pan, add the bouquet garni, reduce the heat to low, partially cover, and barely simmer until almost tender, about 1 hour.
Meanwhile, bring a saucepan of water to a boil, add the onions, and boil for 3 minutes. Drain and immerse in cold water. Drain again. Trim and cut an X in the root end of each onion, then slip off the skins.
When the veal has simmered for 1 hour, add the onions, tomatoes, carrots, and salt and pepper to taste to the pan. Continue to simmer until the veal is tender, another 30–45 minutes. Discard the bouquet garni. If the stock is thin, stir a little into the cornstarch mixture, then stir the cornstarch mixture into the stew until slightly thickened. Add the coarsely chopped sage and a few drops of lemon juice. Simmer for 5 minutes.
Spoon the stew onto warmed individual plates. Garnish with the chopped parsley and sage and serve at once.

LAMB STEW WITH RAISINS

SERVES 4

A traditional stew that reflects the blending of cultures in American cooking, this dish takes its seasoning from the kitchens of North Africa. I have used leeks in place of onions as they add an extra edge of sweetness that, along with that of the raisins, complements the lamb. The stew can be served with rice or noodles.

 Feel free to adjust any of the strong spices to suit your taste. It is important to let the spices cook in the oil for a minute or two to bring out their flavor before you add any liquid.

2 lb (1 kg) boneless lamb shoulder, cut into 1-inch (2.5-cm) cubes
½ cup (2½ oz/75 g) all-purpose (plain) flour
3 tablespoons extra-virgin olive oil or vegetable oil
2 cloves garlic, chopped (1 tablespoon)
1 teaspoon ground cinnamon
½ teaspoon ground cumin
½ teaspoon ground coriander
pinch of cayenne pepper
1 bay leaf
1½ cups (12 fl oz/375 ml) hot tap water
2 leeks
3 or 4 medium carrots, peeled and thinly sliced (1½ cups/6 oz/185 g)
½ cup (3 oz/90 g) golden raisins (sultanas)
1 teaspoon salt, or to taste
freshly ground black pepper
1 lemon

Remove all excess fat from the lamb pieces. Put the flour on a plate. Toss the lamb in the flour to coat lightly, then shake off any excess. In a large, heavy pot or sauté pan over medium-high heat, warm the oil. When hot, add the lamb cubes in batches and lightly brown

on all sides, 5–6 minutes. Transfer to a plate and set aside.

 Add the garlic to the same pan over low heat, stir for a few seconds, then stir in the cinnamon, cumin, coriander, cayenne pepper, and bay leaf and cook for 1–2 minutes. Add the hot water and stir to scrape up any browned bits. Return the meat to the pan and simmer, stirring, until the liquid thickens, about 2 minutes. Cover and simmer over low heat, stirring every now and then, for 1 hour.

 Meanwhile, trim the leeks, leaving some tender green tops intact. Make a lengthwise slit along each leek to within 2 inches (5 cm) of the root end. Hold under running water to wash away any dirt lodged in the leaves. Cut into slices ½ inch (12 mm) thick; you should have about 2 cups (8 oz/250 g). Set aside.

 When the lamb has simmered for 1 hour, blanch the leeks: bring a saucepan three-fourths full of water to a boil,

add the leeks, and boil for 2 minutes. Drain and add to the lamb along with the carrots, raisins, salt, and black pepper to taste. Simmer, covered, until the meat is tender when pierced with a fork, 40–50 minutes longer. Taste and adjust the seasoning.

 Transfer the stew to a warmed serving dish. Using a zester or fine-holed shredder, and holding the lemon over the stew, shred the zest from the lemon as directed on page 287. Serve at once.

A

LAMB SHANKS WITH POTATOES

SERVES 4

I'm surprised by how seldom people think to cook such a homey, uncomplicated dish as this one. The preparation is truly simple, and all you need is some time for the cooking to make sure the lamb shanks become absolutely tender.

❧ If you haven't tried Yukon gold potatoes before, seek them out for the mashed potatoes. They have a lovely color, a rich flavor, and a wonderfully smooth consistency when mashed.

1 bunch small leeks, trimmed and cleaned (see page 291)

4 whole lamb shanks, 3–3½ lb (1.5–1.75 kg) total weight

3 tablespoons olive oil

4 or 5 cloves garlic, sliced

2 teaspoons chopped fresh rosemary, plus rosemary sprigs for garnish

salt and freshly ground pepper

¾ cup (6 fl oz/180 ml) dry white wine

1½–2 lb (750 g–1 kg) Yukon gold or other white potatoes, peeled and cut lengthwise into quarters

¼ cup (2 fl oz/60 ml) heavy (double) cream, or as needed

Slice the leeks crosswise ½ inch (12 mm) thick. Set aside.

❧ Trim the lamb of any fat and wipe with damp paper towels. In a large, deep frying pan over medium-high heat, warm the oil. When hot but not smoking, add the shanks and brown on all sides, 10–12 minutes. Transfer to a plate.

❧ Reduce the heat to medium-low, add the garlic and sauté for 30–40 seconds. Add the leeks and sauté until translucent, 6–8 minutes.

❧ Return the shanks to the pan, scatter the chopped rosemary over them, and sprinkle with salt and pepper. Add the wine, raise the heat to medium-high, and bring to a simmer. Reduce the heat to low, cover, and simmer until the shanks are very tender when pierced with a knife, 2–2½ hours, turning once or twice during the cooking and adding water to the pan to maintain the original level of liquid.

❧ About 30 minutes before the shanks are ready, place the potatoes in a saucepan with water to cover by 2 inches (5 cm). Add 2 teaspoons salt and bring to a boil over medium heat. Boil, uncovered, until the potatoes are tender when pierced with a sharp knife, 25–30 minutes. Strain, reserving the cooking water. Pass the potatoes through a potato ricer or food mill held over the saucepan. Alternatively, mash them with a potato masher in the pan until free of lumps. Place the pan over medium-low heat and, using a wooden spoon, vigorously beat in ¼–½ cup (2–4 fl oz/

60–125 ml) of the cooking water, a little at a time, until the potatoes are smooth and of a good consistency. Beat in the ¼ cup (2 fl oz/60 ml) cream and salt and pepper to taste until well blended. For a thinner consistency, beat in more cream. Cover to keep warm.

❧ When the lamb shanks are tender, season the sauce with salt and pepper if necessary. Spoon the potatoes onto 4 warmed plates. Place 1 shank on each plate and spoon the leeks and juices over them. Garnish with rosemary sprigs and serve. F ❧

BRAISED VEAL SHANKS

SERVES 4

This recipe for Italy's classic osso buco was given to me in the mid-1960s by a friend named Valentina, an Italian couturier and exceptionally good cook whose salon was across the street from Williams-Sonoma's first San Francisco store. She didn't use the typical seasoning ingredients for this dish, relying instead on flaming the meat with good cognac after browning, then adding an onion and a little well-flavored beef stock for slowly simmering the veal. The results are at once delicate and richly flavored.

❧ Seek out a good butcher who specializes in quality veal. The veal shanks must come from a very young animal and preferably from the front shanks, which are smaller and more tender. Only the center two pieces of the shank should be used; the end pieces contain too much bone. The veal should be pale pink and have no fat.

❧ This dish is excellent served with a simple risotto or egg noodles. Try it with Saffron Risotto (follow the recipe on page 183, leaving out the Marsala, crab, and lemon juice).

½ cup (2½ oz/75 g) all-purpose
   (plain) flour
8 veal shank pieces from foreleg, each
   2½ inches (6 cm) thick and weighing
   6–8 oz (185–250 g) each, or 4 veal
   shank pieces from hind leg, each
   2 inches (5 cm) thick and weighing
   10–12 oz (315–375 g) each
2 tablespoons unsalted butter
2 tablespoons olive oil
¼ cup (2 fl oz/60 ml) cognac
½ cup (4 fl oz/125 ml) beef stock
1 yellow onion
½ teaspoon salt
freshly ground pepper
1 teaspoon cornstarch (cornflour),
   if needed
1 lemon

Spread out the flour on a plate. Coat each veal shank piece evenly with the flour, shaking off any excess. Select a large sauté pan or deep frying pan in which the veal pieces will fit in a single layer. Place over medium-high heat and melt the butter with the olive oil. When hot, add the veal pieces, cut side up, and sauté until lightly browned on all sides, 6–8 minutes total. Arrange the pieces cut side up and in a single layer, then remove from the heat.

❧ In a small pan over medium-low heat, warm the cognac. Remove from the heat. Well away from the heat, ignite the cognac with a long match. Carefully pour the flaming cognac over the veal pieces. Let the flame burn itself out, then return the pan to low heat. Add the stock, onion, salt, and pepper to taste. Cover and barely simmer until the veal is tender when pierced with a fork, 1¼–1½ hours if using shank pieces from the foreleg and 1½–2 hours if using pieces from the hind leg, turning the veal pieces over halfway through cooking. When done, transfer the veal pieces, cut side up, to a serving platter. Set aside and cover to keep warm.

❧ Remove the pan from the heat and, using a spoon, skim off any fat from the surface of the liquid. Return the pan to high heat and boil the liquid until thickened and reduced to about ½ cup (4 fl oz/125 ml). (Or thicken with cornstarch mixed with a little cold water.) Taste and adjust the seasoning. Pour the sauce over the veal pieces.

❧ Using a zester or a fine-holed shredder, shred the zest (yellow part only) from the lemon directly onto the veal (see page 287). Serve at once.

"Good food has a magic appeal. You may grow old, even ugly, but if you are a good cook, people will always find the path to your door."

–James Beard

$\mathcal{P}$ASTA & RISOTTO

Pasta and risotto have the mild, wholesome flavors that welcome a great variety of ingredients. As a result, these kitchen staples provide cooks with canvases for creating endless arrays of culinary masterpieces.

Italy has a centuries-old love of pasta and the creamy rice dish known as risotto. Among the following recipes, you'll find such Italian kitchen classics as Cheese and Basil Ravioli (page 185), Saffron Risotto with Crab (page 183), and Baked Semolina Gnocchi (page 179). But you'll also discover evidence of the international possibilities for those ingredients, as in a variation on an American favorite, Macaroni and Cheese with Broccoli (page 181).

Whether served as a starter, a main course, or a side dish, these easy-to-cook recipes showcase pasta and risotto as true comfort foods.

FARFALLE WITH TUNA AND BLACK OLIVES

SERVES 4

This southern Italian pasta dish is one of the best of the region. The butterfly-shaped farfalle are especially pretty, but you can substitute other pasta of similar size. Look for imported Italian tuna packed in olive oil in well-stocked food stores or Italian markets, or use one of the good-quality Alaskan or north Atlantic brands.

Fresh dill or mint can take the place of the basil. For extra color, add red bell pepper (capsicum) to the sauce: cut the pepper into ½-inch (12-mm) squares and blanch in boiling water for 5 minutes before sautéing it with the green onions.

¼ cup (2 fl oz/60 ml) olive oil
4 or 5 green (spring) onions, including
    some tender green tops, chopped
    (about ¼ cup/¾ oz/20 g)
1 lemon
12 large fresh basil leaves, finely
    shredded, plus extra basil leaves
    for garnish
20 European black olives, such as Gaeta,
    Kalamata, or Spanish, preferably pitted
1 can (12½ oz/390 g) solid-pack tuna
    in olive oil, preferably imported
    Italian, drained and flaked
salt and freshly ground pepper
¾ lb (375 g) dried farfalle

In a large saucepan over medium-low heat, warm the olive oil. Add the green onions and sauté, stirring, until translucent, about 2 minutes. Using a zester or fine-holed shredder, shred the zest (yellow part only) from the lemon directly onto the onions (see page 287). Add the shredded basil and the olives and stir to mix. Add the tuna, and then cut the lemon in half and squeeze a little juice over the mixture to taste. Season with salt and pepper and stir until well heated. Set aside and cover to keep warm.

Meanwhile, fill a large pot three-fourths full of water and bring to a rolling boil over high heat. Add the pasta and 1 tablespoon salt, stirring as you do, and boil until al dente (tender but firm to the bite), about 8 minutes, or according to the package instructions.

Drain the pasta and immediately add it to the warm tuna-olive mixture; act quickly so that a little water is still clinging to the pasta. Toss well and briefly reheat for serving. Taste and adjust the seasoning.

Divide among warmed plates, garnish with the whole basil leaves, and serve at once.

PENNE WITH TOMATO AND BROCCOLI

SERVES 4

I can't imagine an easier or tastier pasta dish or one that makes a simpler, prettier picture than this combination of quill-shaped pasta tubes, bright red tomatoes, and small green florets of broccoli. The tomato sauce cooks within 15 minutes, and the pasta and broccoli can be prepared while the sauce finishes simmering. Of course, you'll find the sauce will be at its best in high summer, when tomatoes are at their freshest, firmest, and most flavorful.
If you can't find fresh oregano, use ½ teaspoon dried oregano. And feel free to leave out the bacon, if you prefer.

1½ lb (750 g) ripe plum (Roma)
    tomatoes
1 bunch broccoli, about 1½ lb (750 g)
3 oz (90 g) thickly sliced lean bacon
    (2 or 3 slices), cut crosswise into
    pieces ¼ inch (6 mm) wide
2 cloves garlic, chopped
¼ cup (1 oz/30 g) chopped
    yellow onion
1 teaspoon minced fresh oregano
pinch of red pepper flakes
salt
¾–1 lb (375–500 g) dried penne
    or rigatoni
½ cup (2 oz/60 g) freshly grated
    Italian Parmesan cheese, preferably
    Parmigiano-Reggiano

Core and peel the tomatoes (see page 289). Cut the tomatoes in half cross-wise and carefully squeeze out the seeds. Chop the tomatoes coarsely; you should have about 3 cups (18 oz/560 g). Set aside.

Remove the florets from the broc-coli stalks; reserve the stalks for another use. Break or cut apart the florets so they are uniform in size. Set aside.

In a large saucepan or frying pan over medium-low heat, sauté the bacon until crisp, 3–4 minutes. Pour off the fat, but leave the bacon in the pan. Add the garlic and onion and sauté gently over medium-low heat, stirring occa-sionally, until the onion is translucent, 4–5 minutes. Add the tomatoes, oregano, and red pepper flakes and raise the heat to medium. Continue to cook, stirring occasionally, until the tomatoes have softened, 8–10 minutes longer. Season with salt.

Meanwhile, fill a large pot three-fourths full of water and bring to a rolling boil over high heat. Add the pasta and 1 tablespoon salt, stirring as you do, and cook at a rapid boil for about 4 minutes. Add the broccoli and boil until the pasta and broccoli are al dente (tender but firm to the bite), another 4–5 minutes.

Drain the pasta and broccoli and immediately add to the pan holding the tomatoes; act quickly so that a little water is still clinging to the pasta. Toss well; the pasta will continue to absorb liquid.

Divide the pasta among warmed plates and sprinkle with some of the grated Parmesan cheese. Serve imme-diately, with the remaining cheese in a small bowl alongside.

BAKED SEMOLINA GNOCCHI

SERVES 4

After the publication of Marcella Hazan's first great book, The Classic Italian Cook Book, *in 1976, many people (myself included) learned more than they'd ever expected to know about the marvelous food of northern Italy. One of the things I learned was how to make semolina gnocchi as made in Rome, and for quite a while I was preparing this dish about once a week.*

⏵ *Of all the gnocchi dishes, I think this one is probably the easiest and best. It's splendid as a dinner party first course, or as a brunch main course accompanied with a green salad. The gnocchi can be made in advance and refrigerated; just slip the dish into the oven 15 minutes before serving.*

⏵ *Semolina flour is finely ground from durum wheat—the wheat used for the finest pastas—and it cooks to a velvety consistency. Look for semolina imported from Italy. Or use stone-ground semolina from one of the many small mills in America; they are producing excellent flours that can be found in specialty-food stores.*

4 cups (32 fl oz/1 l) milk
½ teaspoon salt
freshly ground pepper
pinch of freshly grated nutmeg
1 cup (6 oz/185 g) semolina flour
1 tablespoon unsalted butter, plus ¼ cup
  (2 oz/60 g) unsalted butter, melted
⅔ cup (3 oz/90 g) freshly grated
  Italian Parmesan cheese, preferably
  Parmigiano-Reggiano
2 egg yolks, lightly beaten

In a deep, heavy saucepan over medium heat, warm the milk until small bubbles appear around the edges of the pan; do not allow to boil. Add the salt, pepper to taste, and the nutmeg. Using a heavy whisk or wooden spoon to whisk or stir constantly, pour in the semolina slowly (to avoid lumping). Reduce the heat to low and continue to cook, stirring, until the mixture is very thick and stiff, 10–12 minutes. Be sure to scrape the bottom thoroughly while stirring, to avoid lumping or sticking.

⏵ Remove from the heat and add the 1 tablespoon butter; stir until fully melted and absorbed. Stir in ⅓ cup (1½ oz/45 g) of the Parmesan cheese until combined. Add the egg yolks and stir vigorously to keep the yolks from coagulating. Stir until well blended and smooth.

⏵ Using cold water, wet a jelly-roll pan or a 10-by-15-inch (25-by-37.5-cm) baking pan (this keeps the dough from sticking). Using a wet spatula or spoon, spread out the semolina mixture evenly in the pan. It should be approximately ¼ inch (6 mm) thick. Let cool completely, 40–50 minutes. On a warm day it is best to cover and refrigerate.

⏵ Position a rack in the upper part of an oven and preheat to 425°F (220°C). Generously butter a round 10-inch (25-cm) baking dish or a 9-by-11-inch (23-by-28-cm) rectangular or oval baking dish.

⏵ Using a round cutter 1½–2 inches (4–5 cm) in diameter, cut out rounds of the firm semolina. Place the rounds in a single layer in the baking dish, overlapping them slightly. Gather up the scraps, cut out additional rounds, and add to the dish. Using a spoon, distribute the melted butter evenly over the rounds. Sprinkle the remaining ⅓ cup (1½ oz/45 g) Parmesan cheese evenly over the top.

⏵ Bake until the top is golden and the butter is bubbly, about 15 minutes. Transfer the gnocchi to warmed plates and serve immediately. ⏵

MACARONI AND CHEESE WITH BROCCOLI

SERVES 4

For some reason or other, even though pasta has become a favorite in recent years, we have forgotten how good America's own pasta dish, macaroni and cheese, can be. With a few innovations, macaroni and cheese can stand up to many of the most popular pasta dishes. It enjoys the distinct advantage of advance preparation, making it a great informal meal, and the leftovers can be reheated successfully. Serve it with a green salad.

❧ *When I was a child, we always added other ingredients to our macaroni and cheese. By including broccoli, tomatoes, cauliflower, or leftover chicken, shrimp, or scallops, you can turn the simple dish into something special.*

❧ *I've chosen white cheddar cheese for this recipe because I wanted the sauce to remain white. Use New England white cheddar, if possible, as it is one of the best natural cheeses made in the United States. Take care not to allow the sauce to become too thick. And use freshly made bread crumbs for the topping.*

2 slices French or Italian bread
1½ cups (12 fl oz/375 ml) milk
¼ white onion (or 1 small onion), stuck
   with 2 whole cloves
1 bunch broccoli, about 1½ lb (750 g)
2 tablespoons unsalted butter
2 tablespoons all-purpose (plain) flour
1½ cups (6 oz/185 g) shredded aged
   white cheddar cheese
salt and freshly ground pepper,
   preferably white pepper
freshly grated nutmeg
2 teaspoons dry sherry
1 cup (3½ oz/105 g) small elbow
   macaroni

Position a rack in the upper part of an oven and preheat the oven to 325°F (165°C). Butter a shallow 2-qt (2-l) baking dish.

❧ Remove the crusts from the bread. Cut the bread into small pieces and put into a food processor fitted with the metal blade or into a blender. Pulse a few times to make coarse crumbs; you should have 1 cup (2 oz/60 g). Set aside.

❧ In a saucepan over medium heat, combine the milk and the clove-pierced onion. Warm to a simmer. Remove from the heat; set aside for 10–15 minutes.

❧ Meanwhile, cut or break the florets off the broccoli stalks. Peel the stalks and cut into small chunks. Cut any large florets in half. Set aside.

❧ In a saucepan over low heat, melt the butter. Using a whisk or wooden spoon, stir in the flour and cook, stirring, for 30–40 seconds; do not brown. Remove from the heat. Using a slotted spoon, remove the onion from the milk and discard. Gradually pour the milk into the flour mixture, stirring briskly. Return to the heat and slowly bring to a boil, stirring constantly (scrape the pan bottom and sides to avoid lumping and scorching) until the sauce thickens and is smooth, 3–4 minutes. Add ½ cup (2 oz/60 g) of the cheese and stir until blended. Add salt and pepper to taste, a sprinkling of nutmeg, and the sherry. Remove from the heat and keep warm.

❧ Bring a large pot three-fourths full of water to a boil. Add 1 teaspoon salt and the broccoli. Bring back to a boil and cook until not quite tender, 4–5 minutes. Using a slotted spoon or tongs, transfer the broccoli to a colander; immediately place under cold running water to stop the cooking. Drain and set aside. To the still-boiling water, add the macaroni and cook until slightly underdone, 6–8 minutes or according to the timing on the package. Drain well.

❧ Place the broccoli in the prepared dish and scatter on the macaroni. Spoon on the sauce, then scatter with the remaining cheese and the bread crumbs. Bake, uncovered, until lightly browned and bubbling, 25–30 minutes. Serve at once. A ❧

SAFFRON RISOTTO WITH CRAB

SERVES 4

At a good restaurant in Italy, risotto can be absolute heaven—silky smooth and creamy, with a slight bite to each rice grain and the distinctive influence of other ingredients. No wonder people are willing to endure the 25–30 minutes of stirring required to coax the starch from the plump grains of Arborio rice.

✦ *For this risotto, it is best to use Arborio rice imported from Italy. I've included saffron and crab—two flavors that blend well with the rich, creamy rice. Plan your menu so that other dishes can be cooked ahead, freeing you to pay full attention to the risotto for the last half hour or so. The dish must be served and eaten at the moment the rice reaches the* al dente *stage—tender and cooked through, yet still pleasingly chewy.*

✦ *For the best taste and consistency, purchase fresh-cooked crabmeat. If there is no crab at the market, buy medium-sized shrimp (prawns), then peel, devein, and cook them before adding to the risotto.*

1 bunch of small leaf spinach,
   4–5 oz (125–155 g)
2 cups (16 fl oz/500 ml) bottled
   clam juice
2 cups (16 fl oz/500 ml) water
½ teaspoon saffron threads
salt
¼ cup (2 oz/60 g) unsalted butter
1 small yellow onion, finely chopped
   (about ½ cup/2 oz/60 g)
1½ cups (10½ oz/330 g) Italian Arborio
   rice or medium-grain white rice
1 cup (8 fl oz/250 ml) dry white wine
1 tablespoon dry Marsala
freshly ground pepper

½ lb (250 g) fresh-cooked crabmeat,
   picked over for any cartilage or
   shell fragments and flaked
2 tablespoons fresh lemon juice
chopped fresh flat-leaf (Italian)
   parsley (optional)

Wash the spinach carefully, drain well, and remove the stems. Pick out about 20 of the smallest leaves; reserve the rest for another use. Wrap the leaves in a damp kitchen towel and set aside. Combine the clam juice and water in a saucepan to form a broth and heat to just below boiling. Keep hot.

✦ To draw out the flavor of the saffron, place the saffron threads and a pinch of salt in a large metal spoon and hold over heat until warmed, just a few seconds. Using a teaspoon, crush the saffron threads to a powder. Place in a small bowl, add ½ cup (4 fl oz/ 125 ml) of the hot broth and set aside.

✦ In a large, heavy saucepan over medium-low heat, melt the butter. Add the onion and sauté, stirring, until translucent, 4–5 minutes. Add the rice and stir until coated with the butter and becoming opaque, about 2 minutes. Reduce the heat to low, add the white wine, and stir until the liquid has been absorbed, 3–4 minutes. Stir in the saffron broth and cook until absorbed, another 2 minutes.

✦ Start adding the hot clam broth, ½ cup (4 fl oz/125 ml) at a time, while stirring. Cook slowly, stirring frequently, until the liquid has been completely absorbed before adding the next batch of broth. The risotto is ready when it is creamy and the grains are tender but slightly al dente (firm to the bite) in the center. This will take 25–30 minutes; you may not need all of the liquid.

✦ Stir in the Marsala and salt and pepper to taste. Then gently stir in the crab and finally the lemon juice. Adjust the seasoning. Add more broth if necessary.

✦ To serve, arrange the spinach leaves on warmed plates or in shallow bowls, creating a bed for the risotto. Spoon the risotto in a mound on the spinach. Garnish with the parsley, if desired, and serve immediately.

SPINACH RISOTTO

SERVES 6–8

Starting in the late 1890s, risotto, a creamy rice dish that had been part of the northern Italian table since the 17th century, became a featured item on the menus of most Italian restaurants in the United States. Although short-grained Arborio rice is the most common Italian rice available, other varieties such as Carnaroli or Vialone Nano may also be used.

½ lb (250 g) spinach
4½ cups (36 fl oz/1.1 l) chicken stock
6 tablespoons (3 oz/90 g) unsalted
   butter
2 cups (14 oz/440 g) Arborio rice
½ cup (4 fl oz/125 ml) dry white wine
salt and freshly ground pepper
½ cup (2 oz/60 g) freshly grated
   Italian Parmesan cheese, preferably
   Parmigiano-Reggiano

Pick over the spinach, discarding any old or damaged leaves. Remove the stems and rinse well. Place in a saucepan with just the rinsing water clinging to the leaves. Cover and place over medium heat. Cook, turning once or twice, just until the leaves are wilted, 1–2 minutes. Transfer to a colander and drain, pressing out any excess water. Chop coarsely and set aside.

Place the stock in a saucepan and heat to just below boiling. Keep hot.

In a large, heavy saucepan over medium-low heat, melt 4 tablespoons (2 oz/60 g) of the butter. Add the rice and stir until coated with the butter and becoming opaque, about 2 minutes. Reduce the heat to low, add the white wine, and stir until the liquid has been absorbed, 2–3 minutes. Start adding the hot stock, ½ cup (4 fl oz/125 ml) at a time, while stirring. Cook slowly, stirring frequently, until the liquid has been completely absorbed and the grains are tender but slightly firm to the bite in the center. This will take 20–25 minutes; you may not need all of the liquid. Stir in the remaining 2 tablespoons butter and the chopped spinach. Season with salt and pepper, then remove from the heat.

Spoon the risotto into warmed individual bowls and top with the cheese. Serve immediately.

CHEESE AND BASIL RAVIOLI

MAKES 48–64 RAVIOLI; SERVES 4–6

On my yearly buying trips to Paris and London in the early 1960s, I enjoyed many pleasant evenings sharing a bottle of wine and talking about food with the now-departed great English food writer Elizabeth David. On one of those evenings, she explained to me the essentials of this recipe. I've never forgotten them, and have always found the ravioli excellent.

⌇ The use of boiling water, instead of egg, makes a more pliable dough that is much easier to roll out. I think you will find these ravioli very easy to make.

⌇ A good cheese shop will carry at least one of the softer cheeses you will need— provolone, fontal, or fontina—as well as high-quality Parmesan.

⌇ The ravioli can be made a few hours ahead and refrigerated, if necessary. Drape a piece of plastic wrap over them to keep them from drying out.

½ cup (2 oz/60 g) walnut pieces,
  coarsely chopped
1 egg
1½ cups (6 oz/185 g) freshly grated
  Italian Parmesan cheese, preferably
  Parmigiano-Reggiano
1½ cups (6 oz/185 g) shredded
  provolone, fontal or fontina cheese
1½ tablespoons chopped fresh basil, plus
  10–12 basil leaves, finely shredded,
  for garnish
freshly ground pepper
2 pinches of freshly grated nutmeg
¼–⅓ cup (2–3 fl oz/60–80 ml) milk
ravioli dough (recipe on page 284)
2 tablespoons unsalted butter
1 cup (8 fl oz/250 ml) heavy
  (double) cream
salt

Preheat an oven to 325°F (165°C). Spread the walnuts on a baking sheet and bake until the nuts begin to change color and are fragrant, about 10 minutes; do not allow to brown too much. Remove from the oven and let cool.

⌇ In a bowl, beat the egg until blended. Add 1 cup (4 oz/125 g) of the Parmesan cheese; the provolone, fontal, or fontina cheese; the 1½ tablespoons chopped basil; pepper to taste; and the nutmeg. Mix well. Stir in ¼ cup (2 fl oz/ 60 ml) milk to make a creamy but not runny mixture, adding more milk as needed to achieve the correct consistency. Set aside.

⌇ Prepare the ravioli dough, then roll out and fill as directed on page 284, using the cheese mixture.

⌇ In a large frying pan over medium heat, melt the butter. Add the cream and heat, stirring, until slightly thickened. Season with salt and pepper. Set aside and cover to keep warm.

⌇ Fill a large pot three-fourths full of water and bring to a rapid boil over high heat. Add 1 tablespoon salt and carefully slide in the ravioli. Cook until the ravioli rise to the surface and puff, 3–4 minutes. Using a slotted spoon, transfer the ravioli to the sauce in the frying pan.

⌇ Return the frying pan to medium heat and spoon the sauce over the ravioli until well coated and the sauce is thickened. Transfer to a warmed serving platter or warmed individual plates. Top evenly with the walnuts and shredded basil. Sprinkle with some of the remaining ½ cup (2 oz/60 g) Parmesan cheese and pass the rest at the table. ⌇

FETTUCCINE WITH ASPARAGUS AND ARUGULA

SERVES 4

Both asparagus and arugula are beloved by northern Italians, who have created many different ways to serve them. In this recipe they are married in an excellent sauce for the popular pasta ribbons known as fettuccine. The slight bitterness of the arugula leaves provides a nice balance to the sweetness of the asparagus and cream. A touch of lemon juice and zest, added just before serving, contributes an extra dimension of freshness.

➷ *I have found that pasta is best when served quite hot. See page 288 for other tips on draining, saucing, and serving pasta.*

1 lb (500 g) asparagus, preferably small, slender spears

1 bunch arugula (rocket), 4–5 oz (125–155 g)

2 tablespoons olive oil

4 or 5 green (spring) onions, including some tender green tops, coarsely chopped (about ¼ cup/1¼ oz/37 g)

¾ cup (6 fl oz/180 ml) heavy (double) cream

freshly grated nutmeg

salt and freshly ground pepper

¾–1 lb (375–500 g) dried fettuccine

2 lemons

Break or cut off any tough white ends of the asparagus spears and discard. If medium-sized or larger, peel the spears as well: using a vegetable peeler or an asparagus peeler and starting about 2 inches (5 cm) below the tip, peel off the thin outer skin from each spear. Cut on the diagonal into 1-inch (2.5-cm) lengths. You should have 2–2½ cups (8–10 oz/250–315 g). Set aside.

➷ Pick over the arugula, discarding any old leaves and the stems. Rinse and drain well. Pat dry 4 leaves to use for garnish and set aside. Tear or cut the remaining leaves into bite-sized pieces. You should have 2–2½ cups (2–2½ oz/ 60–75 g), loosely packed. Set aside.

➷ In a large saucepan over medium-low heat, warm the olive oil. Add the green onions and sauté gently, stirring, until translucent, 1–2 minutes. Add the cream, a sprinkling of nutmeg, and salt and pepper to taste. Set aside; cover to keep warm.

➷ Meanwhile, fill a large pot three-fourths full of water and bring to a rolling boil over high heat. Add the fettuccine and 1 tablespoon salt, stirring as you do. Boil for about 2 minutes. Add the asparagus and arugula and continue to boil until the fettuccine and asparagus are al dente (tender but firm to the bite), another 6–7 minutes. Drain and immediately add to the pan holding the cream mixture; act quickly so that a little water is still clinging to the pasta. Toss well. Taste and adjust the seasoning.

➷ Divide the pasta among warmed plates. Using a zester or fine-holed shredder, shred the zest (yellow part only) from 1 of the lemons directly onto the pasta (see page 287).

➷ Sprinkle a little nutmeg over each plate of pasta and garnish with the 4 reserved arugula leaves, tearing each leaf into small pieces. Cut the remaining lemon into wedges and place in a small bowl. Serve the pasta immediately, accompanied with the lemon wedges.

"Pasta is the single most universally captivating dish any cuisine has put on the table."

–Marcella Hazan

EGGS

Eggs are not meant for breakfast or brunch alone. Each of the following dishes is also perfectly suited to being the main attraction for lunch or a light evening meal.

A classic French Cheese Soufflé (this page), served here with an aromatic tomato-basil sauce, is a prime example. This airy creation makes a beautiful presentation and is relatively easy to prepare, belying the reputation of soufflés as being difficult to make.

For the very essence of ease, look no further than an Artichoke Flat Omelet (page 190). Although French in origin, it does not demand the dexterity called for when preparing traditional folded omelets. For another egg dish that is as satisfying as it is simple, try the Italian Swiss Chard and Poached Eggs with Polenta (page 191). The tender simmered eggs nestle on a bed of flavorful greens, tucked alongside a mound of polenta, making a one-plate meal that will satisfy morning, noon, or night.

CHEESE SOUFFLÉ WITH TOMATO-BASIL SAUCE

SERVES 4

It is often said in France that guests must wait for a soufflé; a soufflé will never wait for them. You must, indeed, serve it immediately so that it may be appreciated in all its well-risen glory.

A cheese soufflé is probably the easiest to make of all baked soufflés. Its success will depend upon the sauce being made properly, the egg whites being beaten to the correct degree, and the two being folded together but not overmixed.

When you put the soufflé mixture into the prepared dish, the top of the mixture should be about 1 inch (2.5 cm) below the rim. If the mixture is higher than that, you will need to wrap a paper collar around the rim to prevent the soufflé from running over during baking. To make a collar, cut a piece of waxed paper long enough to wrap around the dish. Fold it in half lengthwise and wrap it around the dish with the paper extending 1–2 inches (2.5–5 cm) above the rim. Tie firmly in place with kitchen string.

tomato-basil sauce (recipe on page 285)
1 cup (8 fl oz/250 ml) milk
2 tablespoons unsalted butter
2 tablespoons all-purpose (plain) flour
4 egg yolks, at room temperature
½ cup (2 oz/60 g) shredded
    Gruyère cheese
½ cup (2 oz/60 g) freshly grated
    Parmesan cheese
salt and freshly ground black pepper
cayenne pepper
1 tablespoon Madeira wine
5 egg whites, at room temperature
pinch of cream of tartar

Make the tomato-basil sauce and set aside. Position a rack in the middle of an oven and preheat to 350°F (180°C).

In a small saucepan, heat the milk until small bubbles appear around the edges of the pan. In another saucepan over medium heat, melt the butter. When foaming, add the flour and, using a whisk, stir until blended. Cook, stirring, for 1 minute; do not allow to brown. Gradually add the milk, whisking constantly. Continue whisking, regularly scraping the bottom and sides of the pan, until the mixture thickens and comes to a boil, 2–3 minutes. Cook for a few seconds more until thickened and smooth, then remove from the heat. Let cool a little.

In a bowl, whisk the egg yolks until pale yellow, 1–2 minutes. Gradually whisk the hot sauce into the yolks, then add the cheeses, salt and black pepper to taste, a sprinkling of cayenne, and the Madeira. Stir to mix well. Set aside.

Place the egg whites in a large, clean, dry bowl. Add the cream of tartar and, using a clean whisk or beaters, beat until soft peaks form and hold their shape. Spoon about one-fourth of the egg whites into the sauce and, using a rubber spatula, stir gently to blend. Gently fold the remaining egg whites into the sauce just until incorporated. Spoon the mixture into an ungreased 1½-qt (1.5-l) soufflé dish and bake until puffed and lightly browned, 35–40 minutes.

Warm the tomato-basil sauce gently over medium-low heat.

Remove the soufflé from the oven and carry it immediately to the table before it begins to fall. Spoon onto warmed plates and top each serving with a spoonful of the sauce. Pass the remaining sauce.

ARTICHOKE FLAT OMELET

SERVES 4

Not all of the omelets made in France are the traditional fluffy kind folded around a filling. Some, like this one, are more rustic pancakelike omelets in which the eggs and filling are combined. I find these omelettes plates easier to prepare and equally good. This is a splendid dish to serve at a weekend lunch accompanied by a green salad.

🎜 *For best results, make sure the pan is very hot before adding the butter. Test by flicking a few drops of water into the pan. The drops should sizzle and dance on the surface and immediately evaporate. When you add the soft butter, it should melt right away, spread out, and foam.*

juice of 1 lemon

salt

1 lb (500 g) baby artichokes, each about 1½ inches (4 cm) in diameter or less

8 thick slices lean smoked bacon, about ½ lb (250 g) total weight

6 eggs

1 tablespoon chopped fresh tarragon

2 tablespoons milk

freshly ground pepper

3 tablespoons unsalted butter, at room temperature

2–3 tablespoons heavy (double) cream

Fill a large saucepan three-fourths full of water. Add the lemon juice and 2 teaspoons salt. Working with 1 artichoke at a time, trim off the stem even with the bottom. Starting at the base, remove 3 or 4 layers of leaves until you reach tender, pale green leaves. Using a sharp knife, cut off the top half of the artichoke, then cut lengthwise into quarters and plunge them into the lemon water. When all of the artichokes have been trimmed, place the pan over medium-high heat and bring to a boil. Boil gently, uncovered, until the artichokes are tender, 10–15 minutes. Drain and set aside.

🎜 In a large frying pan over medium heat, gently fry the bacon slices until evenly golden and crisp on both sides, about 4 minutes total. Using tongs or a slotted utensil, transfer to paper towels to drain. Set aside and cover to keep warm.

🎜 Preheat a broiler (griller). In a bowl, combine the eggs, half of the tarragon, the milk, and salt and pepper to taste. Whisk quickly until blended.

🎜 Place a heavy, flameproof 10-inch (25-cm) omelet pan or frying pan, preferably nonstick, over medium heat and heat until hot. When hot, immediately add the butter and allow it to melt, tilting the pan until the bottom is completely coated and the butter foams. Pour in the egg mixture and immediately reduce the heat to medium-low. Cook slowly, shaking the pan occasionally. When the eggs are lightly golden on the bottom, in 2–3 minutes, arrange the quartered artichokes over the surface. Spoon the cream to taste evenly over the surface and place the pan under the broiler about 5 inches (13 cm) from the heat source. Broil (grill) until there is a touch of browning but the eggs are still soft and a little runny, 2–3 minutes. Immediately remove from the broiler.

🎜 Using a wide spatula, slide the omelet onto a warmed serving plate. Garnish with the remaining chopped tarragon. Cut into wedges and serve with the bacon. F 🎜

SWISS CHARD AND POACHED EGGS WITH POLENTA

SERVES 4

If you're used to eating poached eggs on toast or with potatoes, this Italian approach will come as a splendid surprise for your next Sunday brunch or lunch. Although young Swiss chard is preferable for this dish, you can use another green vegetable such as asparagus or spinach.

๑ *The eggs can be fried, if you like, but do so only lightly: cover them for a minute or two to steam until the whites are opaque and set.*

2 bunches green or red Swiss chard,
   about 2 lb (1 kg) total weight
salt
¼ cup (2 fl oz/60 ml) water
Polenta with Parmesan Cheese (recipe
   on page 226)
2 tablespoons cider vinegar
8 very fresh eggs
freshly grated nutmeg
freshly ground pepper

Rinse the chard leaves well and drain. Trim the white stems from the chard, including the first 2 inches (5 cm) that protrude into each leaf. Discard the stems. Stack the leaves in 2 piles on a cutting surface and, using a sharp knife, cut into strips 1 inch (2.5 cm) wide.

๑ Place the chard in a large sauté pan or large saucepan, sprinkle with a little salt, and add the water. Cover and set aside.

๑ Begin to cook the polenta as directed. While the polenta is cooking, place the chard over medium-high heat and cook, turning it several times, until wilted and tender, about 10 minutes. Transfer to a colander and, using a spoon, press against the chard to remove all the liquid. Fluff up with a fork. Place the colander over a pan of hot water and cover to keep warm.

๑ Meanwhile, poach the eggs: Fill a large, shallow pan with warm water, cover to keep warm, and set aside. In a large sauté pan or deep frying pan, pour in water to a depth of 1½ inches (4 cm). Add the vinegar and 1 teaspoon salt. Bring to a simmer over medium heat. Working in 2 or 3 batches, break the eggs, one at a time, into a saucer and, holding the saucer close to the surface of the water, slip each egg into the barely simmering water. Using a kitchen spoon, ease the whites as close to the yolks as possible. When the whites have firmed up a little, spoon the barely simmering water over the eggs and continue to cook until the whites are just set and the yolks are just glazed over but still liquid, 3–5 minutes. Using a slotted spoon or spatula, carefully transfer the eggs to the shallow pan of warm water. Poach the remaining eggs in the same way.

๑ To serve, fluff up the chard again and divide among 4 warmed plates. Sprinkle with a little nutmeg. Using a slotted spoon, pick up 1 poached egg at a time, press a paper towel against the underside of the spoon to soak up the excess moisture, and then place the egg on top of the chard, putting 2 eggs on each plate. Sprinkle the eggs with a little salt and pepper. Spoon the hot polenta onto each plate. Top the polenta with some of the remaining Parmesan cheese and serve at once. Pass the rest of the cheese in a bowl. ๑

Side Dishes

$\mathcal{V}$EGETABLES

When picked at the peak of their season, fresh vegetables are the picture of perfection. But as these recipes make clear, it's a simple matter to improve upon perfection when all you need to add is a pinch of herbs or a touch of cream.

Summertime beans burst with flavor when combined with a refreshing herb and lemon zest in Italian Green Beans with Mint (page 222). Dairy products enrich a wide range of classic recipes, from French Broccoli Gratin (page 217) to American-style Baked Peppers with Cream (page 197) to Italian Braised Fennel in Milk (page 202).

One of the simplest ways a cook can bring out the best in vegetables is to choose a cooking method that highlights an ingredient's inherent qualities. The French bake their beets (page 218) rather than boiling them, producing a more intense taste and texture. Fresh green peas gain enormously in sweetness when they are puréed (page 223).

GLAZED CARROTS WITH MARSALA AND HAZELNUTS

SERVES 4

Wine has been used in Italian cooking since the days of ancient Rome. One of the most popular choices of recent times is Marsala, an amber, aromatic wine used in many meat dishes and desserts, as well as with some vegetables.

Carrots and Marsala go together especially well. Rich, crunchy hazelnuts seem to add just the right finishing touch to this easy but memorable side dish.

½ cup (2½ oz/75 g) hazelnuts (filberts)
1 lb (500 g) carrots (6 or 7)
1 cup (8 fl oz/250 ml) water
½ teaspoon salt
3 tablespoons unsalted butter
2 shallots, minced (2 tablespoons)
½ cup (4 fl oz/125 ml) dry Marsala, preferably Italian
⅓ cup (3 oz/90 g) sugar
bouquets of fresh aromatic herbs, such as mint, rosemary, basil, oregano, and dill, preferably with blossoms, for garnish

Position a rack in the middle of an oven and preheat to 325°F (165°C). Spread the hazelnuts on a baking sheet and bake until the nuts begin to change color, are fragrant, and the skins split and loosen, 5–10 minutes. Let cool for a few minutes. When cool enough to handle, wrap the nuts in a clean kitchen towel and rub them with the palms of your hands to remove most of the skins. Transfer to a coarse-mesh sieve and shake the nuts to separate them from their skins. Do not worry if small bits of the skins remain. Chop the nuts coarsely and set aside.

Peel the carrots and cut in half crosswise. Cut the upper (thicker) portions in half lengthwise so that all the pieces are more or less uniform in size (this ensures that they will cook evenly and quickly). In a sauté pan or large saucepan over medium-high heat, combine the carrots, water, salt, and 1 tablespoon of the butter. Bring to a boil, reduce the heat to low, cover tightly, and barely simmer until the carrots are tender when pierced with the tip of a sharp knife, 10–15 minutes. If the liquid begins to cook away, add a few tablespoons water. Drain, transfer to a plate, and set aside.

In the same pan over medium-low heat, melt the remaining 2 tablespoons butter. Add the shallots and sauté gently, stirring, until translucent, 4–5 minutes. Add the Marsala and sugar and simmer, stirring, until the sugar dissolves. Continue to simmer, stirring occasionally, until thickened to a medium syrup consistency, 4–5 minutes. Return the carrots to the pan, add the chopped hazelnuts, and carefully turn the carrots in the syrup until well coated.

Transfer the carrots to a warmed serving dish or warmed individual plates. Spoon the glaze and hazelnuts over the carrots. Garnish with the herb bouquets and serve immediately.

WARM POTATO SALAD

SERVES 4

A French favorite, warm potato salad makes an exceptional accompaniment to hot cooked sausages or to cold meats served at room temperature. It is also very good served on its own.

I find that Yukon gold potatoes have the best flavor for this salad, and their texture holds together when tossed with the dressing. They are readily available in many markets now. If you cannot find them, use other white potatoes such as white rose or red new potatoes. The potatoes may be left unpeeled, if you like.

1½ lb (750 g) small boiling potatoes, preferably Yukon gold
2 teaspoons salt
3 oz (90 g) thickly sliced smoked lean bacon (about 3 slices)

FOR THE DRESSING:
2 tablespoons tarragon white wine vinegar
⅛ teaspoon salt
freshly ground pepper
⅓ cup (3 fl oz/80 ml) extra-virgin olive oil

2 tablespoons chopped green (spring) onion, including some tender green tops (3 or 4 onions)
2 tablespoons chopped fresh parsley, preferably flat-leaf (Italian)
1 teaspoon chopped fresh tarragon

Scrub the potatoes, but do not peel. Place them in a saucepan with water to cover and add the salt. Bring to a boil over medium-high heat, cover partially, and cook until just tender when pierced with the tip of a sharp knife, 20–30 minutes. Drain and let cool slightly.

Meanwhile, cut the bacon crosswise into pieces ¼ inch (6 mm) wide. Place in a heavy frying pan over medium-low heat and fry, stirring occasionally, until golden and crisp, 3–4 minutes. Do not allow to brown too much. Using a slotted spoon, transfer to paper towels to drain. Pour off the fat from the pan, wipe clean with a paper towel, and set aside.

To make the dressing, in a small saucepan, combine the vinegar, salt, and pepper to taste and stir until the salt dissolves. Gradually add the olive oil, whisking until well blended. Place over low heat and heat until warm. Set aside and cover to keep warm.

When the potatoes are cool enough to handle, peel them and cut into slices about ½ inch (12 mm) thick. Place in a warmed serving bowl and add the green onion, parsley, and tarragon. Toss lightly.

Return the bacon to the reserved pan and place over medium heat to warm. Whisk the warm dressing again and add about three-fourths of it to the potatoes. Toss lightly, adding more dressing if needed. Taste and adjust the seasoning. Garnish with the bacon and serve. F

BAKED PEPPERS WITH CREAM

SERVES 4

Cream works wonders with vegetables. Red bell peppers (capsicums), for example, become rich, tender, and wonderfully sweet when baked in a little cream, making a beautiful side dish for a special meal featuring grilled steak, chops, or fish. You can substitute yellow or orange bell peppers, or prepare a mixture. Don't use green peppers, however, as they lack the necessary sweetness. The ingredients can be prepared well in advance up to the point of assembling everything in the baking dish.

⅔ *Fresh basil now seems to be widely available, and it is at the peak of season at the same time as red peppers. Dried basil doesn't have the same flavor; if you can't find fresh, just omit the basil altogether.*

1½ lb (750 g) red bell peppers
    (capsicums) (4 or 5)
2 tablespoons minced shallot
6–8 large fresh basil leaves, thinly
    shredded (2–3 tablespoons), plus
    whole basil leaves for garnish
¾ cup (6 fl oz/180 ml) heavy
    (double) cream
salt and freshly ground pepper

Roast and peel the bell peppers (see page 290): Preheat a broiler (griller) or an oven to 500°F (260°C). Cut the peppers in half lengthwise and remove the stems, seeds, and ribs. Lay the peppers, cut side down, on a baking sheet. Place under the broiler or in the oven. Broil (grill) or roast until the skins blister and blacken. Remove the peppers from the oven and cover with aluminum foil. Let steam until cool enough to handle, 10–15 minutes. Then, using your fingers or a knife, peel off the skins. Set aside.

⅔ Position a rack in the middle of the oven and reduce the temperature to 375°F (190°C). Butter a 1½-qt (1.5-l) shallow baking dish.

⅔ Scatter half of the shallot and half of the shredded basil over the bottom of the prepared dish. Add the pepper halves, cut side down, arranged in a single layer or slightly overlapping. Scatter the remaining shallot and shredded basil over the peppers. Pour the cream over the peppers, making sure they are all evenly moistened. Season with salt and pepper.

⅔ Place in the oven and bake uncovered, basting several times with the cream to keep the peppers moist, until the cream thickens and the peppers are tender when pierced with a fork, 30–35 minutes.

⅔ Garnish with the basil leaves and serve at once. A ⅔

"If pale beans bubble for you in a red earthenware pot, you can often decline the dinners of sumptuous hosts."

—Martial

FLAGEOLET BEANS WITH CREAM

SERVES 4

Prepared in this way, flageolets are delicious alongside grilled lamb, chicken, or fish. You can also serve them on their own as a warm first course.

❧ *Now grown in the United States, dried domestic flageolet beans can be found along with imported varieties in specialty-food shops and the international section of some large food stores. I have found that the domestic beans are smaller and not as old as some of the imported varieties, and thus cook in less time.*

1½ cups (10½ oz/330 g) dried
  flageolet beans
2 fresh thyme sprigs
2 fresh parsley sprigs
1 bay leaf
1 celery stalk, cut crosswise into
  4 equal pieces
1 small sweet white onion, stuck with
  2 whole cloves
salt
1 tablespoon sour cream
1½–2 teaspoons Dijon mustard
½–¾ cup (4–6 fl oz/125–180 ml) heavy
  (double) cream
2 teaspoons chopped fresh tarragon,
  plus more to taste, if needed
freshly ground pepper

Sort through the beans, discarding any damaged beans or small stones. Rinse and drain. Place in a large saucepan and add water to cover by 2 inches (5 cm). Bring to a boil over high heat, remove from the heat, cover, and set aside to soak for 1 hour.

❧ Drain, rinse, and return the beans to the saucepan with water to cover by 1 inch (2.5 cm). Place the thyme and parsley sprigs and bay leaf inside the celery pieces and tie securely with kitchen string to form a bouquet garni. Add to the pan along with the clove-studded onion and ½ teaspoon salt. Bring to a boil over medium-high heat, reduce the heat to low, cover partially, and simmer gently until the beans are tender, 30–45 minutes; the timing will depend upon the size and age of the beans.

❧ Remove and discard the bouquet garni and the onion. Let cool for 10 minutes, then drain the beans and return them to the pan. In a small bowl, combine the sour cream and mustard to taste and mix well. Add the heavy cream to taste, stir until well blended, and then stir in 1 teaspoon of the tarragon. Add the cream mixture to the beans, stir gently to blend, and place over medium-low heat. Warm gently to serving temperature. Season to taste with salt, pepper, and more mustard, cream, or tarragon if needed. Do not stir too much or the beans will become mushy.

❧ Transfer to a warmed serving dish or spoon onto warmed plates. Sprinkle evenly with the remaining tarragon and serve immediately. F ❧

ROASTED RED PEPPERS WITH OREGANO

SERVES 4

Roasted red peppers (capsicums) like these are a classic item on menus in Italy, and for good reason. Deliciously sweet when roasted, the peppers make an excellent hot accompaniment to a main course. They can also be served cold as a first course or as part of an antipasto table.

Today, with air transport, red peppers are available from some part of the world year-round. But the dish is likely to be at its best, and cost the least, if you make it in summertime—when local peppers are plentiful and in peak condition.

You can prepare the peppers ahead of time, right up to their final baking. Leave them covered at room temperature for up to 2 hours before putting them in the oven.

If fresh oregano is unavailable, substitute fresh marjoram, basil, dill, or mint.

1½–2 lb (750 g–1 kg) red bell peppers (capsicums)

3 tablespoons olive oil

2 cloves garlic, minced

1 small sweet white onion, chopped (about ½ cup/2 oz/60 g)

2 teaspoons chopped fresh oregano

2 tablespoons balsamic vinegar

salt and freshly ground pepper

coarsely chopped fresh flat-leaf (Italian) parsley for garnish

Roast and peel the bell peppers (see page 290). Cut the peppers lengthwise into strips ½ inch (12 mm) wide. Set aside.

Position a rack in the middle of an oven and preheat to 375°F (190°C). In a small saucepan over medium-low heat, warm 1 tablespoon of the olive oil. When hot, add the garlic and sauté gently, stirring, for 30–40 seconds. Add the onion and sauté slowly, stirring, until the onion is translucent, 4–5 minutes; do not allow it to brown. Remove from the heat, add the oregano, and stir to blend. Transfer to a rectangular or oval baking dish, spreading the mixture evenly over the bottom. Arrange the peppers evenly in the dish.

In a small bowl, combine the balsamic vinegar and a little salt and pepper. Using a small whisk, stir until well blended, then whisk in the remaining 2 tablespoons olive oil. Spoon evenly over the peppers. Cover the dish with aluminum foil and bake for 10 minutes. Remove the foil and continue to bake until the peppers are very tender, another 5–10 minutes.

Garnish with the parsley and serve immediately.

"Lunch is going to be a feast. Our red peppers are to be impaled on the electric spit and roasted until their skins are charred. Then we shall peel them, cut them in strips, dress them with the good olive oil we have bought. Over them we strew chopped parsley and garlic and leave them to mature in their dressing."

—Elizabeth David

BRAISED FENNEL IN MILK

SERVES 4

Those people who have encountered fresh fennel only as part of a salad in Italian restaurants are often surprised by how good it can be when cooked. It develops a delightful flavor, with only subtle hints of anise. In Italy, you'll find fennel grilled, fried, sautéed, roasted, and prepared as a gratin. I prefer cooking the vegetable in milk, which further mellows its flavor.
🙟 *Take care to cook the fennel just until tender. Any longer, and it can fall apart and lose its appeal.*

2–3 small fennel bulbs, about
  1½ lb (750 g) total weight
¾ cup (6 fl oz/180 ml) milk
2 tablespoons unsalted butter, cut into
  small cubes
salt and freshly ground pepper
¼ cup (1 oz/30 g) freshly grated
  Italian Parmesan cheese, preferably
  Parmigiano-Reggiano

Trim off any stems and bruised stalks from the fennel bulbs; save any feathery sprigs for garnish. Trim the root end but leave the core intact. Cut each bulb in half lengthwise and then cut each half lengthwise into 4 wedges; the portion of the core with each wedge will hold it together.

🙟 In a large sauté pan or frying pan, arrange the fennel wedges, in a single layer if possible. Add the milk, then dot the surface with the butter cubes, and sprinkle with salt and pepper to taste. Bring to a simmer over medium heat, reduce the heat to medium-low, cover partially, and simmer for 15 minutes; watch carefully that the milk does not boil over. Turn the wedges over once during cooking. Uncover, raise the heat slightly and cook until the fennel is just tender when pierced with a sharp knife and the milk is reduced to 1–2 tablespoons, about 15 minutes longer.

➷ Meanwhile, position a rack in the middle of an oven and preheat to 400°F (200°C). Butter a baking dish in which the fennel wedges will fit comfortably. Using a spatula, carefully transfer the fennel, with its liquid, to the baking dish, arranging the wedges in a single layer. Top with the Parmesan cheese. Bake until golden on top, 10–15 minutes.

➷ To serve, chop any reserved feathery fennel sprigs and use for garnish. Serve at once. ◻ ➷

Trim the green beans, discarding any old or large ones, and put them in a shallow dish or pan in which they lie flat. Add ice water to cover and set aside to crisp, 10–15 minutes.

➷ In a sauté pan or deep frying pan in which the beans will lie flat, pour in water to a depth of 2–3 inches (5–7.5 cm). Bring to a boil over high heat. When the water is boiling vigorously, drain the beans and plunge them into the boiling water. Add 2 teaspoons salt. When the water returns to a boil, continue to boil until the beans are just tender but still crisp, 4–5 minutes. Drain and immediately plunge into cold water to stop the cooking; then drain again. Set aside.

➷ Pour off the water from the pan if you have not already done so and place the pan over medium-low heat. Add the butter; when it is melted and foaming, add the shallots. Sauté, stirring, until translucent, 1–2 minutes; do not allow them to brown. Add the beans and squeeze on a few drops of the juice from the lemon half. Season with salt and pepper. Toss until the beans are evenly seasoned and hot.

➷ Using tongs, arrange the beans on a warmed serving plate. Spoon the shallots over the beans. Garnish the plate with the lemon wedges and mint sprigs and serve at once. ◻F ➷

GREEN BEANS WITH SHALLOTS

SERVES 4

I find that green beans cook better if they are first put into ice water to crisp and then cooked as quickly as possible. Spreading the beans out in rapidly boiling water helps cook them faster.

➷ *If you like mint, try mixing 1 tablespoon of the chopped fresh herb with the beans just before serving. It's a delicious way to enjoy them.*

1 lb (500 g) young, tender green beans, preferably a uniform 4–5 inches (10–13 cm) long

ice water to cover

salt

1 tablespoon unsalted butter

2 oz (60 g) shallots (3 or 4 shallots), thinly sliced crosswise

½ lemon, plus 4 lemon wedges for garnish

freshly ground pepper

4 fresh mint sprigs

"*Cauliflower is nothing but cabbage with a college education.*"

—*Mark Twain*

CAULIFLOWER WITH CHERRY TOMATOES

SERVES 4

American cooking has gradually absorbed the spices and herbs of many other cuisines, enhancing even the simplest preparations of vegetables and meats. The mild Anaheim (New Mexican) chile, or the Hungarian wax variety, goes well with some of our blander vegetables, like the cauliflower in this recipe. Cilantro, too, adds bright flavor, although this fresh form of coriander needs to be used with discretion because not everyone likes it.

Cauliflower is one of the easiest and quickest vegetables to steam, and I think its strong flavor is made milder by steaming. Small, sweet cherry tomatoes are the perfect companion in both taste and color.

1 head of cauliflower, about 2 lb (1 kg)
1 fresh green Anaheim chile or Hungarian wax pepper
¾ lb (375 g) small ripe cherry tomatoes (about 2 cups)
2 tablespoons unsalted butter
½ yellow onion, chopped (½ cup/2 oz/60 g)
2 tablespoons water
2 teaspoons chopped fresh cilantro (fresh coriander)
salt and freshly ground pepper

Remove the florets from the head of cauliflower. Cut any large ones in half, so they are all the same size. Set aside.

Slice the chile in half lengthwise. Remove the seeds and ribs and discard. Cut crosswise into slices ⅛ inch (3 mm) thick. Set aside.

Remove the stems from the cherry tomatoes. Slice one-third of the tomatoes in half and leave the remainder whole. Set aside.

Bring a saucepan three-fourths full of water to a boil. Add the cauliflower and bring back to a boil. Reduce the heat to medium and cook, uncovered, at a gentle boil until just tender but still crisp, 5–6 minutes. Drain and keep warm. Alternatively, put the cauliflower in a steamer basket and place in a saucepan over simmering water. Cover and steam until tender, 6–7 minutes. Set aside.

Meanwhile, in a sauté pan over medium-low heat, melt the butter. Add the onion and sauté, stirring, for 1 minute. Add 1 tablespoon of the water, cover, and cook, stirring occasionally, until translucent, 3–4 minutes. Add the chile slices and the remain-ing 1 tablespoon water, cover, and cook, stirring occasionally, for another 3–4 minutes. Uncover, add all the tomatoes, ½ teaspoon of the cilantro, and salt and pepper to taste. Sauté uncovered, stirring and tossing, until the halved tomatoes begin to break down and release their juices, 1–2 minutes. Taste and adjust the seasoning. Remove from the heat.

Arrange the cauliflower in a serving dish and spoon the tomato mixture over it. Sprinkle with the remaining 1½ teaspoons cilantro. A

FRENCH CARROTS

This side dish is also known as carrots Vichy. Vichy water, from the French spa of the same name, was supposed to have made the difference in the cooking. But actually any water will do in this glazing process, which slowly cooks the carrots until the liquid reduces to a spoonful or so of syrup. The addition of lemon zest is my contribution to tradition.

1 lb (500 g) large carrots (6 or 7)
3–4 tablespoons (1½–2 oz/45–60 g) unsalted butter
2 tablespoons sugar
½ teaspoon salt
1 cup (8 fl oz/250 ml) water
1 lemon
4 or 5 fresh mint sprigs

Peel the carrots, then slice on the diagonal about ⅛ inch (3 mm) thick. You should have about 3 cups. Put them into a heavy saucepan together with the butter, sugar, salt, and water. Place over medium heat and bring to a boil. Reduce the heat to medium–low and boil gently, uncovered, until the liquid is reduced to 1–2 tablespoons syrup, 20–25 minutes; check the carrots occasionally to be sure they are not scorching. Transfer to a serving dish.

❧ Remove the zest from the lemon (see page 287): Using a zester or fine-holed shredder, and holding the lemon over the carrots, shred the zest (yellow part only) from the skin evenly over the carrots.

❧ Garnish with the mint sprigs and serve at once. ▣❧

ASPARAGUS MIMOSA SALAD

SERVES 4

Take care not to overcook the asparagus; the stalks should be tender-crisp. I think the best way to cook slender young asparagus stalks is in a sauté pan or frying pan large enough to hold them perfectly flat and fully covered in boiling water. For medium to large stalks, I like to use a vertical asparagus pot. It holds the stalks upright, allowing the tender tips to steam while the tougher bottoms boil in water.

The chopped egg whites and sieved yolks that garnish the asparagus are said to resemble mimosa flowers, giving the salad its name. Some people have trouble keeping the hard-cooked yolks from taking on a greenish color. I've found the secret to keeping them bright yellow is to start with very fresh eggs and, once they are boiled, transfer them immediately to a bowl of cold water.

For the dressing, choose an extra-virgin olive oil with a mild flavor that won't mask the delicacy of the tarragon-flavored white wine vinegar.

1 red bell pepper (capsicum)

2 eggs, at room temperature

1½ lb (750 g) asparagus

salt

2 tablespoons tarragon white wine vinegar

½ cup (4 fl oz/125 ml) mild extra-virgin olive oil

2 tablespoons minced green (spring) onion, including some tender green tops

freshly ground pepper

¼ cup (2 oz/60 g) well-drained capers

Roast and peel the bell pepper as directed on page 290. Cut the pepper into long, narrow strips and set aside.

To hard-cook the eggs, make a tiny hole in one end of the shell with a pin or needle to help avoid cracking. Place the eggs in a saucepan and add water to cover. Place over medium heat and bring to a boil; reduce the heat to low and simmer for 15 minutes. Immediately plunge the eggs into cold water. When cool enough to handle, crack each shell and then roll each egg around in the palm of your hand to crack it evenly all over. Peel off the shell. Separate the whites from the yolks. Coarsely chop the whites; cover and set aside. Using the back of a wooden spoon, force the yolks through a coarse-mesh sieve into a bowl; cover and set aside.

Cut or break off the tough white ends of the asparagus. Trim all to the same length. If the asparagus are large, peel the tough skin from the stalk as well: using a vegetable peeler and starting 2 inches (5 cm) below the tip, peel off the thin outer skin. Bring a large sauté pan or frying pan half full of water to a boil. Add 1 teaspoon salt and the asparagus, return to a boil, reduce the heat slightly, and simmer, uncovered, until tender but still crisp, 6–9 minutes, depending upon their size. Drain and immediately plunge into cold water to stop the cooking. Drain again, pat dry with paper towels, and set aside.

In a small bowl, stir together the vinegar and ⅛ teaspoon salt until the salt dissolves. Add the olive oil and whisk until well blended. Stir in the green onion and pepper to taste.

Arrange the asparagus on a serving plate or individual plates. Carefully spoon the dressing over the asparagus, particularly over the tips and the upper part of the spears. Spoon the chopped egg whites over the asparagus, in a crosswise band, and then spoon the yolks on top of the whites. Arrange the red pepper strips over the asparagus and garnish the egg yolks with the capers.

SAUTÉED ZUCCHINI AND MUSHROOMS

SERVES 4

Often referred to as Italian squash, zucchini (courgettes) have invaded the world's food markets and home gardens, probably because they are incredibly easy to grow, are prolific in their yield, and are highly versatile in the kitchen. The Italians, certainly, make good and frequent use of them in their cuisine.

The vegetables you select for this recipe must be young and fresh. The mushrooms, in particular, should be small and very firm, with no brown gills showing beneath their caps.

The zest of the lemon brings out the flavors of the vegetables and herbs. Have everything else ready to serve before you begin cooking this dish, so that the zucchini and mushrooms arrive at the table hot and crisp.

1 lb (500 g) small zucchini (courgettes)
salt
1 lb (500 g) small, firm fresh mushrooms
5 tablespoons (3 fl oz/80 ml) olive oil
2 cloves garlic, chopped
¼ cup firmly packed, finely shredded
  fresh basil leaves
freshly ground pepper
1 lemon

Trim off the ends of the zucchini and cut on the diagonal into slices ½ inch (12 mm) thick. Place in a colander and sprinkle with salt, tossing to distribute the salt evenly. Spread the zucchini out in the colander. Let stand over a bowl or in the sink for 40–50 minutes to drain off excess moisture and bitterness. Rinse and pat dry with a clean kitchen towel. Set aside.

Using a soft brush or a clean kitchen towel, clean the mushrooms of any bits of soil; do not wash. Trim the stems. Cut the mushrooms into slices ¼ inch (6 mm) thick. Place in a bowl and set aside.

In a large sauté pan or frying pan over medium heat, warm 2 tablespoons of the olive oil. Add the zucchini and sauté, tossing often, until tender but still firm, 8–10 minutes. Transfer to a bowl and set aside.

Add another 2 tablespoons olive oil to the same pan over medium-high heat. Add the mushrooms and sauté, tossing often, until the mushrooms begin to soften, 6–7 minutes. Transfer to the bowl with the zucchini.

Add the remaining 1 tablespoon olive oil to the pan, reduce the heat to medium-low, and add the garlic. Sauté gently, stirring, until the garlic just begins to change color, 30–40 seconds.

Return the mushrooms and zucchini to the pan and add the basil and salt and pepper to taste. Raise the heat and toss until the vegetables are hot.

Transfer to a warmed serving dish. Using a zester or fine-holed shredder, shred the zest (yellow part only) from the lemon directly onto the vegetables (see page 287). Serve immediately.

"Small and firm—almost crisp, zucchini can be a great delicacy, but to remain so they should never touch water in the course of cooking."

–Richard Olney

LEEKS IN TOMATO SAUCE

SERVES 4

Try serving this hot or at room temperature as a first course, or accompany it with rice to make a light main course. You can also serve the leeks chilled; but in that case you may wish to increase the seasonings slightly, since they will be muted by the cooler temperature.

It's a shame that leeks are often overlooked in the market. Easy to prepare, they lend themselves well to many recipes. You can substitute them for onions, or include them along with onions, to give a decidedly different flavor. Be sure to rinse the leeks thoroughly to rid them of any sand or grit lodged between the leaves, following the instructions in the recipe.

1 lb (500 g) ripe plum (Roma)
  tomatoes (4 or 5)
4 medium leeks
1 bay leaf
2 whole cloves
½ cup (4 fl oz/125 ml) dry white wine,
  or as needed
½ cup (4 fl oz/125 ml) chicken stock,
  or as needed
3 tablespoons extra-virgin olive oil or
  vegetable oil
¼ cup (1 oz/30 g) diced sweet red
  (Spanish) onion or other sweet onion
⅛ teaspoon salt
scant ¼ teaspoon red pepper flakes

Core and peel the tomatoes (see page 289): Bring a saucepan three-fourths full of water to a boil. Core the tomatoes and then cut a shallow X in the opposite end. Put them into the boiling water for 20–30 seconds to loosen the skins. Using a slotted spoon, transfer the tomatoes to a bowl of cold water. Using your fingers or a paring knife, immediately remove the skins. Cut in half crosswise and carefully squeeze out the seeds. Coarsely chop; you should have about 2 cups (12 oz/375 g). Set aside in a bowl.

Trim the leeks, leaving some of the tender green tops intact and cutting them all to the same length. Make a lengthwise slit along each leek to within about 2 inches (5 cm) of the root end. Place under running water to wash away any dirt lodged between the leaves.

To blanch the leeks, select a large sauté pan or frying pan that will accommodate the leeks lying flat. Fill three-fourths full of water and bring to a boil. Add the leeks and boil for 2–3 minutes. Drain carefully and, when cool enough to handle, finish cutting the leeks in half lengthwise.

In the same pan, place the bay leaf and cloves. Arrange the leek halves on top of the spices in a single layer, cut side up.

Add the wine, chicken stock, oil, onion, salt, and red pepper flakes to the bowl holding the tomatoes and stir well to blend. Spoon the tomato mixture evenly over the leeks.

Bring the leeks to a simmer, reduce the heat to low, and cook uncovered at a bare simmer (just a few bubbles), basting occasionally, until the leeks are tender, 45–60 minutes; add more chicken stock or wine if too dry.

Taste and adjust the seasoning. Serve hot or at room temperature. A

STUFFED ZUCCHINI

SERVES 4

With a filling of bread crumbs and ham and a fragrant tomato sauce on top, this pleasing recipe reminds me of the kind of French country cooking found in a village restaurant. Serve it as a side dish with roasted or grilled meats, poultry, or seafood; or offer it on its own for a light lunch or supper, accompanied with a green salad.

꙰ *Purchase a piece of good-quality smoked ham from your butcher.*

6 zucchini (courgettes), 5–6 oz
   (155–185 g) each and not longer
   than 8 inches (20 cm)
2 tablespoons unsalted butter
¼ cup (¾ oz/20 g) minced green
   (spring) onion, including tender
   green tops (6 or 7 onions)
½ lb (250 g) smoked ham, trimmed of
   any fat and minced
1 cup (4 oz/125 g) fine dried bread
   crumbs (see page 217)
salt and freshly ground pepper

FOR THE TOMATO SAUCE:

1 lb (500 g) ripe plum (Roma)
   tomatoes
2 tablespoons unsalted butter
1 large clove garlic, minced
¼ cup (1½ oz/45 g) minced yellow
   onion
½ teaspoon minced fresh oregano or
   ¼ teaspoon dried oregano
½ small green bell pepper (capsicum),
   seeded, deribbed, and minced

Fill a large saucepan three-fourths full of water and bring to a boil. Add the zucchini and parboil for 2–3 minutes. Drain, cool, and slice in half lengthwise. Scoop out the pulp from each half, leaving walls ¼ inch (6 mm) thick; reserve the pulp. Lightly salt the cut sides and invert on a rack to drain for 30 minutes. Finely chop the pulp and drain in a sieve, pressing with a spoon. Set aside.

꙰ Position a rack in the top third of an oven and preheat the oven to 375°F (190°C). Butter a 9-by-13-inch (23-by-33-cm) rectangular baking dish.

꙰ In a sauté pan over medium-low heat, melt the butter. Add the green onion and sauté until translucent, 1–2 minutes. Add the ham and sauté for 4–5 minutes. Add the zucchini pulp and sauté until the moisture evaporates, 4–5 minutes. Remove from the heat and stir in half of the bread crumbs. Season with salt and pepper.

꙰ Pat the zucchini halves dry with paper towels and place in the prepared dish, cut side up. Fill the cavities with the ham mixture, rounding the tops if necessary. Cover evenly with the remaining bread crumbs and bake until the crumbs are golden and the zucchini is tender when pierced with a knife tip, 30–40 minutes.

꙰ Meanwhile, make the tomato sauce: Core, seed, and peel the tomatoes (see page 289). Chop coarsely. In a saucepan

over medium-low heat, melt the butter. Add the garlic and yellow onion and sauté until translucent, 3–4 minutes. Add the tomatoes, oregano, and bell pepper, raise the heat to medium and sauté until the tomatoes are soft, 20–25 minutes. Season with salt and pepper.

❧ Place the zucchini on warmed plates and top with the sauce. F ❧

BAKED EGGPLANT AND TOMATO

SERVES 4

This simple side dish is found almost everywhere in the south of France. You might recognize it as a version of the familiar vegetable stew known as ratatouille, of which there are many variations. It is equally good served at room temperature.
❧ *If you cannot find fresh thyme and oregano, substitute ¼ teaspoon of each of them dried.*

1 eggplant (aubergine), about
   1 lb (500 g)
olive oil for brushing, plus 2 tablespoons
   olive oil
1 lb (500 g) ripe plum (Roma)
   tomatoes
1 tablespoon chopped garlic
   (about 3 cloves)
1 yellow onion, finely diced (about
   1 cup/5 oz/155 g)
1 green bell pepper (capsicum), seeded,
   deribbed, and cut lengthwise into
   slices ½ inch (12 mm) wide
½ teaspoon chopped fresh thyme
½ teaspoon chopped fresh oregano
salt and freshly ground pepper

Preheat a broiler (griller). Cut the eggplant in half lengthwise and place on an oiled baking sheet, cut side down.

Brush the skin of each eggplant half with olive oil and, using a fork, pierce the skin in 6 or 7 places. Place under the broiler with the top of the eggplant about 4 inches (10 cm) from the heat source. Broil (grill) until the skin is blistered and beginning to blacken, 15–20 minutes. Remove, cover loosely with aluminum foil, and set aside to cool. The eggplant will continue to steam for a few minutes.

❧ Core, peel, and seed the tomatoes (see page 289). Chop coarsely; you should have about 2 cups (12 oz/ 375 g). Set aside.

❧ When the eggplant halves are cool enough to handle, using your fingers, carefully remove the skin. Cut the eggplant halves crosswise into slices ½ inch (12 mm) thick. Place the slices in an oiled oval or rectangular baking dish in a single layer or layered slightly, depending upon the size of the dish. Set aside.

❧ Position a rack in the upper third of an oven and preheat to 350°F (180°C). In a sauté pan or frying pan over medium-low heat, warm the 2 tablespoons olive oil. When hot but not smoking, add the garlic and sauté, stirring, until it begins to change color, 20–30 seconds. Add the onion and sauté, stirring, until translucent, 6–7 minutes. Add the tomatoes, bell pepper, thyme, and oregano, cover partially, and cook, stirring occasionally, until the tomatoes have broken down, 10–15 minutes. Season with salt and pepper.

❧ Spoon the tomato mixture evenly over the eggplant, cover loosely with aluminum foil, and bake until bubbly, 25–30 minutes. Serve immediately directly from the dish. F ❧

MASHED POTATOES WITH ROSEMARY AND LEMON

SERVES 4

If you've ever eaten mashed or puréed potatoes in Italy or France, you'll probably understand why I specify Yukon gold or Yellow Finn potatoes—varieties that are similar to those used by Italian and French cooks. These small, waxy, golden potatoes can be mashed or puréed smoothly and quickly, producing results that are superior in flavor and consistency to most other potatoes. If you can't find them, use russet or other waxy boiling potatoes. I find that red new potatoes are not the best choice for mashed potatoes.

A potato ricer (see page 293) is the easiest and most efficient way to mash potatoes. The pulp is easily forced through the small holes to produce a fine texture. And a ricer also eliminates the need to peel the potatoes—a real time-saver—as the skins remain in the ricer when the pulp is forced through.

2 lb (1 kg) Yukon gold or Yellow Finn
  potatoes
3 fresh rosemary sprigs, plus extra
  for garnish
salt
1 tablespoon mild extra-virgin olive oil
1 cup (8 fl oz/250 ml) milk, heated
freshly ground pepper
1 lemon

If you will be mashing the potatoes with a ricer, simply cut them into 1–1½-inch (2.5–4-cm) pieces. If you will be using a food mill or a hand masher, first peel the potatoes and then cut into 1–1½-inch (2.5–4-cm) pieces.

Place the potatoes in a saucepan and add water to cover by 1 inch (2.5 cm). Place the 3 rosemary sprigs in a square of cheesecloth (muslin), gather the edges together to form a sachet, and tie with kitchen string. Add to the pan along with 1 tablespoon salt. Place over medium-high heat and bring to a boil. Reduce the heat slightly, cover partially, and gently boil until the potatoes are just tender when pierced with the tip of a sharp knife, 15–20 minutes.

Remove the rosemary and discard. Drain the potatoes. Place the potatoes in a potato ricer held over the saucepan and push the handle to purée. Alternatively, after draining, return the potatoes to the saucepan and mash them with a potato masher until they are free of lumps. Or you can purée the potatoes using a food mill fitted with the fine disk.

Return the saucepan to very low heat, add the olive oil, and beat vigorously with a wooden spoon until well blended. Add the warm milk, a little at a time, continuing to beat and scraping the sides and bottom of the pan each time, until the potatoes are smooth and fluffy. You may not need all of the milk to achieve the correct consistency. Add salt and pepper to taste and continue to stir over low heat until very hot.

Spoon the potatoes into a warmed serving dish. Using a zester or fine-holed shredder, shred the zest (yellow part only) from the lemon directly onto the potatoes (see page 287). Garnish with fresh rosemary and serve immediately.

BROCCOLI GRATIN

SERVES 4

Gratins are among France's most appealing dishes, from first course to last. The word translates as "crust," describing the golden, often crisp surface that develops when a relatively thin layer of food is baked with a sauce and topping in a broad, shallow baking dish.

The gratin offered here is an excellent way to serve broccoli. It can be prepared in advance up to the point when it goes into the oven. If you like, add to the baking dish 1½ pounds (750 g) tiny pearl onions, blanched for 3 minutes and peeled.

2 or 3 slices coarse country French or
   Italian bread
1 bunch broccoli, about 1¼ lb (625 g)
salt
2 cups (16 fl oz/500 ml) milk
2 tablespoons unsalted butter
2 tablespoons all-purpose (plain) flour
½ cup (2 oz/60 g) shredded Gruyère
   cheese
freshly ground pepper
freshly grated nutmeg

Position a rack in the top third of an oven and preheat to 200°F (95°C). Remove the crusts from the bread and discard. Tear the bread into small pieces and place in a food processor fitted with the metal blade or in a blender. Pulse to form fine crumbs. You should have 2 cups (4 oz/125 g). Spread the crumbs on a baking sheet and place in the oven to dry out; do not allow to brown. This will take 4–6 minutes, depending upon how moist the bread is. Remove from the oven and set aside to cool. Raise the oven temperature to 375°F (190°C).

Cut the florets from the broccoli stems. Cut the large florets so that they are all the same size. Using a vegetable peeler or paring knife, peel off the tough skin from the larger main stems. If the stems are very large, cut in half or into quarters lengthwise, and then cut crosswise into 1-inch (2.5-cm) pieces.

Fill a large saucepan three-fourths full with water and bring to a boil. Add the broccoli and 2 teaspoons salt and boil, uncovered, until the florets and stems are just tender, 4–5 minutes. Drain immediately and spread out on a plate to cool.

In a small saucepan, heat the milk until small bubbles appear around the edges of the pan. Set aside. In another saucepan over medium heat, melt the butter. Add the flour and, using a whisk, stir until blended with the butter. Cook, stirring, for 1 minute; do not allow to brown. Gradually add the milk, whisking or stirring constantly. Continue whisking or stirring, regularly scraping the bottom and sides of the pan, until thickened, 3–4 minutes. Add ⅛ teaspoon salt and cook gently for another 1–2 minutes. Add the cheese and stir until the cheese melts and is blended. Season with salt, pepper, and a little nutmeg. Set aside.

In a 1½-qt (1.5-l) baking dish, arrange the broccoli in a single layer. Spoon the sauce evenly over the broccoli and then scatter the bread crumbs over the top. Bake until the crumbs are golden and the sauce is bubbly, 10–15 minutes. Serve at once directly from the dish. F

"There is nothing that is comparable to it, as satisfactory or as thrilling, as gathering the vegetables one has grown."

—Alice B. Toklas

CORN AND GREEN BEANS, CIRCA 1935

SERVES 4

I learned to cook this dish when I was about 17, soon after I moved to California. I suppose it's a variation on the classic American Indian succotash, a mixture of lima beans and corn. In the 1930s, California's kitchens were beginning to change the way Americans cooked, as we all learned about and experimented with an abundance of fresh vegetables. Of course, the tendency then was to cook some of them far too long, green beans being a good example.

⊃⊃ *I find small, young green beans to be best for this dish; they have a fine flavor and a delicate texture, and they cook in minutes. And if you can find just-picked corn, by all means buy it.*

4 ears of yellow corn, husks and silk removed, trimmed of any defects
½ red bell pepper (capsicum), seeded and deribbed
1 tablespoon unsalted butter
1 slice cooked ham, ¼ lb (125 g) and ¼ inch (6 mm) thick, cut into strips 1½ inches (4 cm) long and ¼ inch (6 mm) wide
1 or 2 cloves garlic, depending upon your taste and the size of cloves, minced
½ lb (250 g) young green beans, trimmed and cut on the diagonal into 1½-inch (4-cm) lengths
salt and freshly ground pepper
4 tablespoons (2 fl oz/60 ml) chicken stock or dry white wine, or a mixture, plus more as needed

Firmly hold each ear of corn, stem end down, on a cutting surface and, using a sharp knife, carefully cut off the kernels; you should have about 3 cups (18 oz/ 560 g). Set aside.

⊃⊃ Cut the bell pepper into strips 1½ inches (4 cm) long and ¼ inch (6 mm) wide. Set aside.

⊃⊃ In a large sauté pan over low heat, melt the butter until it bubbles. When hot, add the ham and garlic and sauté, stirring, 2–3 minutes. Do not allow to brown. Add the corn, green beans, bell pepper, salt and pepper to taste, and 3 tablespoons of the stock and/or wine. Stir to combine, cover tightly, and cook over medium-high heat for 2–3 minutes. Stir and check liquid; add another 1 tablespoon stock and/or wine. Re-cover and cook for another 2–3 minutes. Stir again and, if the pan seems dry, add another 1 tablespoon stock and/or water. Re-cover, cook for 1–2 minutes longer and check doneness of green beans; they should be tender but still crisp and green. If not tender, re-cover and cook longer, adding more stock and/or wine as needed to prevent sticking.

⊃⊃ Taste and adjust the seasoning. Serve at once. A ⊃⊃

BAKED BEETS WITH ONION AND CREAM

SERVES 4

The French have always baked their beets, and for good reason: the resulting taste and texture are much more intense and complex than those of boiled beets. Do try them. You will find this an excellent companion to a simple grilled steak or chop.

6 beets, about 3 lb (1.5 kg) total weight
2 tablespoons unsalted butter
1 sweet white onion, cut into small dice
2–3 tablespoons water
1 cup (8 fl oz/250 ml) heavy
   (double) cream
salt and freshly ground pepper
chopped fresh parsley

Position a rack in the middle of an oven and preheat to 450°F (230°C).
☙ Cut off the tops of the beets, leaving about ½ inch (12 mm) of stem intact. Do not cut off the root ends or peel or otherwise cut into the beets. Rinse well and pat dry with paper towels. Place the beets on a large piece of aluminum foil, bring the foil up around the beets to enclose fully and fold over the top to seal. Using a knife, make a small slit in the top of the packet for steam to escape and place in a baking pan, folded side up.
☙ Bake until the beets are tender when pierced with the tip of a sharp, thin-bladed knife, 50–60 minutes or more, depending upon the size and age of the beets. Test for doneness after about 45 minutes of baking. Remove from the oven and open the package partway to let the beets cool a little. Reduce the oven temperature to 375°F (190°C).
☙ When cool enough to handle, cut off the stem and root end from each beet. Using your fingers, or with the aid of a paring knife, peel off the skins; they should slip off easily. Cut the beets crosswise into slices about ⅛ inch (3 mm) thick and arrange, layered in straight rows or in concentric circles, in a baking dish. Set aside.

☙ In a sauté pan or frying pan over medium-low heat, melt the butter. When foaming, add the onion and sauté gently, stirring, until translucent, 6–7 minutes. Add the water, cover, and steam over low heat until the onion is tender, 8–10 minutes. Watch carefully so that the onion does not burn or brown. When the moisture has evaporated, add the cream and salt and pepper to taste.

Raise the heat to medium, bring the cream to a boil, and then cook for 1 minute. Remove from the heat and pour the cream-onion mixture evenly over the beets. Bake, uncovered, until the sauce is bubbly, 10–15 minutes.
☙ Sprinkle with chopped parsley and serve immediately directly from the dish. F ☙

"What I say is that, if a man really likes potatoes, he must be a pretty decent sort of fellow."
–A.A. Milne

POTATO AND ONION GRATIN

SERVES 4

The potatoes, onions, and garlic in this crusty gratin require a good deal of baking time for absolute tenderness. Make sure the baking dish you choose is large enough for the top of the potatoes to be well below the rim; otherwise, the milk and cream may bubble over.

The potatoes should be sliced to a uniform thickness so they cook evenly. A mandoline is a good tool for slicing the potatoes.

Any leftovers can be reheated in a 300°F (150°C) oven for 8–10 minutes.

2 teaspoons minced garlic (about 2 cloves)
2 lb (1 kg) baking potatoes (about 4), peeled and thinly cut crosswise into slices of uniform thickness
salt and freshly ground pepper
freshly ground nutmeg
1 sweet white onion, peeled, halved lengthwise and each half thinly sliced lengthwise
1 cup (8 fl oz/250 ml) milk
1 cup (8 fl oz/250 ml) heavy (double) cream

Position a rack in the middle of an oven and preheat to 375°F (190°C). Butter a 1½- or 2-qt (1.5- or 2-l) oval or rectangular baking dish.

Sprinkle the garlic over the bottom of the baking dish. Layer half of the potato slices, in overlapping rows, over the garlic. Sprinkle lightly with salt, pepper, and nutmeg. Spread the onion slices evenly over the potatoes, then layer the remaining potato slices over the top, arranging them attractively. Carefully pour the milk over the potatoes, moistening all of the potato slices as you do. Then pour ½ cup (4 fl oz/ 125 ml) of the cream over the potato slices, also being careful to moisten all of the slices. Sprinkle to taste with salt, pepper, and nutmeg.

Bake until the potatoes are very tender when pierced with the tip of a knife, golden brown on top and have absorbed most of the milk and cream, 1–1½ hours. During the first 40 minutes of baking, baste the potatoes every 10 minutes by tipping the dish a little and scooping up the liquid with a large spoon. Be sure to baste all of the potato slices so that an even golden coating forms. During the last 20–40 minutes of baking, baste the potatoes every 10 minutes with the remaining ½ cup (4 fl oz/125 ml) cream, again being sure to coat all of the slices. You may not need all of the cream.

Remove from the oven and serve directly from the dish.

ITALIAN GREEN BEANS WITH MINT

SERVES 4

For a short time every summer, markets carry green beans known as Italian or romano beans. They are wider and flatter than most common varieties, and are similar to runner beans. I find their flavor excellent, and when young (about 4 inches/10 cm long) they generally have a tender texture and cook quickly, usually in only 3–4 minutes. Be sure the beans are small and very fresh; otherwise they are not worth preparing this way.

You can, of course, make this recipe with any variety of tender, fresh young green beans, although the cooking time will be closer to 4–5 minutes. The secret to the dish is the mint, an herb that has been popular since Roman times and goes very well with other vegetables as well.

⅓ cup (2 oz/60 g) pine nuts
1 lb (500 g) young Italian green beans
   or other young, tender green beans
salt
3 tablespoons olive oil
1 small sweet white onion, chopped
   (about ½ cup/2 oz/60 g)
2 tablespoons water
2 tablespoons chopped fresh mint
greshly ground pepper
1 lemon

In a heavy frying pan over medium heat, toast the pine nuts, stirring, until lightly colored and fragrant, 1–2 minutes. Set aside.

Trim off the ends of the beans and cut the beans in half crosswise; each piece should be about 2 inches (5 cm) long. Fill a large saucepan three-fourths full of water and bring to a rapid boil over high heat. Add 2 teaspoons salt and the beans, quickly bring back to a boil and cook, uncovered, until the beans are just tender to the bite, 3–4 minutes. Drain immediately and plunge into cold water to stop the cooking. Set aside.

In a large sauté pan or frying pan over medium-low heat, warm the olive oil. Add the onion and sauté gently, stirring, until translucent, 4–5 minutes. Add the water, cover, and cook for another 3–4 minutes; do not allow to brown.

Add the beans, mint, and toasted pine nuts, raise the heat to medium-high and heat, tossing the beans gently, to serving temperature. Season with salt and pepper.

Transfer to a warmed serving dish. Using a zester or fine-holed shredder, shred the zest (yellow part only) from the lemon directly onto the beans (see page 287). Serve at once. I

PURÉE OF MINTED GREEN PEAS

SERVES 4

I'm always looking for new ways to cook peas, especially because they can be so inconsistent in the cooking time they take to reach tenderness. A purée, I have found, irons out those inconsistencies and highlights the sweet flavor of the peas. Another advantage is that you can prepare the purée ahead of time—something you can't really do when you serve whole peas. A small amount of cream enhances the dish's taste; if you prefer, use milk instead.

Pulsing the purée in a food processor gives you fingertip control over its fineness. Alternatively, pass the peas through a food mill to get a consistent fine or medium texture, depending on which disk you insert.

3–4 lb (1.5–2 kg) green peas (amount depends upon fullness of pods)
1 tablespoon unsalted butter
1 white Bermuda onion, coarsely chopped (1 cup/4 oz/125 g)
3 tablespoons water
½ teaspoon salt
2 teaspoons finely chopped fresh mint
freshly ground pepper
¼ cup (2 fl oz/60 ml) heavy (double) cream

Shell the peas. You should have about 4 cups (1¼ lb/625 g). Set aside.

In a saucepan over medium-low heat, melt the butter. Add the onion and 1 tablespoon of the water, cover tightly, and steam, stirring occasionally, until translucent, about 10 minutes. Do not allow to brown or burn; add more water if necessary.

Add the peas, the remaining 2 tablespoons water, and the salt. Raise the heat slightly, cover, and cook, stirring the peas from the bottom every now and again until they are tender and bright green, another 8–10 minutes. The liquid in the pan may increase; but watch that it doesn't boil dry, adding more water if necessary.

Drain the peas and onion, reserving the liquid. Put the peas and onion in a food processor fitted with the metal blade. Add the mint, 1 tablespoon of the cooking liquid, and pepper to taste. Process to form a soft purée. Add more cooking liquid if necessary to achieve the correct consistency. Alternatively, pass the mixture through a food mill (see page 292): Fit the food mill with the fine or medium disk (depending upon how fine you want the purée to be) and rest the mill over a large bowl. Ladle the peas and onion into the mill; add the mint, 1 tablespoon of the cooking liquid, and pepper to taste. Turn the handle to purée.

Return to the pan and stir in the cream. Reheat, while stirring, for a few seconds, until hot. Taste and adjust the seasoning and serve. A

GREEN LENTIL SALAD

SERVES 4

An excellent first course for a weekend brunch, this salad also makes a wonderful luncheon main course or side dish to almost any entrée. It can be made several hours ahead and refrigerated. Bring to room temperature and stir before serving.
Small dark green lentils, exported from France and also known as Puy lentils, are essential for this recipe. Green lentils are now being grown in the United States as well. You'll find them in specialty-food stores and in the international-food sections of large markets.

1 cup (7 oz/220 g) dried green lentils
3 cups (24 fl oz/750 ml) water
1 small white sweet onion, stuck with
  2 whole cloves
1 bay leaf
1 orange zest strip, 1 inch (2.5 cm)
  wide and 2 inches (5 cm) long
  (see page 287)

FOR THE DRESSING:
2 tablespoons tarragon white wine
  vinegar
⅛ teaspoon salt
freshly ground pepper
1 teaspoon Dijon mustard
⅓ cup (3 fl oz/80 ml) extra-virgin
  olive oil

1 carrot, peeled and shredded
½ green bell pepper (capsicum), seeded,
  deribbed, and cut into small dice
  (½ cup/2½ oz/75 g)
1 tablespoon minced green (spring)
  onion, including some tender green
  tops (2 or 3 onions)
8 tender romaine (cos) lettuce leaves,
  carefully washed and dried

Sort through the lentils, discarding any misshapen lentils or small stones. Rinse, drain, and place in a saucepan. Add the water, onion, bay leaf, and orange zest and place over medium-high heat. Bring to a boil, reduce the heat to medium-low, cover partially and simmer until the lentils are tender, 30–35 minutes. Remove from the heat and remove and discard the onion, bay leaf, and orange zest. Drain the lentils well and transfer them to a bowl. Set aside to cool completely.

To make the dressing, in a small bowl, combine the vinegar and salt and stir until the salt dissolves. Add pepper to taste and the mustard and whisk until blended. Gradually add the olive oil, whisking until well blended and emulsified. Taste and adjust the seasoning. Set aside.

Add the carrot, bell pepper, and green onion to the cooled lentils. Toss until well mixed. Drizzle with the dressing and toss again. Taste and adjust the seasoning.

To serve, spoon the lentils on top of the lettuce leaves. Serve at room temperature.

BAKED STUFFED TOMATOES WITH BASIL

SERVES 4

The success of this recipe depends entirely upon finding firm, flavorful, vine-ripened tomatoes, so it is advisable to make it only at the height of summer. You will also need fresh basil, which is most plentiful and inexpensive at that time of year.

Choose tomatoes that are more or less the same size and shape, being sure they sit upright in the dish.

Although the tomatoes must be baked until they are very tender, be careful not to overcook them or they will become mushy. If you like, mix a little freshly grated Parmesan cheese with the bread crumbs.

3 or 4 slices coarse country Italian or
   French bread, preferably day-old
4 large, firm but ripe tomatoes, about
   ¾ lb (375 g) each
¼ cup (2 fl oz/60 ml) extra-virgin
   olive oil
2 or 3 cloves garlic (depending upon
   your taste), minced
¼ cup chopped fresh basil
2 tablespoons chopped fresh flat-leaf
   (Italian) parsley
salt and freshly ground pepper
¼ cup (1½ oz/45 g) pine nuts

Position a rack in the middle of an oven and preheat to 400°F (200°C).
Tear the bread slices into small pieces and place in a food processor fitted with the metal blade or in a blender. Process to form fine crumbs. Measure out 2 cups (4 oz/125 g) and set aside.
Cut off the top one-fourth of the stem end of each tomato so that the seed cavities are exposed. Using a very small spoon (such as a coffee spoon), scoop out all of the seeds and liquid

from each cavity; do not break down the flesh dividing the seed cavities. Sprinkle the inside of the tomatoes with salt and turn upside down in a colander or on a rack. Let stand for 30 minutes to drain off some of their liquid.
In a frying pan over medium-low heat, warm the olive oil. Add the garlic and sauté gently, stirring, for 30–40 seconds. Remove from the heat and stir in the basil and parsley. Then add the bread crumbs, stirring until well mixed. Season to taste with salt and pepper and stir again.
Spoon the bread crumb mixture into the tomatoes, filling each cavity full

and mounding the filling slightly on top. Spread the leftover mixture in the bottom of a small baking dish in which the tomatoes will fit comfortably. Place the tomatoes upright in the dish and sprinkle the pine nuts evenly over them. Bake until the tomatoes are light golden on top, tender, and cooked through, 30–45 minutes; the time will depend upon the ripeness of the tomatoes.
Transfer the tomatoes to warmed plates. Spoon the bread crumb mixture from the baking dish alongside. Serve immediately.

Grains

Grains are a foundation of most of the world's cuisines. They are versatile enough to be served on their own or dressed up for special occasions.

Polenta, the popular Italian porridge of coarsely ground cornmeal, offers one of the most satisfying grain options imaginable. Polenta with Parmesan Cheese (this page) presents the grain in its most familiar guise. But it gains new dimension as Polenta with Mushrooms and Fontina (page 232).

As popular in Italy, France, and America as it is in Asia, rice is another side dish stalwart. It's virtues are seen here in recipes for Jasmine Rice with Shredded Zucchini (page 228) and Basmati Rice with Cashews and Raisins (page 231).

POLENTA WITH PARMESAN CHEESE

MAKES ABOUT 8 CUPS (4 LB/2 KG); SERVES 4–6

A richly textured, flavorful dish of cooked cornmeal, polenta is one of the great traditions of northern Italian cooking. To be truly first-rate, however, it needs to be cooked slowly, with almost constant stirring, resulting in a soft, creamy consistency. The addition of butter and good Parmesan cheese enhances the richness and smoothness of the polenta, yielding a dish that is as perfect with a rustic stew as it is with fried eggs and ham at a weekend brunch.

Imported Italian long-cooking polenta is the best. It is evenly and finely ground and cooks to a smooth, even consistency.

I also offer two variations for cooked polenta—baked polenta crostini and fried polenta squares.

7 cups (56 fl oz/1.75 l) water
2 teaspoons salt
2 cups (12 oz/375 g) Italian polenta
¼ cup (2 oz/60 g) unsalted butter, cut into small cubes
1 cup (4 oz/125 g) freshly grated Italian Parmesan cheese, preferably Parmigiano-Reggiano

In a deep, heavy saucepan over high heat, bring the water to a rapid boil. Add the salt and, while stirring continuously with a long-handled wooden spoon, gradually add the polenta in a thin, steady stream until all has been incorporated. Continuing to stir constantly to keep lumps from forming, reduce the heat until the mixture only bubbles occasionally. Continue to cook, stirring, until thick, smooth, and creamy, 20–25 minutes; be careful to scrape the bottom and sides of the pan to avoid sticking or lumping. The polenta will start to come away from the sides of the pan and the spoon should stand upright alone.

Remove from the heat and stir in the butter, a few cubes at a time, until fully absorbed. Then stir in ½ cup (2 oz/60 g) of the Parmesan cheese. Return the pan to the heat for a few seconds, continuing to stir, until the polenta is piping hot.

Transfer to a warmed bowl or platter and serve immediately, with the remaining Parmesan cheese in a small bowl alongside.

TO MAKE POLENTA CROSTINI:
On a baking sheet, spread out the cooked hot polenta about ¼ inch (6 mm) thick. Set aside until cold and firm, 30–40 minutes, or refrigerate. Preheat a broiler (griller). Cut the polenta into 1½-by-2½-inch (4-by-6-cm) rectangles or 2-inch (5-cm) rounds. Brush each side with olive oil and place on a baking sheet. Place under the broiler until golden and crispy, 3–4 minutes on each side. Serve as an appetizer or to accompany soup or salad.

TO MAKE FRIED POLENTA SQUARES:
On a baking sheet, spread out the cooked hot polenta about ½ inch (12 mm) thick. Set aside until cold and firm, 30–40 minutes, or refrigerate. Cut into 3- or 4-inch (7.5- or 10-cm) squares. In a sauté pan over medium heat, warm 3 tablespoons olive oil. When hot, add several polenta squares and fry until golden, 4–5 minutes on each side. Sprinkle with coarse salt. Transfer to a serving plate, then fry the remaining squares. Serve as an accompaniment to meat, poultry, or fish.

> "It may be safely averred that good cookery is the best and truest economy, turning to full account every wholesome article of food, and converting into palatable meals what the ignorant either render uneatable or throw away in disdain."
>
> —Eliza Acton

JASMINE RICE WITH SHREDDED ZUCCHINI

SERVES 4

Jasmine rice, a long-grain white rice grown in Thailand, has a fragrant and slightly nutty aroma and flavor, a smooth and shiny surface, and a firm body. Paired here with mild zucchini courgettes, it gains a delightful taste by the addition of coconut milk and fresh ginger.

Once you have shredded, salted, and drained the zucchini, you will find the flavor and texture so much improved that you'll want to repeat the method often. Although the steps sound time-consuming, they really aren't, and removing the vegetable's bitterness and emphasizing its crispness merits the extra effort.

1 lb (500 g) small zucchini (courgettes)
salt
½ cup (4 fl oz/125 ml) coconut milk, stirred well before using
1¼ cups (10 fl oz/310 ml) water
1 teaspoon peeled and grated fresh ginger
1 cup (7 oz/220 g) jasmine rice, rinsed and drained
3 tablespoons unsalted butter
1 tablespoon minced green (spring) onion, including some tender green tops
freshly grated nutmeg
1 tablespoon fresh lemon juice
1 lemon

Trim the zucchini and shred on a medium-holed shredder; you should have about 3½ cups. In a colander set over a bowl, layer half of the zucchini. Sprinkle with salt, top with the remaining zucchini, and sprinkle again with salt. Set aside for 25–30 minutes to drain off the bitter juice. Then, pick up the drained zucchini by small handfuls and squeeze out the released juice. Return the zucchini to the colander and rinse under cold running water to wash out the salt. Again, squeeze out the moisture by handfuls, then set aside.

In a heavy saucepan, stir together the coconut milk, water, ginger, and ½ teaspoon salt. Bring to a rapid boil and gradually add the rice. Reduce the heat to very low, cover, and barely simmer until just tender and the water has been absorbed, 15–20 minutes. Remove from the heat and let stand, covered, for an additional 5 minutes. Uncover and carefully fluff the rice with a fork. Re-cover to keep warm until ready to serve.

In a sauté pan or frying pan over medium-high heat, melt the butter. Add the zucchini, green onion, and a little nutmeg. Cook, stirring and tossing, until tender but still opaque, 4–5 minutes, adding a little of the lemon juice toward the end of cooking. Adjust the seasoning with more lemon juice or salt.

Arrange the rice around the edge of a warmed serving plate, forming a ring. Spoon the zucchini mixture into the center.

Remove the zest from the lemon (see page 287): Using a zester or fine-holed shredder, and holding the lemon over the zucchini mixture, shred the zest (yellow part only) from the skin evenly over the zucchini. Serve at once.

BASMATI RICE WITH CASHEWS AND RAISINS

SERVES 4–6

The Indian long-grain rice variety known as basmati has become very popular in American kitchens since the late 1980s, prized for its delicate fragrance and light, fluffy texture. In this recipe, it is the basis for a golden pilaf made aromatic with Indian seasonings and enriched with coconut milk.

 You can find imported basmati rice, and even American-grown varities, in most well-stocked food stores. Canned, ready-to-use coconut milk is also easy to find and is always a staple in Asian and Caribbean markets. Just be sure to buy unsweetened coconut milk and not the sweetened coconut cream sold for use in bar drinks.

1¾ cups (14 fl oz/430 ml) water

¾ teaspoon salt

½ teaspoon ground turmeric

1 cup (7 oz/220 g) basmati rice, rinsed
   and drained

2 tablespoons unsalted butter

¼ cup (1 oz/30 g) diced yellow onion

¼ cup (1½ oz/45 g) golden raisins
   (sultanas)

¼ cup (1¼ oz/37 g) roasted cashews

1 teaspoon ground cardamom

⅓ cup (3 fl oz/80 ml) coconut milk

In a heavy saucepan, combine the water, salt, and turmeric. Bring to a rapid boil and gradually add the rice. Reduce the heat to low, cover, and barely simmer just until tender and the water is absorbed, 15–20 minutes.

 Meanwhile, in a sauté pan over medium heat, melt the butter. When hot, add the onion and sauté until translucent, 2–3 minutes. Add the raisins, cashews, and cardamom and cook, stirring, for 2 minutes longer. Stir in the coconut milk and cook for 2 minutes longer.

 When the rice is ready, remove from the heat, uncover, and fluff with a fork. Add the onion-raisin mixture and toss gently with the fork until mixed. Taste and adjust the seasoning. Spoon into a warmed serving bowl. Serve immediately.

A

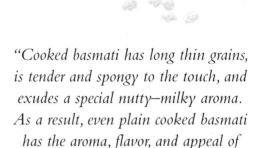

"Cooked basmati has long thin grains, is tender and spongy to the touch, and exudes a special nutty–milky aroma. As a result, even plain cooked basmati has the aroma, flavor, and appeal of an exquisite pilaf."

–Julie Sahni

POLENTA WITH MUSHROOMS AND FONTINA

SERVES 6 AS A MAIN COURSE, 10 AS A SIDE DISH

Be sure the polenta is very soft (almost pourable) when spreading it in the baking dish. If necessary, thin with a little hot water. It will firm up as it is assembled and baked. Serve the polenta as a main dish with a green salad for a luncheon or light supper, or as an accompaniment to roasted meat or poultry.

½ cup (4 oz/125 g) unsalted butter
1 lb (500 g) fresh mushrooms,
    brushed clean and cut into slices
    ¼ inch (6 mm) thick
salt
freshly grated nutmeg
7 cups (56 fl oz/1.75 l) water
2 cups (10 oz/315 g) Italian polenta
½ lb (250 g) imported fontina cheese,
    thinly sliced

In a large sauté pan or frying pan over medium heat, melt ¼ cup (2 oz/60 g) of the butter. When bubbly, add the mushrooms, raise the heat to medium-high, and sauté, tossing often, until tender, about 5 minutes. Do not let brown. Season with salt and a little nutmeg and remove from the heat. Cover to keep warm.

꒰꒱ Position a rack in the center of an oven and preheat to 425°F (220°C). Butter a 2–2½-qt baking dish.

꒰꒱ In a deep, heavy saucepan over high heat, bring the water to a rapid boil. Add 2 teaspoons salt and, while stirring continuously with a long-handled spoon, gradually add the polenta in a thin, steady stream until all has been incorporated. Continuing to stir constantly to keep lumps from forming, reduce the heat until the mixture only bubbles occasionally. Continue to cook, stirring, until smooth and creamy, about 20 minutes; be careful to scrape the bottom and sides of the pan to avoid sticking or lumping. Remove from the heat. Cut the remaining ¼ cup (2 oz/60 g) butter into small cubes and add to the polenta, a few cubes at a time, stirring until melted after each addition. The polenta should be soft and spreadable.

꒰꒱ Spread one-third of the polenta over the bottom of the prepared baking dish. Spread half of the mushrooms in a layer on top, then cover with a layer of half of the cheese slices. Repeat with half of the remaining polenta, then all of the remaining mushrooms and cheese. Top with the remaining polenta.

꒰꒱ Place in the oven and bake until lightly browned, about 20 minutes. Cut into squares and serve immediately directly from the dish. ⬚

"The dish is so important in Lombardy today that every properly equipped family owns a special copper pot reserved solely for the cooking of polenta, along with a similarly dedicated long stick for stirring it."

—Waverley Root

$\mathscr{B}$READS

While good-quality bread can be found today in boutique bakeries and well-stocked food stores alike, the art of making bread has never strayed far from the home kitchen. And readily available products ranging from baking powder to fast-acting yeasts, which considerably shorten leavening time, put good bread within easy reach of more home cooks than ever before.

The quickest breads to make are those that rely on the carbon dioxide gas released by baking powder. American cooks are especially fond of such recipes, typified by Cranberry-Orange Muffins (page 243) and Toasted Walnut Quick Bread (page 237). If you have that little bit of extra time necessary to wait for bread to rise, it is worth exploring the wonders of more traditional European-style loaves such as Parmesan Cheese Bread (page 239) or Grape Focaccia (page 236). You will be richly compensated in taste, texture, and the aroma of fresh-baked bread.

POLENTA BREAD

MAKES 1 ROUND OR OVAL LOAF

If you have found bread making intimidating or too much work, try baking this simple loaf. I think you will change your mind. It is a delicious, richly textured bread. You'll especially like it warm or toasted, at breakfast time or with soups, salads, meats, or seafoods.

Purchase one of the fast-acting dry yeasts now sold in most food stores. They are much stronger and quicker than conventional active dry yeast; under ideal conditions, rising time can be shortened to less than an hour.

I have found that when you are ready to put the dough in a bowl to rise, it is a good idea to warm the bowl first with warm to moderately hot tap water; then dry the bowl, brush lightly with oil, add the dough, and cover. The warmth of the bowl starts the dough rising much faster, decreasing total rising time.

If you have one, an electric mixer fitted with a dough hook can also be used to knead the dough.

3 cups (15 oz/470 g) unbleached
   bread flour
½ cup (2½ oz/75 g) finely ground,
   quick-cooking Italian polenta, plus
   extra for the baking sheet
2 teaspoons quick-rise yeast
1 teaspoon salt
1⅓ cups (11 fl oz/330 ml) warm tap
   water (110°F/43°C)
1 tablespoon extra-virgin olive oil
1 egg beaten with 1 tablespoon water

In a large bowl, combine the flour, the ½ cup (2½ oz/75 g) polenta, the yeast, and salt. Using a wooden spoon, stir to mix well. Add the warm water and olive oil and stir until all of the flour has been absorbed and a dough has formed.

Using your hands, gather the dough into a ball and transfer to a well-floured work surface. Knead until soft and elastic and no longer sticky, about 10 minutes. Work more flour into the dough if needed to reduce stickiness; be sure to keep the work surface well floured. The dough should remain in a rounded shape and not flatten out when left on the work surface for a minute or two. If not, work a little more flour into the dough. Place the dough in a warmed, lightly oiled bowl, turning several times to coat it with oil. Cover with plastic wrap and let rise in a warm place until doubled in bulk, 45–75 minutes.

Sprinkle a little polenta on a baking sheet and set aside. Punch down the dough, return to the lightly floured work surface, and knead a few times. Form into a round ball or an oval shape and place on the prepared baking sheet. The dough should retain its shape and not flatten out. Cover loosely with plastic wrap and let rise in a warm place until doubled in bulk, 30–40 minutes.

While the dough is rising, position a rack in the middle of an oven and preheat to 425°F (220°C).

When the dough has risen, using a very sharp, thin-bladed knife or single-edge razor blade, carefully make a slash ½ inch (12 mm) deep across the top. Brush the surface with the egg mixture. Bake for 15 minutes. Reduce the oven temperature to 375°F (190°C); continue to bake until golden, and crusty, 30–35 minutes longer.

Transfer the loaf to a wire rack and let cool.

GRAPE FOCACCIA

MAKES ONE 10-BY-15-INCH (25-BY-38-CM) SHEET;
SERVES 6–8

*Italy's popular flat bread, focaccia, is another
of the country's culinary treasures that is
gaining permanent popularity abroad—and
for good reason. Tasty and easy to prepare,
it is, in simplest terms, nothing more than a
pizza without the topping.*

*This version includes fresh rosemary,
a little sugar, olive oil, and white grapes
to produce a marvelously light, mild, sweet
bread. Serve it warm with coffee on a
Sunday morning, with tea in the afternoon,
or for a lunch dessert. It is a delightful
substitute for coffee cake or Danish pastry.*

*Please take a look at the suggestions
about working with yeast and mixing and
rising dough in the note on page 234
and on page 288.*

focaccia dough (recipe on page 283)
2 tablespoons sugar

FOR THE GRAPE TOPPING:
3 tablespoons extra-virgin olive oil
4 fresh rosemary sprigs
1½ cups (9 oz/280 g) ripe seedless
  white grapes, rinsed and dried
¼ cup (2 oz/60 g) sugar

Make the focaccia dough as directed,
adding the 2 tablespoons sugar with the
salt and decreasing the amount of olive
oil in the bread to 1 tablespoon.

While the dough is rising, begin to
make the topping: In a small saucepan
over low heat, warm the 3 tablespoons
olive oil until hot. Add 2 of the rosemary sprigs, pushing down on them to
submerge completely. Remove from the
heat and set aside for the oil to absorb
the rosemary flavor.

Prepare a baking pan as directed
in the focaccia recipe, line it with the
dough, and let rise as directed. Preheat
an oven as directed.

Remove the rosemary sprigs from
the oil and discard. Brush the risen
dough generously with the rosemary-
flavored oil. Scatter the grapes evenly
over the surface and carefully push each
one into the dough. Sprinkle the sugar
evenly over the surface. Remove the
leaves from the 2 remaining rosemary
sprigs (about 2 teaspoons). Leave them
whole or chop them; then sprinkle
them over the surface.

Bake until golden brown, 30–40
minutes. Transfer the pan to a rack and
let cool for a few minutes.

Cut into squares and serve warm,
preferably, or at room temperature.
To reheat, place in a preheated 350°F
(180°C) oven for 3–4 minutes.

TOASTED WALNUT QUICK BREAD

MAKES 1 LOAF

Since the introduction of soda bread by the first Irish immigrants, quick breads have been an important part of American baking. The development of baking powder brought a still greater variety of breads, cakes, and muffins to the country's kitchens. Most quick breads resemble cake as much as bread, and they are at their best eaten right after baking. But dried fruit or nut breads such as this one keep very well for up to 3 days and are excellent for sandwiches or with salads or cold meats. To store, wrap tightly with plastic wrap and keep in a cool place or in the refrigerator.
❧ *I believe this bread tastes best the day after it is baked. The walnuts contribute a wonderful texture, and the inclusion of whole wheat flour adds still more crunch. Try the bread lightly toasted and spread with lemon curd (recipe on page 284) or apricot-orange preserves (page 282).*

1 cup (4 oz/125 g) coarsely chopped walnuts

1½ cups (7½ oz/235 g) all-purpose (plain) flour

1 cup (5 oz/155 g) whole wheat (wholemeal) flour

1 tablespoon baking powder

1 teaspoon salt

1 orange

1 egg, at room temperature

1 cup (8 fl oz/250 ml) milk, at room temperature

¼ cup (2 fl oz/60 ml) pure maple syrup

3 tablespoons unsalted butter, melted

Position a rack in the middle of an oven and preheat the oven to 325°F (165°C). Butter and flour an 8½-by-4½-by-2½-inch (22-by-12-by-6-cm) loaf pan.
❧ Spread out the walnuts on a baking sheet. Place in the oven and bake until they begin to change color, 6–8 minutes. Watch carefully so they do not burn. Remove from the oven and set aside to cool. Raise the oven temperature to 350°F (180°C).
❧ In a large bowl, combine the all-purpose flour, whole wheat flour, baking powder, salt, and toasted walnuts; stir together to mix well. Remove the zest from the orange (see page 287): Using a zester or fine-holed shredder, and holding the orange over the bowl containing the flour mixture, shred the zest (orange part only) from the skin. Stir and toss together the flour mixture and zest until well blended.
❧ In another bowl and using a whisk, beat the egg lightly. Add the milk, maple syrup, and melted butter and beat until smooth. Add the milk mixture to the dry ingredients and stir quickly to combine. Pour into the prepared pan and smooth the top.
❧ Bake until well risen and golden, 40–45 minutes. To test for doneness, insert a wooden toothpick into the center of the loaf; it should come out clean. Transfer to a wire rack and let cool in the pan for about 3 minutes. Turn out of the pan and leave on the rack, right side up, to cool completely.
❧ Cut into slices to serve. A ❧

PARMESAN CHEESE BREAD

MAKES 12 ROLLS

Make this bread for a party, serving it while still warm and breaking off individual rolls at the table. If necessary, you can reheat it in a 300°F (150°C) oven; but don't use a microwave oven, which will toughen the bread.

∾ *The dough can also be made by hand: Stir together the ingredients in a bowl and then knead the dough on a lightly floured board until smooth and elastic, about 15 minutes.*

∾ *Use freshly grated Parmesan cheese, preferably imported, for the best flavor. And you will achieve better results in bread making if you seek out one of the professional-quality active dry yeasts, such as Engedura from Holland or SAF from France. Both are available at specialty-food stores.*

∾ *I use a 9-inch (23-cm) round cake pan with 1½-inch (4-cm) straight sides for this bread, but any pan of approximate equal capacity can be used.*

3¾ cups (19 oz/590 g) unbleached
   bread flour, or as needed
1 tablespoon active dry yeast
2 teaspoons salt
1⅓ cups (11 fl oz/330 ml) warm water
   (110°F/43°C)
½ cup (2 oz/60 g) freshly grated
   Parmesan cheese
extra-virgin olive oil

In the bowl of a heavy-duty stand mixer, combine the 3¾ cups (19 oz/590 g) flour, the yeast, and salt. Add the warm water and stir with a wooden spoon until just mixed together. Sprinkle ¼ cup (1 oz/30 g) of the Parmesan cheese over the dough. Fit the mixer with the dough hook and begin mixing and kneading on very low speed. When the mixture pulls away from the sides of the bowl, increase the mixer speed to medium-low and continue to knead until the dough is smooth and elastic, 12–15 minutes, adding more flour if too sticky. Transfer the dough to a floured work surface and knead by hand for 1–2 minutes.

∾ Form the dough into a ball, brush it with a little olive oil and return it to the bowl. Cover with a towel and let rest in a warm, draft-free place until doubled in bulk, 1–1½ hours.

∾ Position a rack in the lower part of an oven and preheat the oven to 425°F (220°C). Brush a 9-inch (23-cm) round pan with olive oil. Place the remaining ¼ cup (1 oz/30 g) Parmesan cheese on a plate. Punch down the dough. Return it to the floured work surface and knead a few times. Then, using your palms, roll to form the dough into a log about 12 inches (30 cm) long. Cut the log in half crosswise, then cut each half crosswise into 6 equal pieces. Knead each dough piece a couple of times, roll it between the palms of your hands into a ball, and then roll it in the cheese to coat lightly and evenly, shaking off any

excess. As each ball is coated, place it in the prepared pan, resting it against the rim and pressing down slightly to form a 2-inch (5-cm) disk. Arrange 9 balls around the rim and 3 balls in the center. Cover loosely with plastic wrap and let rise again in a warm place until doubled in bulk, 30–40 minutes.

∾ Sprinkle the top with the cheese remaining on the plate. Using a razor blade or sharp knife, cut a slash ¼ inch (6 mm) deep in the top of each ball. Bake for 10 minutes. Reduce the oven temperature to 375°F (190°C) and continue baking until brown and crusty, 20–30 minutes longer. Transfer to a wire rack and let rest in the pan for 1–2 minutes, then remove from the pan; the rolls will come out in a single loaf.

∾ Serve the loaf warm, breaking off the rolls at the table. Or let cool, top side up, on the rack. ∾

GINGER BISCUITS

MAKES 12–14 BISCUITS

Biscuits are about as American as bread can get, a part of our cooking culture from colonial times. Easily and quickly prepared, they make a fine addition to almost any meal. I have added freshly grated ginger to this particular recipe, but you can leave it out if you wish. You can also substitute butter for the shortening, although shortening does make a flakier biscuit.

Anyone who has never eaten biscuits as they are made in the American South has a treat in store. The secret lies in the flour, which is milled from soft, locally grown winter wheat that rises higher and produces light, crunchy results.

Serve the biscuits with lemon curd (recipe on page 284) or apricot-orange preserves (page 282).

2 cups (10 oz/315 g) all-purpose
   (plain) flour
¼ teaspoon salt
1 tablespoon baking powder
¼ cup (2 oz/60 g) vegetable shortening
⅔ cup (5 fl oz/160 ml) milk
1 tablespoon sugar
½ teaspoon peeled and finely grated
   fresh ginger

Position a rack in the middle of an oven and preheat the oven to 450°F (230°C).
In a large bowl, combine the flour, salt, and baking powder. Stir until well blended. Add the shortening and, using a pastry blender, 2 knives, or your fingertips, cut it into the dry ingredients until the mixture resembles coarse crumbs.
Measure the milk in a glass measuring pitcher. Add the sugar and ginger to the milk and stir until the sugar dissolves and the ginger is mixed in. Using a fork, slowly stir the milk mixture into the flour mixture to form a soft but not sticky dough. You may not need all of the milk. The dough should pull away from the sides of the bowl.
Gather up the dough and place on a lightly floured work surface. Knead gently 8–10 times, using extra flour as needed to keep the dough from sticking. Roll out, or pat out with your hands, into a rectangle measuring about 6 by 8 inches (15 by 20 cm) and ½ inch (12 mm) thick. Dust a plain or fluted biscuit cutter 2 inches (5 cm) in diameter with flour and cut out the biscuits.

Press straight down and do not twist the cutter, to ensure evenly shaped, straight-sided biscuits when baked.
Transfer the cutouts to an ungreased baking sheet, spacing them about 1 inch (2.5 cm) apart. Gather the dough scraps together and again roll or pat them out ½ inch (12 mm) thick. Cut out more biscuits and transfer to the baking sheet.
Bake until golden brown, 8–10 minutes. Serve warm. A

SPOON CORN BREAD

SERVES 4

Also known as spoon bread, spoon corn bread is a great specialty of the American South—a cross between corn bread, pudding, and a soufflé. Dish it out with a spoon, as its name suggests, to accompany family-style main courses. If you like, drizzle each serving with roasted red pepper sauce (recipe on page 285), thinned with a little chicken stock or water.

🌀 *In the earliest recipes for spoon bread, the eggs were beaten vigorously to incorporate air to help the spoon bread rise. After baking powder became popular, most cooks added a little to ensure lightness.*

🌀 *You can use white or yellow cornmeal, although I prefer the flavor and color of the yellow. Imported Parmesan cheese gives the best taste to the mixture; if you prefer a stronger cheese flavor, sprinkle the top with 2 or 3 more tablespoons. For a little hotness, add 1 or 2 small fresh chiles, seeded and chopped, to the batter.*

3 cups (24 fl oz/750 ml) milk
pinch of freshly grated nutmeg
1 teaspoon salt
1 cup (5 oz/155 g) yellow cornmeal
2 tablespoons unsalted butter, cut into small cubes
4 eggs
2 teaspoons baking powder
¼ cup (1 oz/30 g) freshly grated Parmesan cheese

Position a rack in the middle of an oven and preheat the oven to 425°F (220°C). Butter a 1½-qt (1.5-l) soufflé dish or other deep baking dish.

🌀 In a large, heavy saucepan over medium heat, add the milk and heat until small bubbles form along the edges of the pan; do not allow it to boil. Remove from the heat and add the nutmeg and salt. Then, while vigorously stirring (preferably with a whisk), slowly add the cornmeal. (The vigorous stirring is necessary to avoid lumping.) Continue to beat until smooth.

Return the pan to low heat and, while stirring continuously, add the butter, a few pieces at a time, until melted and mixed in, about 1 minute. Remove from the heat.

🌀 In a bowl, combine the eggs and baking powder and, using a fork or whisk, beat until light and frothy, 3–4 seconds. Stir the egg mixture into the cornmeal mixture just until blended. Stir in the Parmesan cheese. Pour into the prepared dish.

🌀 Bake until puffed and golden, 35–40 minutes. To test for doneness, insert a wooden toothpick into the center; it should come out clean. Serve at once.

A

WALNUT RING LOAF

MAKES 1 RING LOAF

When Williams-Sonoma opened the first Il Fornaio bakery in San Francisco in 1980, I learned to make this fragrant, flavorful loaf from one of the bakers we brought over from Italy.

❧ *I have explained making the bread by hand, but the dough can also be made in an electric mixer equipped with a dough hook. Knead at medium-low speed for about 10 minutes. And please take a look at the suggestions about working with yeast and mixing and rising dough in the note on page 234 and on page 288.*

❧ *You can also bake this bread in an 8-inch (20-cm) ring mold.*

2 cups (10 oz/315 g) whole wheat (wholemeal) bread flour
1 cup (5 oz/155 g) unbleached bread flour
2 teaspoons quick-rise yeast

2 teaspoons salt
1 cup (8 fl oz/250 ml) warm tap water (110°F/43°C)
1 tablespoon extra-virgin olive oil
2 tablespoons honey
½ cup (2 oz/60 g) walnut pieces, plus 10 walnut halves
1 egg beaten with 1 teaspoon water

In a large bowl, combine both flours, the yeast, and the salt. Using a wooden spoon, stir to mix well. Add the warm water, olive oil, and honey and stir until all of the flour has been absorbed and a dough forms. Gather the dough into a ball and transfer to a well-floured work surface. Knead until soft and smooth and no longer sticky, about 10 minutes. Work in more bread flour if needed to reduce stickiness. Place in a warmed, lightly oiled bowl, turning several times to coat it with oil. Cover with plastic wrap and let rise in a warm place until doubled in bulk, 45–75 minutes.

❧ Meanwhile, position a rack in the middle of an oven and preheat to 325°F (165°C). Spread the ½ cup (2 oz/60 g) walnut pieces on a baking sheet and bake until the nuts begin to change color, about 10 minutes. Let cool.

❧ Oil an 8-inch (20-cm) round cake pan with 1½-inch (4-cm) sides, or a baking sheet. Punch down the dough and turn out onto a well-floured surface; knead a couple of times. Using your palms, form the dough into a log 10 inches (25 cm) long. Cut crosswise into 10 equal pieces and let rest for 5 minutes. Flatten each piece into a 3-inch (7.5-cm) round. Place a few toasted walnut pieces in the center of each round. Gather the edges of each round and pinch together to form a ball. Place the balls, seam side down and touching one another, around the perimeter of the cake pan, or on the baking sheet in a circle 8 inches (20 cm) in diameter. Cover loosely with plastic wrap and let rise in a warm place until doubled in bulk, 30–45 minutes. While the dough is rising, reposition the rack to the lower part of the oven and preheat to 375°F (190°C).

❧ When the buns have risen, brush them with the egg mixture; do not let it run onto the pan or the buns may stick. Place a walnut half on each bun and press slightly to anchor firmly. Bake for 15 minutes, then reduce the heat to 350°F (180°C). Cover loosely with aluminum foil to keep the nuts from burning and continue to bake until golden, 20–25 minutes longer.

❧ Immediately unmold onto a rack. Serve warm, preferably, or at room temperature. Place the loaf on a serving plate and let guests pull the buns apart.

CRANBERRY-ORANGE MUFFINS

MAKES 12

One of the secrets to making good muffins is to assemble and combine all the ingredients as quickly as possible, with a minimum of stirring, and then bake immediately. This ensures that the carbon dioxide gas released by the baking powder causes the muffins to rise in the oven rather than dissipating into the air; and the minimal stirring prevents overdevelopment of the flour's gluten, which would produce less tender results. The muffins are best eaten as soon as they cool to warm; but they're also excellent reheated the next day for 5–6 minutes in a 325°F (165°C) oven.
The small amount of cornmeal in the batter gives these muffins a crunchy texture. Dried cherries can be substituted for the cranberries, and lemon for the orange. Serve with lemon curd (recipe on page 284) or apricot-orange preserves (page 282), if you like.

⅓ cup (1½ oz/45 g) dried cranberries, coarsely chopped
2 tablespoons plus ⅓ cup (3 oz/90 g) sugar
3 tablespoons boiling water
1 medium orange
1¾ cups (9 oz/280 g) all-purpose (plain) flour
½ cup (2½ oz/75 g) yellow cornmeal
2½ teaspoons baking powder
½ teaspoon baking soda
½ teaspoon salt
2 eggs, at room temperature
1 cup (8 fl oz/250 ml) milk, at room temperature
⅓ cup (3 oz/90 g) unsalted butter, melted

Position a rack in the middle of an oven and preheat the oven to 400°F (200°C). Butter the cups of one 12-cup or two 6-cup standard-sized muffin tins.
In a small bowl, stir together the dried cranberries and the 2 tablespoons sugar. Stir in the boiling water and set aside for 15 minutes to allow the cranberries to absorb the water and soften.
Meanwhile, remove the zest from the orange (see page 287): Using a zester or a fine-holed shredder, and holding the orange over a saucer, shred the zest (orange part only) from the skin. You should have about 1 tablespoon. Set aside.
In a large bowl, combine the flour, cornmeal, the ⅓ cup (3 oz/90 g) sugar, baking powder, baking soda, and salt. Stir until well blended. Set aside. In

another bowl and using a whisk, beat the eggs lightly. Add the milk and melted butter and beat until smooth. Stir in the cranberries and their remaining liquid and the orange zest.
Quickly stir the liquid mixture into the flour mixture; do not overmix. Divide the batter evenly among the prepared muffin tin(s), filling each cup about three-fourths full.
Bake until risen and the tops are golden, 20–25 minutes. To test for doneness, insert a wooden toothpick in the center of a muffin; it should come out clean. Transfer to a wire rack and let cool in the tin(s) for 2–3 minutes. Remove from the tin(s) and serve warm. The muffins can be stored in an airtight container overnight.

Desserts

Pies & Pastries

Lovers of good food never cease to be delighted by the myriad treats that result from baking some combination of flour, sugar, butter, milk, and eggs. Even the simplest of such preparations can tempt us almost daily. Take the all-American Lime-Pecan Butter Cookies (page 248), which are easy to make and store well. French Walnut Wafers (page 248) come together even more quickly and make a wonderful accompaniment to a cup of café au lait. Almond Biscotti (page 254) may take a little longer to make, only because they are baked twice, the source of both their incomparable crispness and their Italian name.

Take a basic dough or batter, partner it with fruit, and the result will always be a dessert of distinction. An American Golden Apple Cobbler (page 251) crowns harvest apples with a sweet, buttery crust, yet it is among the simplest to make of all pies.

Pear Tart with Walnuts

SERVES 4

I especially like this style of French tart, in which a shallow layer of fruit tops thinly rolled pastry. For best results in pastry making, be sure the dough is pliable and not sticky when you gather it into a ball. If it is too soft and sticky, knead on a floured board a couple of times.

I use Comice pears in the recipe, but the firmer Bosc variety is also excellent. You may find, however, that you will have to poach the Bosc pears a little longer or bake the tart for a few more minutes than what is indicated here.

The tart makes a perfect end to a small dinner party. Any leftovers are delightful the next day with coffee.

1 cup (5 oz/155 g) all-purpose (plain) flour
½ cup (2 oz/60 g) cake (soft-wheat) flour
1 tablespoon plus 1½ cups (12 oz/375 g) sugar
¼ teaspoon salt
½ cup (4 oz/125 g) unsalted butter, chilled, cut into small cubes
2–3 tablespoons ice water
3 cups (24 fl oz/750 ml) cold water, or as needed
3 ripe but firm pears such as Comice or Bosc, peeled, halved, cored, and tossed in a bowl with the juice of 1 lemon
½ cup (5 oz/155 g) apricot preserves, forced through a sieve
1 cup (4 oz/125 g) walnut pieces
whipped cream topping (recipe on page 262 or 276)

Position a rack in the lower third of an oven and preheat to 400°F (200°C).

In a bowl, mix together the flours, the 1 tablespoon sugar, and the salt. Using a pastry blender, 2 knives, or your fingertips, cut the butter into the flour mixture until it resembles oatmeal. Tossing the mixture with a fork, slowly add the ice water just until the mixture holds together. Gather into a ball, flatten into a round, and place between 2 pieces of plastic wrap. Roll out into a round 12 inches (30 cm) in diameter. Peel off the top sheet of plastic wrap. Invert the dough round over a 9-inch (23-cm) fluted tart pan with a removable bottom. Peel off the other piece of plastic wrap and fit the dough into the pan. Cut off the excess even with the rim. Refrigerate to chill.

In a deep frying pan over medium heat, combine the cold water and the 1½ cups (12 oz/375 g) sugar. Bring to a boil and stir to dissolve the sugar. Add the pears and lemon juice and bring back to a simmer; add water as needed just to cover the pears. Reduce the heat to medium-low and simmer, turning once, until almost tender, about 15 minutes. Transfer the pears to a rack placed over a baking pan. Let cool.

Spread most of the apricot preserves over the bottom of the tart shell. Cut each pear half crosswise into thin slices, keeping them together. Transfer the pears to the shell with the stem ends facing the center. Brush with the remaining preserves. Fill the spaces between them with the walnuts.

Bake until the crust is golden, 1–1¼ hours. Let cool on a rack, then remove the outer ring and slide the tart onto a flat plate. Serve warm or at room temperature with the whipped cream.

F

WALNUT WAFERS

MAKES 80–85 COOKIES

Thin nut wafers are a perfect accompaniment to fruit desserts. One easy-to-make batch yields an abundance.

The cookies should crisp up right after baking. Let the first batch cool for a few minutes, then check to see if they are crisp. If not, bake the second batch a little longer.

Being crisp sugar cookies, they attract moisture, so store them in airtight containers to keep them fresh and brittle. They will keep for up to three or four days in a cool, dry place.

2 tablespoons all-purpose (plain) flour

½ teaspoon salt

½ teaspoon baking soda (bicarbonate of soda)

½ cup (4 oz/125 g) unsalted butter, at room temperature

1 cup (8 oz/250 g) sugar

2 eggs

1 teaspoon vanilla extract (essence)

1½ cups (6 oz/185 g) chopped walnuts

Position a rack in the middle of an oven and a second one in the upper part; preheat to 375°F (190°C). Line 2 or more baking sheets with parchment (baking) paper or waxed paper and set aside.

In a bowl, sift together the flour, salt, and baking soda and set aside.

In another bowl, combine the butter and sugar and, using an electric mixer set on medium speed, beat until light and creamy, 5–6 minutes, scraping the sides of the bowl occasionally with a rubber spatula. Add 1 of the eggs and continue to beat at medium speed until fully incorporated. Add the remaining egg and again beat in thoroughly. Beat in the vanilla extract. Using a rubber spatula, fold in the flour mixture and then the walnuts.

Using a teaspoon, place spoonfuls of the batter about 3 inches (7.5 cm) apart on the prepared baking sheets; the wafers will need space to spread. Bake until brown around the edges, 8–10 minutes. Using a thin spatula, immediately remove the wafers from the paper and place on a wire rack to cool. They should be very crisp. Store in airtight containers. F ⟲

LIME-PECAN BUTTER COOKIES

MAKES 60–65 COOKIES

For the best results, weigh or measure your ingredients carefully. For instance, when using any size measuring cup to measure flour, scoop up the flour with a smaller cup or a scoop and place it loosely in the measuring cup until the cup is full. Then, using the back of a straight-bladed knife or a spatula, evenly scrape off the top. Scooping out the flour with the measuring cup itself would pack it down, giving you too much.

The texture of the cookies also depends on beating enough air into the dough. Start by thoroughly beating together the butter and sugar, scraping down the bowl several times. Then add the egg white and lime juice and beat again thoroughly until light and fluffy. Do not make the cookies too big: form balls of dough no more than 1 inch (2.5 cm) in diameter.

2 cups (10 oz/315 g) all-purpose (plain) flour

¼ cup (1 oz/30 g) cornstarch (cornflour)

¼ teaspoon salt

¾ cup (6 oz/185 g) sugar

1 cup (3½ oz/105 g) pecans, coarsely chopped

1 lime

¾ cup (6 oz/185 g) unsalted butter, cut into cubes

1 egg white

Position a rack in the middle of an oven and preheat the oven to 350°F (180°C). Butter 2 baking sheets.

In a bowl, sift together the flour, cornstarch, and salt. Set aside.

❧ In a food processor fitted with the metal blade or in a blender in two batches, combine ¼ cup (2 oz/60 g) of the sugar and the pecans. Pulse until finely chopped. Set aside.

❧ Remove the zest from the lime (see page 287): Using a small fine-holed grater and holding the grater over a saucer, grate the zest (green part only) from the skin of the lime. Be sure to include all the zest clinging to the grater. You should have about ½ teaspoon. Cut the lime in half and squeeze the juice into a small bowl. Set the zest and juice aside.

❧ In a bowl, combine the remaining ½ cup (4 oz/125 g) sugar and the butter. Using a heavy-duty electric mixer set on medium speed, beat until light, about 5 minutes, scraping down the sides of the bowl as needed. Add the egg white, the lime zest, and 2 teaspoons of the lime juice and continue beating until fluffy, another 8–10 minutes, again scraping down the sides of the bowl as needed. Reduce the speed to low and carefully beat in the flour mixture, a little at a time. Add the pecans and beat until well blended.

❧ Using a small spoon, scoop up spoonfuls of the dough and, using your hands, form into balls about 1 inch (2.5 cm) in diameter. Place on the prepared baking sheets about 1 inch (2.5 cm) apart. Using your thumb, press down on each ball to flatten it to about ⅜ inch (1 cm) thick, leaving a thumbprint in the dough.

❧ Bake until the cookies just begin to color at the edges, 18–20 minutes. Transfer the baking sheets to wire racks to cool for 3–4 minutes, then transfer the cookies to the racks to cool completely. Store in airtight containers for up to 1 week. A ❧

GOLDEN APPLE COBBLER

SERVES 6–8

The flaky crusts characteristic of pie making are sadly becoming a lost art, but that does not mean that delectable pies must become a thing of the past. If you find pastry making too difficult, try preparing other types of "pies" such as this deep-dish cobbler.

❧ *I use Golden Delicious apples here for their wonderful flavor. Also, their firm texture doesn't break down during cooking, so there's less chance of their juice boiling over in the oven. You can also use Fuji apples, which are sweet and have crisp white flesh. Partially cooking the apples before assembling the cobbler cuts down on the baking time and ensures that the apples are thoroughly cooked.*

FOR THE FILLING:

½ cup (4 oz/125 g) sugar

1½ tablespoons all-purpose (plain) flour

¼ cup (2 oz/60 g) unsalted butter

3 lb (1.5 kg) Golden Delicious apples, peeled, cored, and thinly sliced

2 tablespoons fresh lemon juice

1 teaspoon vanilla extract (essence)

FOR THE CRUST:

2 cups (10 oz/315 g) all-purpose (plain) flour

¼ cup (2 oz/60 g) sugar

2 teaspoons baking powder

¼ teaspoon salt

2 tablespoons unsalted butter, chilled and cut into small cubes

⅓ cup (2 oz/60 g) coarsely chopped crystallized ginger

1 orange

1 cup (8 fl oz/250 ml) heavy (double) cream, plus cream for brushing top

whipped cream sauce (recipe on page 285)

Position a rack in the middle of an oven and preheat to 425°F (220°C). Butter a 1½-qt (1.5-l) pie dish 10 inches (25 cm) in diameter and 2 inches (5 cm) deep.

❧ To make the filling, in a bowl, stir together the sugar and flour. In a large sauté pan over medium heat, melt the butter. Stir in the apples, lemon juice, and sugar mixture. Cover partially and cook, stirring, until tender, 15–20 minutes. Stir in the vanilla. Let cool for 15–20 minutes. Transfer to the prepared dish.

❧ To make the crust, mix together the flour, sugar, baking powder, and salt in a bowl. Add the butter and, using a pastry blender, 2 knives, or your fingertips, cut in the butter until the mixture resembles coarse crumbs. Stir in the ginger.

❧ Using a fine-holed grater, grate the zest from the orange into a separate bowl as directed on page 287. Be sure to include all the zest clinging to the grater. Stir in the cream. Then, using a fork, stir the cream–zest mixture into the flour mixture, just until it holds together. Gather the dough into a ball. On a floured work surface and with floured hands, knead briefly until soft, then roll out a little larger than the pie dish. Transfer the round to the dish; trim off the excess. Cut a small hole in the center for steam to escape. Cut any pastry scraps into fanciful shapes. Brush the top with cream where you wish to decorate, then press the pastry shapes in place. Lightly brush the crust and decorations with cream.

❧ Bake for 10 minutes. Reduce the oven temperature to 375°F (190°C) and bake until golden, 20–25 minutes longer. Cool on a wire rack. Serve warm, topped with whipped cream sauce. A ❧

"If you are cold, tea will warm you.
If you are too heated, it will cool you.
If you are depressed, it will cheer you.
If you are excited, it will calm you."

–William Gladstone

CREAM SCONES

MAKES 15 SCONES

An old English teatime favorite, scones came to the United States with the early settlers. Only in recent years have they become a nationwide favorite. Finely grated orange zest flavors this particular version. They are wonderful served warm with lemon curd (recipe on page 284) or apricot-orange preserves (page 282). Leftover scones can be placed on a baking sheet and warmed in a preheated 350°F (180°C) oven until hot, 6–7 minutes. It's best not to reheat scones in a microwave, as they will become tough and lose their crispness. I find that cake flour—milled from soft winter wheat, which has less gluten—produces a lighter, flakier scone. If you are a novice at pastry making, I'm sure you'll find that a pastry blender (see page 294) works wonders in helping you achieve the desired results quickly and easily.

2¼ cups (9 oz/280 g) cake
   (soft-wheat) flour
¼ cup (2 oz/60 g) sugar
½ teaspoon salt
2 teaspoons baking powder
2 tablespoons unsalted butter, chilled,
   cut into small cubes
⅓ cup (2 oz/60 g) dried currants
1 orange
1 cup (8 fl oz/250 ml) heavy (double)
   cream, plus cream for brushing tops

Position a rack in the middle of an oven and preheat the oven to 400°F (200°C).

In a bowl, combine the cake flour, sugar, salt, and baking powder. Stir until well blended. Drop the butter cubes into the flour mixture and, using a pastry blender, 2 knives, or your fingertips, cut the butter into the dry ingredients until the mixture resembles coarse crumbs. Stir in the currants.

Remove the zest from the orange (see page 287): Using a fine-holed grater and holding the grater over a bowl, grate the zest (orange part only) from the skin of the orange. Be sure to include all the zest clinging to the grater. Add the 1 cup (8 fl oz/250 ml) cream to the zest and stir to blend. Using a wooden spoon, quickly stir the cream-zest mixture into the flour mixture.

Form the soft dough into a ball and transfer to a lightly floured work surface. With floured hands, knead the dough 4 or 5 times, then roll out (or pat out with your hands) into a 9-inch (23-cm) square about ½ inch (12 mm) thick. Using a sharp knife, cut the square into 3 strips each about 3 inches (7.5 cm) wide. Cut each strip into 5 triangles. Place on an ungreased baking sheet about ½ inch (12 mm) apart. Brush the tops of the triangles with cream.

Bake until golden, 20–25 minutes. Let cool on the baking sheet for 5–6 minutes, then serve warm.

ALMOND BISCOTTI

MAKES 18–20 BISCOTTI

These Tuscan almond cookies have won worldwide popularity. In keeping with tradition, serve them with a glass of dessert wine, such as Tuscany's Vin Santo. The cookies are also excellent served with any fruit dessert, a pudding, or, of course, coffee or tea.

❧ *For the second baking, you may want to use two baking sheets so that you can spread the slices out for more uniform baking and greater crunchiness. I find that the cookies also cool better—to an even crispness—if left in the turned-off oven with the door ajar about 2 inches (5 cm).*

1 cup (5½ oz/170 g) almonds
2 cups (10 oz/315 g) all-purpose
  (plain) flour
1½ teaspoons baking powder
⅛ teaspoon salt
⅛ teaspoon ground cinnamon
1 teaspoon aniseeds, lightly crushed
1 small orange
¼ cup (2 oz/60 g) unsalted butter
½ cup (4 oz/125 g) granulated sugar
¼ cup (2 oz/60 g) firmly packed light
  brown sugar
2 eggs
2 teaspoons almond extract (essence)
½ cup (3 oz/90 g) golden raisins
  (sultanas)
1 egg beaten with 1 tablespoon water

Position a rack in the middle of an oven and preheat to 325°F (165°C). Spread the almonds on a baking sheet and bake until well toasted, about 10 minutes; let cool. Chop very coarsely and set aside. Raise the oven temperature to 350°F (180°C). Butter and flour a baking sheet.

❧ In a bowl, combine the flour, baking powder, salt, cinnamon, and aniseeds and stir well; set aside. Using a fine-holed grater and holding the orange over a saucer, grate the zest (orange part only) from the orange (see page 287). You should have about 1 tablespoon zest. Set aside.

❧ In a bowl, using an electric mixer set on medium speed, beat together the butter and both sugars until light, about 5 minutes, scraping down the bowl at intervals. Add the eggs, one at a time, beating well after each addition. Beat in the almond extract and the orange zest. Reduce the speed to low and gradually beat in the flour mixture until blended. The dough should be stiff. Add the almonds and raisins and knead in with your hands. Gather into a ball, transfer to a well-floured surface, and knead a few times, adding a little flour if too sticky.

❧ Divide the dough in half. Form each half into a flattened log about 2 inches (5 cm) wide and 10 inches (25 cm) long. Place on the baking sheet, spacing them 1 inch (2.5 cm) apart. Brush the tops with the egg mixture. Bake until lightly browned, 20–25 minutes. Place the sheet on a rack to cool for 5 minutes.

❧ Transfer the logs to a work surface. Using a sharp serrated knife, cut on the diagonal into slices 1 inch (2.5 cm) wide. Place the slices upright on the baking sheet (or 2 sheets), spacing them 1 inch (2.5 cm) apart. Return to the oven and bake until golden brown, about 15 minutes. Turn off the oven, open the oven door about 2 inches (5 cm), and let cool for 30–35 minutes. Transfer the baking sheet(s) to a wire rack(s) and let the biscotti cool completely until dry and crisp. ❧

Cakes

The recipes on these pages present a delectable array of cakes you might find in the typical French, Italian, or American home. Each reflects the desire of today's cook for simplicity, ease of preparation, and outstanding results.

One of the simplest approaches to making a cake is to aim for just a single layer; you can turn your cake out of its pan ready to cut into wedges and serve. But that doesn't mean you will sacrifice interest or complexity. An Italian Apple Walnut Cake (page 259) abounds in sliced apples, golden raisins, and chopped walnuts to make every bite intriguing. A French Bittersweet Chocolate Cake (this page) and an American Chocolate-Orange Cheese-cake (page 261) beguile with their rich intensity.

Sometimes a special occasion calls for a little extra effort. The recipe for Lemon-Almond Butter Cake (page 258) shows how a few added steps can lead to the most delightful, impressive results.

Bittersweet Chocolate Cake

MAKES ONE 8-INCH (20-CM) CAKE; SERVES 6–8

True chocolate purists will love this cake. It has a fine flavor without being too rich, and it does not need an icing.

A springform pan is the best choice, but a pan with a solid bottom may also be used. If you settle on the latter, be sure to butter the pan well, cut a piece of waxed paper to fit the bottom precisely, slip it into the pan, butter the paper, and then dust the paper well with flour.

The cake tastes best served warm. Reheat any leftovers in a 200°F (95°C) oven for 4–5 minutes.

3 tablespoons cake (soft-wheat) flour

1 tablespoon unsweetened cocoa powder

2 teaspoons instant espresso powder

5 oz (155 g) bittersweet chocolate, chopped into chunks

6 tablespoons (3 oz/90 g) unsalted butter, cut into small cubes, at room temperature

4 eggs, separated

½ cup (3½ oz/105 g) superfine (caster) sugar

1 teaspoon pure vanilla extract (essence)

FOR THE WHIPPED CREAM TOPPING:

1 cup (8 fl oz/250 ml) heavy (double) cream

2 tablespoons sour cream

2 tablespoons confectioners' (icing) sugar

1 tablespoon finely grated orange zest (see page 287)

1 teaspoon pure vanilla extract (essence)

confectioners' (icing) sugar for dusting

Position a rack in the middle of an oven and preheat to 350°F (180°C). Butter and flour an 8-inch (20-cm) springform pan with 2-inch (5-cm) sides.

In a bowl, sift together the flour, cocoa powder, and espresso powder. Set aside.

Place the chocolate in a heatproof bowl and set over (but not touching) barely simmering water in a saucepan. Melt, stirring occasionally, then remove from the heat and stir in the butter, a little at a time, until blended. Let cool slightly.

In a large bowl, combine the egg yolks and superfine sugar. Using an electric mixer set on medium speed, beat until creamy, 3–4 minutes. Beat in the chocolate mixture until blended. Fold in the flour mixture and then the vanilla.

Beat the egg whites until soft peaks form. Stir one-fourth of the whites into the batter. Fold in the remaining whites just until incorporated.

Pour into the prepared pan and level the top. Bake until the top is risen and crusty and a toothpick stuck into the center comes out almost clean, 30–35 minutes. The center should be soft and moist. Let cool on a wire rack for 10–15 minutes. The top will fall a bit. Remove the pan sides. Loosen the cake's edges with a knife and slide the warm cake onto a serving plate.

In a bowl, whisk together the cream and sour cream until slightly thickened. Beat in the sugar, orange zest, and vanilla until soft folds form. Dust the warm cake with confectioners' sugar. Cut into slices and top with the whipped cream.

LEMON-ALMOND BUTTER CAKE

SERVES 8–10

Although simple to bake and assemble, this is a splendid-looking cake to serve at a special dinner.

⤳ *The keys to producing a light, finely grained cake are measuring or weighing the ingredients carefully and beating thoroughly to ensure that ample air is incorporated. Beat the butter and sugar until they are very creamy, scraping down the sides of the bowl frequently to ensure a smooth mixture. Add a little of the egg and beat thoroughly to create an emulsion that doesn't separate. Then continue to add the eggs a little at a time, beating thoroughly each time until well mixed with no sign of separation before adding more. Continue beating until the volume doubles. Next, carefully fold (do not beat) in the flour mixture, one-third at a time, alternating with the liquid.*

⤳ *For a different look, increase the sliced (flaked) almonds to ¾ cup (3 oz/90 g) and simply scatter the nuts more heavily over the cake to cover the icing.*

½ cup (2 oz/60 g) sliced (flaked) almonds
1¾ cups (5½ oz/170 g) cake (soft-wheat) flour, sifted before measuring
2 teaspoons baking powder
¼ teaspoon salt
2 lemons
½ cup (4 oz/125 g) unsalted butter, at room temperature
1 cup (8 oz/250 g) sugar
2 eggs, beaten
½ cup (4 fl oz/125 ml) milk
lemon curd (recipe on page 284)

Position a rack in the middle of an oven and preheat the oven to 300°F (150°C).

⤳ Butter the bottom and sides of an 8-inch (20-cm) round cake pan with 2-inch (5-cm) sides. Cut out a piece of waxed paper to fit the bottom of the pan precisely and slip into place. Butter the paper and then dust the paper and the pan sides with flour. Tap out any excess flour.

⤳ Spread the sliced almonds on a baking sheet and bake until they begin to change color, 4–5 minutes. Watch carefully so they do not burn. Set aside to cool. Raise the oven temperature to 350°F (180°C).

⤳ In a large bowl, sift together the sifted cake flour, baking powder, and salt. Set aside. Using a fine-holed grater and holding the grater over a saucer, grate the zest from the lemons as directed on page 287. Be sure to include all the zest clinging to the grater. Set aside.

⤳ In a large bowl, combine the butter and sugar. Using an electric mixer set on medium speed, beat until light and creamy, about 5 minutes, scraping down the sides of the bowl 3 or 4 times. Add the beaten eggs, a little at a time, beating

thoroughly after each addition, then continue beating until doubled in volume, 4–5 minutes, again scraping down the sides of the bowl 3 or 4 times. Beat in the lemon zest.

⤳ Using a rubber spatula, carefully fold in the flour mixture, one-third at a time, alternating with the milk. Spoon into the prepared pan, building up the sides higher than the center. Bake until the top is golden, 35–40 minutes. To test for doneness, insert a toothpick into the center; it should come out clean. Remove from the oven and let rest for a couple of minutes. Then, using a thin-bladed knife, loosen the sides of the cake from the pan and turn out, bottom side up, onto a wire rack. Peel off the paper and let cool completely.

⤳ When cool, transfer the cake, bottom side up, to a flat cake plate. Using a long, sharp knife, cut the cake in half horizontally to form 2 layers. Using an icing spatula, spread a thin layer of the lemon curd on the bottom layer. Replace the top layer and spread the remaining curd evenly over the top and sides of the cake. Arrange or scatter the toasted almonds over the top and sides.

A

APPLE WALNUT CAKE

SERVES 8–10

With most Italian dessert baking done in small bakeries, it is only natural that any baking done at home would be simple and easy. This is one of the easiest, and probably the best, Italian home-baked desserts. I have added walnuts and golden raisins to the traditional recipe for more crunch and flavor. Apples that are especially sweet and hold their shape well during baking are preferable: Golden Delicious, Fuji, and Gala are among the best.

If you use one of the newer springform pans with a dark stick-resistant finish, it's a good idea to reduce your oven temperature to 325°F (165°C). Otherwise the dark finish will cause the cake to brown too quickly on the bottom and sides. I also suggest placing a baking sheet on the shelf below to catch any drips or runovers.

Serve the cake with zabaglione (see page 274) or with whipped cream flavored with lemon juice or vanilla extract.

1 lemon

4 juicy, sweet apples, such as Golden Delicious, Fuji, or Gala

1½ cups (6 oz/185 g) cake (soft-wheat) flour

1½ teaspoons baking powder

¼ teaspoon salt

½ cup (4 oz/125 g) unsalted butter

1 cup (8 oz/245 g) sugar, plus extra for sprinkling on top

3 eggs

1 teaspoon vanilla extract (essence)

½ cup (3 oz/90 g) golden raisins (sultanas), softened in boiling water to cover for 8–10 minutes and drained

½ cup (2 oz/60 g) walnuts, coarsely chopped

½ teaspoon ground cinnamon

Position a rack in the middle of an oven and preheat to 350°F (180°C). Butter and flour a 9-inch (23-cm) springform pan; it should be 2¾ inches (7 cm) deep, measured from the inside.

Using a zester or fine-holed shredder, shred the zest (yellow part only) from the lemon directly into a large bowl (see page 287). Then squeeze the juice from the lemon into the bowl.

Peel the apples and cut into quarters. Remove the cores and cut each quarter into thin slices. Place in the bowl with the lemon juice and toss carefully to coat all cut surfaces to prevent them from darkening. Set aside.

In a separate bowl, sift together the flour, baking powder, and salt. Set aside.

In a bowl, using an electric mixer set at medium speed, beat the butter until light, about 2 minutes. Add ¾ cup (6 oz/185 g) of the sugar and beat until fluffy, 4–5 minutes, scraping down the bowl at intervals. Add the eggs, one at a time, beating well after each addition. Continue beating until doubled in volume, 5–6 minutes, scraping down the bowl at intervals. Beat in the vanilla. Using a rubber spatula, fold in the flour mixture, one-third at a time, until just incorporated. Pour the batter into the prepared pan; level the surface with the spatula. Set aside.

Add the raisins and walnuts to the apples and toss well. In a small bowl, stir together the remaining ¼ cup (2 oz/60 g) sugar and the cinnamon. Sprinkle over the apples and toss again. Spoon the apples evenly over the batter and then sprinkle with 1 or more tablespoons sugar. Bake until golden brown and a toothpick inserted into the center comes out clean, 50–60 minutes.

Transfer the pan to a cooling rack and let rest for 8–10 minutes. Run a knife around the pan to loosen the cake. Release the pan sides and remove. Run a knife between the bottom of the cake and the pan bottom and, using a metal spatula, transfer to a serving plate. Let cool to warm, then slice and serve.

CHOCOLATE-ORANGE CHEESECAKE

SERVES 6–8

The flavors of chocolate and orange, which complement each other so well, make wonderful additions to a tangy cheesecake. If possible, use a Dutch-process cocoa powder, which has a smoother flavor than other cocoa powders.

Several important points will help you achieve a good, smooth, light cheesecake. First, cover the outside of the pan with aluminum foil, shiny side out, to slow down the heat absorption and promote even baking. Next, let the cream cheese soften to room temperature and then beat it until very light and fluffy and free of all lumps; scrape down the sides of the bowl often to make sure you haven't missed any lumps. Third, beat in each egg thoroughly before adding the next one. Finally, slowly stir the batter to dispel as many bubbles as possible before pouring it into the baking pan; this step may take a few minutes.

graham crackers for 1½ cups
   (4½ oz/140 g) crumbs
2 tablespoons plus ¾ cup
   (6 oz/185 g) sugar
1 tablespoon unsweetened cocoa
   powder, plus additional cocoa powder
   for dusting top
1 teaspoon ground cinnamon
¼ cup (2 oz/60 g) unsalted butter,
   melted
8 oz (250 g) bittersweet chocolate,
   chopped
1 orange
1 lb (500 g) cream cheese, at room
   temperature
½ cup (4 fl oz/125 ml) sour cream
5 eggs

Position a rack in the middle of an oven and preheat the oven to 350°F (180°C). Cover the outside (bottom and sides) of a 9-inch (23-cm) springform pan with aluminum foil, shiny side out. Butter the inside of the pan generously.

Place the graham crackers between 2 sheets of waxed paper and, using a rolling pin, crush to form fine crumbs. Measure out 1½ cups (4½ oz/140 g) and place in a bowl. Add the 2 tablespoons sugar, the 1 tablespoon cocoa powder, and the cinnamon and mix well. Gradually add the melted butter, stirring constantly, until the crumbs are evenly coated. Place in the prepared pan and, using your fingers, press evenly over the bottom and two-thirds up the sides. Refrigerate until ready to fill.

Place the chocolate in a heatproof bowl or in the top pan of a double boiler. Set the bowl or pan over (but not touching) 1 inch (2.5 cm) of barely simmering water in a saucepan or the bottom pan of the double boiler. Stir until melted and smooth. Remove the bowl or pan from over the water and set aside.

Using a fine-holed grater, grate the zest from the orange as directed on page 287. Be sure to include all the zest clinging to the grater. Set aside. Place the cream cheese in a bowl. Using an electric mixer set on medium speed, beat until smooth and fluffy and no lumps remain, about 10 minutes. Beat in the sour cream, then beat in the ¾ cup (6 oz/185 g) sugar and the orange zest. Add the eggs, one at a time, beating well after each addition. Beat for 1–2 minutes until fully blended.

Using a rubber spatula, gently stir in the melted chocolate until blended; do not beat. Continue to stir slowly for 1–2 minutes to dispel as many bubbles as possible. Pour the batter into the prepared pan. Bake until puffed and no longer shiny, about 50 minutes. The center may still look slightly liquid, but it will firm up when chilled. Transfer to a wire rack to cool. When cold, remove the foil then remove the pan sides. Cover and refrigerate until firm enough to cut easily, 4–5 hours or as long as overnight.

Just before serving, dust cocoa powder generously over the cake.

MIXED BERRY SHORTCAKE

SERVES 4

Whether you consider it a cake, a pastry, or a fruit dessert, American-style berry shortcake is undeniably one of summer's most delicious treats.

❧ *The shortcakes in this recipe are actually scones flavored with orange. Quite crunchy, they go well with the berries, their juice, and the whipped cream. Other soft, juicy fruits such as peaches or nectarines can be used; ice cream can be substituted for the whipped cream; or poached pears can be sliced, sandwiched, and topped with a rich dark chocolate sauce.*

❧ *I specify that the orange zest be shredded over a bowl, so that all the flavorful oil released from the skin during scraping is captured. For the topping, I find that combining a little sour cream with the heavy cream for whipping produces a better flavor, similar to the Devonshire cream of England or the crème fraîche of France.*

3–4 cups (12–16 oz/375–500 g) mixed ripe berries such as strawberries, raspberries, blueberries, and blackberries, in any combination

¼ cup (2 oz/60 g) plus 2 tablespoons granulated sugar

1 cup (4 oz/125 g) cake (soft-wheat) flour

¼ teaspoon salt

1 teaspoon baking powder

1 small orange

1½ cups (12 fl oz/375 ml) heavy (double) cream

2 tablespoons sour cream

2 tablespoons confectioners' (icing) sugar

1 teaspoon vanilla extract (essence)

Position a rack in the middle of an oven and preheat the oven to 400°F (200°C).

❧ Wash the berries and shake dry in a colander. If using strawberries, cut them into halves or quarters. Cut about one-fourth of any other berries into halves. Put all the berries in a bowl and add the ¼ cup (2 oz/60 g) granulated sugar. Toss well. Cover and refrigerate for at least 30–40 minutes or for up to 1½ hours.

❧ In a bowl, stir together the cake flour, the 2 tablespoons granulated sugar, salt, and baking powder. Set aside.

❧ Remove the zest from the orange (see page 287): Using a zester or small fine-holed shredder, and holding the shredder over a bowl, shred the zest (orange part only) from the skin of the orange. Add ½ cup (4 fl oz/125 ml) of the cream to the zest, mixing well, and then stir into the flour mixture until it holds together. Gather into a ball and place on a floured work surface. With floured hands, knead a few times until a soft dough forms, then roll out (or pat out with your hands) into a 6-inch (15-cm) square. Cut into 4 pieces, each 3 inches (7.5 cm) square. Place on an ungreased baking sheet. Bake until golden and crisp, 20–25 minutes. Let cool to warm on the baking sheet.

❧ In a bowl, combine the remaining 1 cup (8 fl oz/250 ml) cream and the sour cream and, using a whisk or an electric or hand beater, beat just until beginning to thicken. Add the confectioners' sugar and vanilla extract and continue to beat until soft folds form. Cover and refrigerate until ready to serve.

❧ Split the warm shortcakes in half horizontally and place the bottom halves on individual plates, cut side up. Spoon some of the berries, with their juices, evenly over the bottoms. Place the tops on them, cut sides down. Spoon on more berries and then the whipped cream. Serve at once. A ❧

CUSTARDS, PUDDINGS & MOUSSES

The down-to-earth appeal of egg-based desserts is undeniable. Moist, rich, and sweet, they bring pleasure to the senses while soothing the soul. No wonder so many people in so many countries consider custards, puddings, and mousses prime examples of comfort food.

In many cultures, such desserts first enjoyed in childhood endure as adults' favorites. An Italian Lemon Rice Pudding (page 269) would be likely to evoke nostalgia just about anywhere in the world. The same would hold true for an American-style Apricot Bread-and-Butter Custard (this page), which relies on good Italian or French bread for body and flavor.

But the desserts that follow are not all intended for family-style or casual dining. French Orange Floating Islands (page 268) and classic Chocolate Mousse (page 271) are sophisticated enough for the most elegant of dinner parties—although they would certainly be devoured at a children's birthday party as well.

APRICOT BREAD-AND-BUTTER CUSTARD

SERVES 6

Bread pudding has long been a favorite in the United States. Lately, however, European-style bread-and-butter custards have been gaining in popularity.

An oval Pyrex baking dish measuring 10½ by 8 by 2¼ inches (26 by 20 by 5.5 cm) works well for this recipe. The key to the success of this pudding is the bread itself. Use a good Italian or French type with a fairly tough crumb that will hold up well in liquid, without getting mushy the way most commercial sandwich-type loaves do.

I prefer to make my own preserves from dried apricots (recipe on page 282), because I can control the sugar and produce a more intense, tart apricot flavor. To my taste, the resulting jam contrasts much better with the soft, rich custard. If you wish, add a little more sugar to the jam. Of course, you can also use any brand of high-quality apricot preserves that is not overly sweet.

6–8 slices Italian or French bread, each ½ inch (12 mm) thick
½ cup (5 oz/155 g) apricot-orange preserves (recipe on page 282)
2–3 tablespoons unsalted butter, at room temperature
1 orange
3 cups (24 fl oz/750 ml) milk
1 cup (8 fl oz/250 ml) heavy (double) cream
½ cup (4 oz/125 g) granulated sugar
3 whole eggs plus 4 egg yolks
confectioners' (icing) sugar

Position a rack in the middle of an oven and preheat the oven to 325°F (165°C). Butter a shallow 2-qt (2-l) baking dish, preferably oval or rectangular. Have ready a baking pan about 3 inches (7.5 cm) deep that is large enough to accommodate the baking dish. Bring a teakettle full of water to a boil.

Arrange 3 or 4 bread slices in the prepared dish; trim as necessary to avoid overlapping. It is not necessary to fill the space completely. Spread the slices evenly with the preserves. Arrange a second layer of bread slices on top. Spread with the butter. Set aside.

Grate the zest from the orange as directed on page 287. In a saucepan over medium heat, combine the milk, cream, and 2 teaspoons of the orange zest. Heat until bubbles form along the edge of the pan; do not boil. Set aside.

In a large bowl, combine the granulated sugar, whole eggs, and egg yolks. Using a whisk, beat until well blended. Gradually add the hot milk, stirring continuously with the whisk just until blended.

Place the baking dish in the baking pan. Carefully pour the hot custard mixture into the dish so that it flows between the bread and the side of the dish, not over the bread. Pour in only enough custard to reach halfway up the bottom layer of bread. Let stand for a few minutes for the bread to absorb some of the custard. Pour in the rest of the custard. Using a large spatula, press the slices down even with the top of the custard and hold them there for a few seconds to help the bread absorb more. Pour water into the baking pan to reach two-thirds up the sides of the baking dish.

Bake until just set, 40–45 minutes. To test, insert a knife into the custard near the center; it should come out clean. Do not overbake, as the custard will separate. Transfer the baking dish to a wire rack to cool slightly. The pudding is best if served warm. Just before serving, dust confectioners' sugar generously over the top.

CHERRY CLAFOUTI

SERVES 4

Clafouti, *a traditional specialty from the Limousin district of France, is dessert making at its simplest. All you need to ensure success are ripe, dark sweet cherries. It is also best to remove their pits with a cherry pitter; cutting them open with a knife results in too much juice being released into the batter.*

❧ *To measure sifted flour, spoon the flour into a sifter while holding the sifter over the appropriately sized measuring cup. Then sift until the cup is full. Use a straight-edged knife to level off the flour even with the rim.*

1 lb (500 g) fresh dark sweet cherries, such as Bing or Lambert
1 cup (8 fl oz/250 ml) milk
¼ cup (2 fl oz/60 ml) heavy (double) cream
½ cup (1½ oz/45 g) sifted cake (soft-wheat) flour
4 eggs, at room temperature
½ cup (4 oz/125 g) granulated sugar
⅛ teaspoon salt
1 tablespoon kirsch or 1 teaspoon pure almond extract (essence)
confectioners' (icing) sugar for dusting
fresh mint leaves

Position a rack in the upper third of an oven and preheat to 350°F (180°C). Butter a 1½-qt (1.5-l) round, oval, or rectangular baking dish with low sides. A 10-inch (25-cm) round pie dish with sides 2 inches (5 cm) deep is a good choice.

❧ Using a cherry pitter, pit the cherries. Arrange the cherries in the prepared baking dish in a single layer. They should just cover the bottom of the dish. Set aside.

❧ In a saucepan over medium-low heat, combine the milk and cream and heat until small bubbles appear along the edges of the pan; do not boil. Remove from the heat and, using a whisk, vigorously whisk in the flour, a little at a time, until well blended and no lumps remain. Set aside.

❧ In a bowl, combine the eggs, granulated sugar, and salt and, using the whisk, beat until light and creamy. Add the milk mixture and the kirsch or almond extract and whisk until well blended and smooth.

❧ Pour over the cherries; it should just cover them. Place the baking dish on a baking sheet and place in the oven. Bake until browned and puffed yet still soft in the center and a sharp, thin-bladed knife stuck into the center of the custard comes out almost clean, 45–55 minutes. Transfer to a rack to cool slightly.

❧ Dust the top generously with confectioners' sugar. Using a large serving spoon, place 2 or 3 spoonfuls on each dessert plate. Dust with more confectioners' sugar and garnish with mint leaves. Serve warm.

ORANGE FLOATING ISLANDS

SERVES 4

Although you'll find similar desserts in many countries, I think the French can take credit for the origin of floating islands. The dessert has always been one of my favorites, and I have regularly sought it out when I've been in France.

⟫ *If you've never made floating islands before, I think you'll be surprised by how relatively simple the directions are, and pleased by the fact that they can be made hours ahead of serving. Poaching the meringues can be a little tricky, however. Poach only a couple of them at a time to start with, until you get the hang of it; be careful not to cook them too long. This recipe will make more meringues than you need; serve only the best ones.*

1 orange
2 cups (16 fl oz/500 ml) milk
5 egg yolks
⅓ cup (3 oz/90 g) sugar
¼ cup (2 fl oz/60 ml) heavy (double) cream

FOR THE MERINGUES:
4 egg whites
⅛ teaspoon cream of tartar
⅓ cup (3 oz/90 g) sugar
Uunsweetened cocoa powder for sprinkling
ground cinnamon for sprinkling

Grate the zest from the orange (see page 287). Measure 1 tablespoon.

⟫ In a saucepan over medium heat, warm the milk until small bubbles appear along the edges of the pan. Remove from the heat. In a bowl, combine the egg yolks and sugar. Whisk until light, 1–2 minutes. Whisk in the cream and orange zest. Then gradually whisk in the hot milk until well blended.

⟫ Return the mixture to the sauce-pan and place over medium-low heat. Stirring with a wooden spoon, heat until thickened and the mixture coats the spoon, about 5 minutes. Do not overcook. To test, run a finger across the back of the spoon; it should leave a trail. Immediately transfer to a shallow serving bowl, set aside to cool a little, then cover and refrigerate to chill.

⟫ To make the meringues, in a large sauté pan or deep frying pan, pour in water to a depth of 1 inch (2.5 cm) and bring to a bare simmer over medium-low heat. Meanwhile, in a large, clean, dry bowl, combine the egg whites and cream of tartar. Using a balloon whisk, beat until stiff peaks begin to form. While continuing to whisk, gradually add about half of the sugar, a little at a time, until the whites are glossy and stand in peaks. Using a large spoon, fold in the remaining sugar, a little at a time. The meringue should remain glossy and stand in peaks.

⟫ Cover a baking pan with paper towels. Using a serving spoon and forming one at a time, scoop up oval mounds of meringue and float them in the simmering water. Poach, turning once, about 45 seconds on each side. Using a slotted spoon, transfer the meringues to the prepared pan to drain. Repeat with the rest of the meringue. Transfer to a plate, cover, and refrigerate for up to 2 hours.

⟫ To serve, spoon the custard into shallow dessert bowls or deep dessert plates and float 2 or 3 meringues on each custard. Sprinkle each meringue with a little cocoa powder and cinnamon and serve. F ⟫

LEMON RICE PUDDING WITH HAZELNUT MERINGUES

SERVES 4–6

The typical Italian dessert pudding, or budino, *is baked. I chose to depart from tradition by leaving out the egg whites and cooking the pudding on the stove top. I then serve it slightly warm or at room temperature, accompanied by crisp hazelnut meringues made with the egg whites.*

❧ *I think you'll find this rice pudding particularly delicious and quite different from any others. Arborio rice gives it a rich, creamy character that is lightened by the lemon. The hazelnut meringues are addictive; you will not have to store them for very long. They are excellent with coffee or tea. The recipe calls for baking and drying the meringues longer than most recipes, to give them better flavor and color.*

hazelnut meringues (recipe on
   page 284)
⅓ cup (2 oz/60 g) golden raisins
   (sultanas)
boiling water, as needed
3 cups (24 fl oz/750 ml) milk
pinch of salt
⅓ cup (2½ oz/75 g) Italian Arborio rice
   or medium-grain white rice
2 lemons
4 egg yolks
¼ cup (2 oz/60 g) sugar
⅛ teaspoon ground cinnamon

Make the hazelnut meringues as directed and let cool for a couple of hours. In a small bowl, combine the raisins and boiling water to cover. Let stand for 8–10 minutes to soften. Drain well and set aside.

❧ In a heavy-bottomed saucepan over medium heat, combine the milk and salt. Heat until small bubbles appear around the edges of the pan; watch carefully that it does not boil. Add the rice in a slow, steady stream, stirring constantly to keep the grains separate. Reduce the heat to low, cover partially, and barely simmer, stirring every few minutes, until the rice is tender and the milk is creamy and thickened, 30–40 minutes; watch carefully that the milk does not boil over. Remove from the heat and let cool for 5 minutes.

❧ Meanwhile, using a fine-holed grater, grate the zest (yellow part only) from 1 of the lemons directly onto a saucer (see page 287); be sure to scrape off all the zest clinging to the grater. You should have about 1 teaspoon zest. Set aside.

❧ In a medium-sized heatproof bowl (or in the top pan of a double boiler), combine the egg yolks and sugar and, using a whisk, beat until light colored and creamy, 2–3 minutes. Beat in the lemon zest and the cinnamon. Using a wooden spoon, stir in the hot rice-milk mixture, a little at a time, until well blended. Stir in the raisins. Place the bowl over a pan of simmering water; do not allow the bottom to touch the water. Stir slowly, scraping the bottom and sides each time, until the mixture thickens and is creamy, 10–15 minutes. It should thickly coat the spoon. Do not allow to boil. Set aside to cool.

❧ When cooled to warm, transfer the pudding to a serving dish. Using a zester or a fine-holed shredder, shred the zest (yellow part only) from the remaining lemon directly onto the top of the pudding.

❧ Serve the pudding, preferably warm, with 4 or 5 hazelnut meringues alongside each serving. Pass extra meringues on a serving plate.

CHOCOLATE MOUSSE

SERVES 4

If you have never eaten chocolate mousse as it is served in a good French bistro or restaurant, you've missed out on an outstanding dessert. The traditional mousse is exceptionally light and very simple. I have added a little espresso powder and cardamom here, which give the mousse a marvelous new dimension of flavor.

⌘ When making the mousse, take care not to overbeat the egg whites, or they will become dry and start to break apart. Whites beaten with a light hand will mix most successfully into the chocolate, without losing much of their loft.

⌘ In France, this mousse is usually served at the table from a large glass or porcelain bowl. You can, however, spoon it into individual dishes. The candied orange peel adds considerably to this dessert, plus it is delicious eaten with after-dinner coffee.

candied orange peel (recipe on
   page 282)
½ teaspoon instant espresso powder
1 tablespoon boiling water
⅛ teaspoon ground cardamom
4 oz (125 g) bittersweet chocolate,
   preferably a dark, rich chocolate,
   broken or chopped into small pieces
2 tablespoons unsalted butter
4 eggs, separated
1 tablespoon sugar
⅛ teaspoon cream of tartar
4 fresh mint sprigs

Make the candied orange peel ahead of time.

⌘ In a cup, dissolve the espresso powder in the boiling water, stir in the ground cardamom, and set aside.

⌘ Place the chocolate and butter in a heatproof bowl and set over (but not touching) 1 inch (2.5 cm) of barely simmering water in a saucepan. Let melt, stirring occasionally. When melted, add the espresso mixture and stir until blended and smooth. Remove from the heat.

⌘ In a separate bowl, combine the egg yolks and the 1 tablespoon sugar and, using a whisk, beat until increased in volume and very light, 3–4 minutes. While stirring the melted chocolate with a wooden spoon or rubber spatula, gradually add the beaten yolks, then beat until the chocolate is thickened.

⌘ Place the egg whites and cream of tartar in another clean, dry bowl. Using a clean whisk or beaters, beat until stiff peaks form that hold their shape but are not dry. Add about one-fourth of the beaten whites to the chocolate mixture and, using a rubber spatula, stir gently to blend. Then add the remaining egg whites and gently fold in just until incorporated. Pour into a serving bowl. Cover the bowl with paper towels (this absorbs any condensation that forms); make sure the towels do not touch the mousse. Refrigerate for several hours until well set.

⌘ At the table, spoon the mousse into shallow dessert bowls or deep dessert plates. Place several strips of candied orange peel alongside each serving. Pass the rest in a bowl at the table. Garnish each serving with a mint sprig.

$\mathcal{F}$RUIT DESSERTS

Peak-of-season fruits provide pure pleasure, needing no effort beyond mere washing and perhaps peeling, cutting, or seeding. Even the simplest embellishments can add to the pleasures of fruit. French cooks will sometimes add a drizzle of black currant syrup and a spritz of fresh lime to seasonal berries and other fruit, creating a Fresh Fruit Compote with Cassis (page 280). A homemade, herb-infused syrup and sliced nuts have a similar effect on the typically Italian Oranges with Mint and Toasted Almonds (page 279). And what could be more eloquent than the way a lemon-scented syrup enhances a favorite American fruit in Poached Pears and Blueberries (this page).

Even when more elaborate preparation is involved, such as diligently stirring up ice crystals for an Italian Pink Grapefruit Granita (page 278), the best fruit desserts always aim to let the character of their featured ingredients shine through.

POACHED PEARS AND BLUEBERRIES

SERVES 4

Poaching is one of the best ways to prepare pears for a simple and delicious dessert, and with little effort a special presentation can be achieved. Make this in the fall when both pears and blueberries are at their peak, or during the early winter, substituting cranberries if blueberries are not available. Raspberries and blackberries can be used as well.

I have found that Comice pears poach extremely well. Select ones that are ripe but still firm. If using the Bosc variety, you may find them difficult to core while retaining the stem. A tip that may help: make a small incision in the side of the pear about 1 inch (2.5 cm) below the stem end, carefully inserting the knife into the center of the pear to sever the hard core just above the seed pocket.

4 cups (32 fl oz/1 l) water
3 cups (24 oz/750 g) sugar
2 lemons
4 firm but ripe pears such as Comice, Bosc, or Bartlett (Williams'), preferably with their stems attached
2 cups (8 oz/250 g) blueberries
whipped cream sauce (recipe on page 285)

In a large saucepan, combine the water, sugar, and the juice of 1 of the lemons. Place over medium-high heat and bring to a boil, stirring to dissolve the sugar. Remove from the heat and set aside.

Working from the bottom of each pear, carefully remove the core, cutting no farther than three-fourths of the way toward the stem end. Do not remove the stem. Peel the pears and, if necessary, cut a thin slice off the bottom of each to make them stand upright. Place the pears in the syrup, return the pan to the heat, and quickly bring back to a boil. Lower the heat and simmer until the pears are tender when pierced with a sharp knife, 20–25 minutes. Turn the pears at intervals so they cook evenly, stay moist, and do not turn brown. Using a slotted spoon, transfer the pears to a dish to cool. Reserve ½ cup (4 fl oz/ 125 ml) of the syrup; refrigerate the remaining syrup for another use.

In a saucepan, combine the blueberries and the ½ cup (4 fl oz/125 ml) reserved poaching syrup. Place over medium heat and bring just to a simmer. Reduce the heat slightly and simmer uncovered until the berries are tender, 10–15 minutes. Set aside to cool.

When ready to serve, transfer the pears, stem end up, to individual dessert plates and spoon the blueberries around them. Dribble some of the blueberries over the pears, as well, if you like. Remove the zest from the remaining lemon (see page 287): Using a zester or fine-holed shredder, and holding the lemon over each pear, shred the zest (yellow part only) from the skin evenly over the top.

Stir the whipped cream sauce and spoon a little over each pear. Serve the remaining cream sauce in a bowl at the table. A

MIXED BERRIES WITH ZABAGLIONE

SERVES 4

The combination of ripe berries and a topping of smooth, creamy zabaglione— a cooked, whipped froth of egg, sugar, and wine blended with whipped cream—is something to savor on a warm summer evening.

This version of zabaglione, a cousin to the traditional one made with Marsala, uses dry white wine and is whisked over ice until cool. (Save the 4 egg whites left over from this recipe to make the hazelnut meringues on page 284.) Lemon-flavored whipped cream is then folded in. A dash or two of cinnamon adds a touch of spice to each serving.

6 cups (1½ lb/750 g) ripe berries
   such as strawberries, raspberries,
   blackberries, and blueberries,
   in any combination

¾ cup (6 fl oz/185 ml) dry white wine
3 tablespoons sugar, plus ⅓ cup
   (3 oz/90 g) sugar
1 lemon
4 egg yolks
½ cup (4 fl oz/125 ml) heavy
   (double) cream
ground cinnamon
fresh mint leaves for garnish

If using strawberries, remove the stems and cut in half lengthwise or, if large, cut into quarters. Place all of the berries in a bowl and toss to mix. Sprinkle with ¼ cup (2 fl oz/60 ml) of the wine and toss with the 3 tablespoons sugar. Cover and refrigerate until chilled, about 1 hour, tossing carefully every 20–25 minutes.

Using a fine-holed grater and holding the lemon over a saucer, grate the zest (yellow part only) from the lemon (see page 287); be sure to scrape off all the zest clinging to the grater. You should have 1 teaspoon. Set aside. Have ready a large bowl of ice cubes with a little water added.

In a medium-sized heatproof bowl (or in the top pan of a double boiler), combine the egg yolks and the ⅓ cup (3 oz/90 g) sugar. Using a whisk, beat until light colored and creamy, 2–3 minutes. Add the remaining ½ cup (4 fl oz/125 ml) wine and whisk until well blended. Place the bowl over a pan of simmering water; do not allow the bottom to touch the water. Whisk continuously, scraping the bottom and sides of the bowl each time, until the mixture has tripled in volume and is quite thick and creamy; the top should stand in soft folds. This will take 10–15 minutes; be careful that the mixture does not get too hot, or it will curdle.

Quickly nest the bowl in the bowl of ice and continue to whisk until the mixture is cold; be sure to scrape the bottom and sides often, as the mixture will thicken when in contact with the cold surface of the bowl. This will take 15–25 minutes; the mixture should be very thick.

In a separate bowl, using a clean whisk or an electric beater, whip the cream until stiff peaks form. Stir in the lemon zest. Then, using a rubber spatula, fold the cream into the egg mixture until thoroughly combined. Use immediately, or cover and refrigerate for 2–3 hours; stir well before serving.

Spoon the berries into bowls and top generously with the zabaglione. Sprinkle a little cinnamon on top and garnish with mint leaves. Any leftover zabaglione can be covered and refrigerated overnight, then whisked briefly to recombine.

SAUTÉED APPLES WITH WHIPPED CREAM

SERVES 4

I first tasted this comforting dessert about 25 years ago and I've never forgotten the perfect combination of flavors—apples, butter, vanilla, and the famed apple brandy calvados. You'll find the recipe a delicious way to prepare apples for a simple yet satisfying finale to nearly any meal.
∽ *Choose full-flavored sweet apples for the best results. I like to use Fuji apples for this dish. Be sure not to let the apples caramelize or burn during cooking.*

1 lemon

6 sweet eating apples such as Fuji, Gala, or Golden Delicious, 2½–3 lb (1.25–1.5 kg) total weight

6 tablespoons (3 oz/90 g) unsalted butter

1 piece vanilla bean, 2 inches (5 cm) long

¼ cup (2 oz/60 g) granulated sugar

FOR THE WHIPPED CREAM TOPPING:

1 cup (8 fl oz/250 ml) heavy (double) cream

2 tablespoons sour cream

1 tablespoon confectioners' (icing) sugar

1 teaspoon pure vanilla extract (essence)

¼ cup (2 fl oz/60 ml) calvados or other apple brandy

4 fresh mint sprigs

Squeeze the juice from the lemon into a large bowl. One at a time, peel, quarter, and core the apples; then, to keep them from turning dark, immediately place in the bowl and turn in the lemon juice until well coated.
∽ In a large sauté pan or frying pan over medium heat, melt the butter. Using a sharp knife, cut a lengthwise slit in the vanilla bean, but do not cut completely through. Open up the pod and add it to the pan, together with half of the apples. Sauté gently, turning the apples from time to time, until golden, 10–15 minutes. Using tongs, transfer the apples to a plate, leaving the vanilla bean and butter in the pan. Sauté the remaining apples in the same manner. Return the first batch of apples to the pan. Spread out the apples in a single layer and sprinkle evenly with the granulated sugar. Cook over medium heat, turning once, until tender when pierced with the tip of a sharp knife, 10–15 minutes longer.
∽ Meanwhile, make the whipped cream topping: In a bowl, combine the cream and sour cream and whisk (or beat with an electric mixer) until the cream starts to thicken. Add the confectioners' sugar and vanilla extract and continue beating until thickened to soft folds. Cover and refrigerate until ready to use.
∽ When the apples are tender, remove from the heat. In a small saucepan, warm the apple brandy. Holding the pan away from the heat, light the brandy, pour it flaming over the apples, and let it burn out. Set aside to cool a little. (If allowed to cool completely, reheat in a 200°F/95°C oven for 4–5 minutes.)
∽ Place 6 warm apple quarters on each dessert plate and top with the whipped cream. Garnish each serving with a mint sprig. F ∽

"Fruit, as it was our primitive, and most excellent as well as most innocent food, whilst it grew in Paradise; a climate so benign, and a soil so richly impregnated with all that the influence of Heaven could communicate to it; so it has still preserved, and retained no small tincture of its original and celestial virtue."

—John Evelyn

PINK GRAPEFRUIT GRANITA

SERVES 4–6

I think Italy has developed some of the world's best frozen desserts, most especially granitas—confections of coarse crystals of flavored ice.

To achieve the appropriate consistency, granitas are made in the freezer compartment of a refrigerator rather than in an ice-cream maker. All you have to do is take the container out of the freezer every 15–20 minutes to stir up the crystals. Use a shallow stainless-steel bowl, which freezes quickly. And make the granita the same day you plan to serve it; if stored longer it will form a solid mass.

For superior color and flavor, I use Ruby grapefruit, but you could substitute any pink variety you like.

6 or 7 pink grapefruits, preferably Ruby

½ cup (4 fl oz/125 ml) water

1 cup (8 oz/250 g) sugar

2 fresh mint sprigs, or as needed, plus extra sprigs for garnish

orange zest strips (see page 287) for garnish (optional)

Be sure your freezer is set at its coldest setting an hour before you begin to make the granita. Squeeze the juice from the grapefruit and strain through a fine-mesh strainer into a bowl to produce a clear juice. You will need 3–3½ cups (24–28 fl oz/750–875 ml). Cover and refrigerate until well chilled.

In a saucepan over medium heat, combine the water and sugar. Bring to a boil, stirring to dissolve the sugar. Using a brush moistened with water, brush down the pan sides to remove any sugar crystals. Add the 2 mint sprigs and boil for 1 minute. Set aside until cool enough to taste, 5–10 minutes, then taste for flavor. If the syrup has a good mint flavor, remove and discard the mint; if not, add more mint and repeat boiling and cooling. Set aside to cool completely.

When the syrup has cooled, stir it into the chilled grapefruit juice until completely blended. Pour this mixture into a shallow stainless-steel bowl or other stainless-steel container. (Ice-cube trays will work if you have nothing else at hand.) Place in the freezer.

After about 20 minutes, check to see if any ice crystals have formed. If they have, stir to break them up with a fork. Continue to check every 15–20 minutes and stir as necessary to prevent the crystals from forming a solid mass. Frequent stirring is important to producing a uniformly textured granita. Be sure to scrape any frozen crystals from the sides and bottom of the container and break them up each time. Under proper conditions, the granita should freeze in 1½–2 hours. However, if your freezer is not cold enough or too full of food, it can take up to 2–3 hours; the timing will depend upon the freezer.

To serve, place 4–6 footed glass goblets in the refrigerator 10–15 minutes before serving. Spoon the granita into the chilled goblets. Garnish with mint sprigs and orange zest strips, if desired. Serve immediately.

ORANGES WITH MINT AND TOASTED ALMONDS

SERVES 4–6

In Italy oranges are served for dessert almost everywhere, as they are especially refreshing after nearly any main course. Their preparation, however, varies from region to region. This bright, mint-scented version recalls an orange dessert made in Venice.

❧ *Navel oranges are an excellent choice here; they have a sweet, full flavor and are seedless. You may find the oranges easiest to eat with a dessert knife and fork. If you prefer, cut the fruit crosswise into thick slices.*

¾ cup (3 oz/90 g) sliced (flaked) almonds, preferably blanched

6 navel oranges

1 cup (8 fl oz/250 ml) water

1 cup (8 oz/250 g) sugar

3 or 4 large fresh mint sprigs, plus mint leaves for garnish

Position a rack in the middle of an oven and preheat to 300°F (150°C). Spread the almonds on a baking sheet and bake until the nuts begin to change color and are fragrant, 4–5 minutes; do not allow to brown too much. Remove from the oven and let cool.

❧ Using a sharp paring knife, peel off the zest (orange part only) of the skin of 2 of the oranges, removing it in long pieces (see page 287). Slice the zest into strips ⅛ inch (3 mm) wide and about 2 inches (5 cm) long. Fill a saucepan half full of water and bring to a boil over medium-high heat. Add the orange zest strips, reduce the heat to medium-low, and simmer, uncovered, for 15 minutes, to remove most of the bitterness. Drain and set aside.

❧ In a saucepan over medium-high heat, combine the water and sugar. Bring to a boil, stirring to dissolve the sugar. Using a brush moistened with water, brush down the pan sides to remove any sugar crystals. Reduce the heat to low, add the 3 or 4 mint sprigs and simmer until the syrup is nicely mint-flavored, 5–6 minutes. Remove the mint sprigs and discard.

❧ Add the reserved orange zest strips and simmer over medium-low heat until the syrup has thickened and the zest is translucent, 12–15 minutes. Brush down the pan sides again if you see any sugar crystals forming. Set aside to cool.

❧ Cut off a thick slice from the top and bottom of the 2 partially peeled oranges, exposing the fruit beneath the peel. Then do the same to the 4 remaining oranges. Working with 1 orange at a time, place upright on a cutting surface and, holding the orange firmly, slice off the peel in strips, cutting off the pith and membrane with it to reveal the fruit beneath. Cut the orange in half crosswise and place in a bowl. When all the oranges have been peeled and cut, cover and refrigerate until chilled.

❧ To serve, place 2 or 3 orange halves on dessert plates. Spoon the syrup and orange strips over the orange halves and sprinkle generously with the toasted almonds. Garnish with the fresh mint leaves and serve at once. ❧

*"Here the currants red and white
In yon green bush at her sight
Peep through their shady leaves, and cry
Come eat me, as she passes by."*

—Robert Heath

FRESH FRUIT COMPOTE WITH CASSIS

SERVES 4

This simple fruit dessert gains distinction from the addition of sirop de cassis, a delicious, non-alcoholic black currant syrup made in France and available in specialty-food shops and in the international section of some large food stores. Do not confuse the syrup with the alcoholic cassis liqueur used in bars for drink making. Other natural berry and fruit syrups will work equally well.

12–16 Walnut Wafers (recipe on page 248)
1 cup (4 oz/125 g) raspberries
1 cup (4 oz/125 g) blueberries
2 oranges
3 tablespoons *sirop de cassis* (see note)
2 large, ripe mangoes
1 large, ripe Comice or Anjou pear
1 lime
4 small fresh mint sprigs

Make the Walnut Wafers ahead of time and set aside.

Sort through the raspberries and blueberries and discard any old or bruised berries. Rinse and drain well. Set aside.

Squeeze the juice from the oranges; you should have about 1 cup (8 fl oz/ 250 ml). Place the juice in a small bowl and stir in the *sirop de cassis*. Set aside.

Peel each mango, then slice off the flesh in one piece from each side of the flat pit. Cut into ¾-inch (2-cm) dice. Place in a serving bowl. Trim the remaining mango flesh from the narrow side of the pits and add to the bowl.

Peel the pear, cut into quarters, and remove the stem and core. Cut each quarter into ¾-inch (2-cm) dice. Add to the diced mango.

Add the raspberries and blueberries to the diced fruit. Pour the orange juice mixture over the fruit and stir gently to blend well. Cover and place in the refrigerator to chill for 30–40 minutes before serving.

To serve, spoon the fruit and their juices into chilled glass compotes. Using a zester or fine-holed shredder and holding the lime over each compote of fruit, shred the zest from the lime directly onto the fruit (see page 287). The released lime oil will spray over the fruit as well. Garnish each serving with a mint sprig. Serve with the Walnut Wafers.

BASIC RECIPES

APRICOT-ORANGE PRESERVES

MAKES ABOUT 1½ CUPS (15 OZ/470 G)

8 oz (250 g) dried apricots, picked over
    and rinsed
1 small orange
1¼ cups (10 fl oz/310 ml) water
⅓ cup (3 oz/90 g) sugar

Place the apricots in a saucepan. Using a zester or fine-holed shredder, shred the zest from the orange (as directed on page 287) over the apricots. Add the water and bring to a boil. Reduce the heat to low and simmer, uncovered, until the apricots are soft and most of the water has been absorbed, about 20 minutes. Transfer to a food processor fitted with the metal blade or to a blender; process to a coarse purée.

❧ Return the purée to the saucepan and add the sugar. Place over low heat and stir until the sugar dissolves, 2–3 minutes. Add a little water if too stiff. Remove from the heat and let cool.

❧ Can be stored tightly covered in the refrigerator for 2–3 weeks.

BASIL AIOLI

MAKES 1 CUP (8 FL OZ/250 ML)

1 small clove garlic, minced
1 egg yolk, at room temperature
1–2 tablespoons fresh lemon juice
salt
½ cup (4 fl oz/125 ml) olive oil or
    vegetable oil
3–4 tablespoons heavy (double) cream
4 tablespoons finely chopped fresh
    basil leaves
freshly ground black pepper or ground
    cayenne pepper

Place the minced garlic in a bowl and mash to a smooth pulp. Add the egg yolk, 1 tablespoon of the lemon juice, and a pinch of salt. Whisk until well blended. Add a few drops of the oil and whisk vigorously until thickened. Add a few more drops of the oil and whisk again until an emulsion forms. Continuing to whisk, add the oil, a little at a time, beating vigorously after each addition before adding more. The mixture should be very thick.

❧ Gradually add the cream until the sauce has the consistency of thick cream. Stir in the basil until well blended. Press some of the basil against the side of the bowl with the back of the spoon to release its flavor. Add black pepper or cayenne pepper to taste. Taste and adjust the seasoning.

❧ Use immediately or transfer to a jar and refrigerate for up to 1 day.

CANDIED ORANGE PEEL

MAKES 1½–2 CUPS (7½–10 OZ/235–315 G)

2 oranges, preferably with thick skin
1 tablespoon sea salt
1 cup (8 oz/250 g) sugar, plus extra
    for coating
½ cup (4 fl oz/125 ml) water
3 tablespoons light corn syrup

Cut around the circumference of each orange, cutting only through the peel. Make a second cut around each orange at a right angle to the first, from the stem through the blossom end, again only cutting through the peel. Carefully remove the peel in 4 segments.

❧ In a small bowl, combine the 4 peel pieces and the salt and add water just to cover. Stir to dissolve the salt and let stand for about 4 hours.

❧ Drain the peel and place in a small saucepan. Add water to cover and bring to a boil over medium-high heat. Reduce the heat to medium-low and simmer, uncovered, for 15 minutes. Drain and repeat the process. Drain again and set aside to cool. Cut the peel into strips ¼ inch (6 mm) wide.

❧ In a small saucepan over medium heat, combine the 1 cup (8 oz/250 g) sugar, water, and corn syrup. Heat, stirring, until the mixture comes to a boil and the sugar is dissolved. Add the peel strips, reduce the heat to low, and cook slowly until the peel is translucent and the syrup registers 230°F (110°C) on a candy thermometer, 45–60 minutes. Do not allow to caramelize.

❧ Transfer the peel to a wire rack to drain, spreading it out so that the strips do not touch. While the strips are still warm, spread sugar on a plate and roll the peels in the sugar until thoroughly coated. Place on a piece of waxed paper to cool completely and to dry. Store in a tightly covered container in a cool place for up to several weeks.

CANNELLINI BEANS

MAKES ABOUT 5 CUPS (2¼ LB/1.1 KG) DRAINED
BEANS; SERVES 4–6

2 cups (14 oz/440 g) dried
    cannellini beans
4 cups (32 fl oz/1 l) hot tap water
1 bay leaf
2 orange zest strips (see page 287),
    each about 2 inches (5 cm) by 1 inch
    (2.5 cm) and stuck with 2 whole
    cloves
3 fresh flat-leaf (Italian) parsley sprigs
2 teaspoons salt
freshly ground pepper

Sort through the beans, discarding any discolored ones or impurities. Rinse the beans, drain, and place in a large saucepan with hot tap water to cover by 3 inches (7.5 cm). Bring to a boil over medium-high heat. Immediately remove from the heat, cover, and let stand for 1 hour.

☙ Drain the beans, rinse, and drain again. Return the beans to the pan and add the 4 cups (32 fl oz/1 l) hot tap water, bay leaf, orange zest strips stuck with cloves, and the parsley sprigs. Bring to a boil over medium-high heat, reduce the heat to medium-low or low, cover and simmer until the beans are just tender, 1–1½ hours. During the last 15 minutes of cooking, add the salt and season with pepper.

☙ When the beans are done, taste and adjust the seasoning. Remove the bay leaf, orange strips, and parsley and discard. Set aside to cool.

☙ The beans can be tightly covered and stored in the refrigerator for 2–3 days. Use any leftover beans in salads, soups, or vegetable side dishes.

COUSCOUS

MAKES 3 CUPS (24 FL OZ/750 ML); SERVES 4 OR 5

1 cup (8 fl oz/250 ml) water
2 tablespoons unsalted butter
½ teaspoon salt
1 cup (6 oz/185 g) instant couscous

In a saucepan over medium-high heat, combine the water, butter, and salt. Bring to a boil and remove from the heat. Stir in the couscous, cover, and let stand for 5 minutes. Fluff up with a fork and serve.

CROSTINI

MAKES 24–30 SLICES

½ crusty French baguette or Italian coarse country bread, 2 inches (5 cm) in diameter and 10–12 inches (25–30 cm) long
extra-virgin olive oil

Position a rack in the upper part of an oven and preheat to 450°F (230°C).

☙ Using a sharp knife or a serrated bread knife, cut the bread on the diagonal into slices ½ inch (12 mm) thick. Brush each side lightly with olive oil and place on a baking sheet. Bake, turning once, until lightly golden, about 2 minutes on each side. Watch carefully and do not allow the crostini to toast until they are hard.

☙ Serve warm. The crostini can be sprinkled with chopped herbs (fresh or dried) or rubbed with a garlic clove. Or top them with such savory spreads as anchovy, black or green olive, artichoke, or ricotta with herbs.

FOCACCIA

MAKES ONE 10-BY-15-INCH (25-BY-37.5-CM) SHEET; SERVES 6–8

3¼ cups (16½ oz/515 g) unbleached bread flour
2 teaspoons quick-rise yeast
1 teaspoon salt
3 tablespoons extra-virgin olive oil, plus extra for brushing
1¼ cups (10 fl oz/310 ml) warm water (110°F/43°C), or as needed
coarse sea salt (optional)

In a large bowl, combine the flour, yeast, and salt. Using a wooden spoon, stir to mix well. Add the 3 tablespoons olive oil. Then, while stirring, gradually add the 1¼ cups (10 fl oz/310 ml)

warm water until all of the flour has been absorbed and a dough forms. You may not need all of the water or you may need a bit more.

☙ Using your hands, gather the dough into a ball and transfer to a well-floured work surface. Knead until soft and elastic and no longer sticky, about 10 minutes. Work more flour into the dough if needed to reduce stickiness; be sure to keep the work surface well floured. Place the dough in a warmed, lightly oiled bowl, turning several times to coat it with oil. Cover with plastic wrap and let rise in a warm place until doubled in bulk, 45–75 minutes.

☙ Position a rack in the lower part of an oven and preheat to 400°F (200°C). Brush a 10-by-15-inch (25-by-37.5-cm) baking pan with ½-inch (12-mm) sides with olive oil and set aside.

☙ Punch down the dough and transfer to the floured surface. Knead a few times, then let rest for 5–6 minutes. With the palms of your hands, form into a rectangle about 4 by 8 inches (10 by 20 cm). Roll out the dough to fit the prepared pan. Transfer the dough to the pan. Stretch and pat the dough to cover the pan bottom completely with an even thickness. Cover with plastic wrap; let rise until about 1 inch (2.5 cm) high, 20–30 minutes.

☙ Using your fingertips, make "dimple" indentations in the dough, spacing them 2 inches (5 cm) apart. Brush with olive oil and sprinkle lightly with coarse sea salt, if desired.

☙ Bake until golden brown, 30–40 minutes. Transfer to a rack and let cool in the pan for a few minutes.

☙ Cut into squares and serve warm, preferably, or at room temperature. To reheat, place in a preheated 300°F (150°C) oven for 6–8 minutes.

GREEN SAUCE

MAKES ¾ CUP (6 FL OZ/180 ML)

2 cloves garlic, minced
¼ cup minced fresh flat-leaf (Italian)
    parsley
1 tablespoon minced fresh sage
2 tablespoons balsamic vinegar
½ cup (4 fl oz/125 ml) extra-virgin
    olive oil
salt

In a small saucepan, combine the garlic, parsley, sage, balsamic vinegar, and olive oil. Stir to blend. Place over low heat and warm, stirring, until heated to serving temperature. Season with a little salt, if desired.

❧ Use immediately or set aside and cover to keep warm until needed.

HAZELNUT MERINGUES

MAKES 60–70 MERINGUES

1¼ cups (6½ oz/200 g) hazelnuts
    (filberts)
¾ cup (6 oz/185 g) superfine
    (caster) sugar
½ teaspoon cream of tartar
pinch of salt
¼ teaspoon ground cinnamon
⅛ teaspoon ground ginger
4 egg whites
1 teaspoon vanilla extract (essence)

Position a rack in the middle of an oven and preheat to 325°F (165°C). Spread the hazelnuts on a baking sheet and bake until the nuts begin to change color and are fragrant, and the skins split and loosen, 5–10 minutes. Let cool for a few minutes, then wrap the nuts in a clean kitchen towel and rub against them with the palms of your hands to remove most of the skins. Place the nuts in a coarse-mesh sieve and shake the nuts to separate them from their skins. Do not worry if bits of the skins remain. Chop the nuts coarsely and set aside.

❧ Reduce the oven temperature to 275°F (135°C). Cover 2 baking sheets with aluminum foil or parchment (baking) paper. Set aside.

❧ In a small bowl, sift together the superfine sugar, cream of tartar, salt, cinnamon, and ginger. Set aside. In a large bowl, combine the egg whites and vanilla. Using a balloon whisk or an electric mixer set on medium speed, whisk or beat until soft folds form. While continuing to beat, add the sugar mixture, a little at a time, beating until stiff, glossy peaks form that hold their shape, 3–4 minutes. Using a rubber spatula, fold in ¾ cup (4 oz/125 g) of the chopped hazelnuts.

❧ Using a teaspoon, form small mounds of the meringue, each ¾–1 inch (2–2.5 cm) in diameter, on the 2 prepared baking sheets, spacing them about ½ inch (12 mm) apart. Sprinkle a few of the remaining nuts on top of each meringue.

❧ Bake until lightly colored, 25–30 minutes. Turn off the oven and prop open the oven door about 1 inch (2.5 cm). Let cool completely, about 2 hours.

LEMON CURD

MAKES ABOUT 1½ CUPS (12 FL OZ/375 ML)

2 or 3 lemons
½ cup (4 oz/125 g) sugar
3 eggs
½ cup (4 oz/125 g) unsalted butter, cut
    into small cubes

Using a fine-holed grater, grate the zest from one of the lemons as directed on page 287. Cut the lemons in half and squeeze enough juice to measure ⅓ cup (3 fl oz/80 ml).

❧ In a heavy saucepan, combine the lemon juice and zest, sugar, and eggs. Whisk until well blended. Place over medium-low heat. While stirring constantly, add the butter, a few cubes at a time, letting the cubes melt before adding more and scraping the bottom of the pan each time. Cook slowly, stirring continuously, until thickened, 10–15 minutes. The curd should be smooth and free of lumps.

❧ Transfer to a bowl and cover with plastic wrap, pressing the wrap directly onto the surface of the curd. Refrigerate or set aside to cool.

❧ Store tightly covered in the refrigerator for up to 1 week.

RAVIOLI DOUGH

MAKES ENOUGH DOUGH FOR 48–64 ROUND RAVIOLI,
EACH 1½ INCHES (4 CM) IN DIAMETER

2 cups (10 oz/315 g) unbleached
    all-purpose (plain) flour
1 teaspoon salt
2 tablespoons unsalted butter, cut into
    small pieces
about ½ cup (4 fl oz/125 ml)
    boiling water

Place the flour and salt in a food processor fitted with the metal blade. Add the butter and, using on-off pulses, process until granular. Continuing to pulse, slowly add the boiling water until a dough just forms; not all of the water may be needed. (Alternatively, mix the dough by hand in a bowl.)

❧ Gather the dough into a ball and place on a floured work surface. Knead a few times until soft and smooth.

Flatten into a rectangle, divide in half, and wrap one-half in plastic wrap.
∾ On a well-floured work surface, roll out the remaining half into a very thin rectangle about 12 by 16 inches (30 by 40 cm). Cut the rectangle in half cross-wise to form 2 rectangles. Lay them on a kitchen towel and top with a second towel. Repeat with the reserved dough.

To Fill Ravioli:

Using a teaspoon, place small mounds of filling in rows on 1 rectangle, spacing ½ inch (12 mm) apart and ¼ inch (6 mm) in from the sides. Lay a second rectangle on top. Using a round cutter 1½ inches (4 cm) in diameter, cut out each mound. (Or cut into squares with a rolling ravioli cutter.)
∾ Press the edges together firmly; place in a single layer on a baking sheet. Cover with a kitchen towel. Repeat with remaining 2 rectangles.

ROASTED RED PEPPER SAUCE

MAKES ABOUT 1½ CUPS (12 FL OZ/375 ML)

1½ lb (750 g) red bell peppers (capsicums)
2 tablespoons extra-virgin olive oil
1 small white Bermuda onion, finely diced (¾ cup/4 oz/125 g)
½ cup (4 fl oz/125 ml) chicken stock or water
¼ teaspoon salt
pinch of red pepper flakes
1 teaspoon minced fresh marjoram

Roast and peel the bell peppers as directed on page 290. Chop coarsely. In a frying pan over low heat, warm the oil. Add the onion and sauté until translucent, about 5 minutes. Add the peppers, stock or water, salt, red pepper flakes, and marjoram; cover and simmer until the onion and peppers are tender, about 20 minutes.
∾ Transfer to a food processor fitted with the metal blade or to a blender. Process to a coarse purée. Return to the pan and reheat gently to serving temperature. Taste and adjust the seasoning.
∾ Can be stored tightly covered in the refrigerator for 2–3 days.

TOMATO-BASIL SAUCE (PISTOU)

MAKES ABOUT 1¼ CUPS (10 FL OZ/310 ML)

2 ripe tomatoes, about ½ lb (250 g) total weight
¼ teaspoon salt
2 cloves garlic
2 cups (2 oz/60 g) tightly packed fresh basil leaves
2 tablespoons extra-virgin olive oil
freshly ground pepper

Core, peel, and seed the tomatoes (see page 289). Cut into small pieces; set aside.
∾ In a food processor fitted with the metal blade or in a blender, combine the salt and garlic. Process until coarsely chopped. Add the basil leaves and continue to process to form a coarse purée, scraping down the sides of the bowl. Add the tomatoes and process until a smooth purée forms. Add the olive oil and pepper to taste and continue to process until well blended and smooth. Taste and adjust the seasoning.
∾ Use immediately or transfer to a jar and refrigerate for up to 1 day.

WHIPPED CREAM SAUCE

MAKES ABOUT 2½ CUPS (20 FL OZ/625 ML)

ice cubes
3 egg yolks
¼ cup (1 oz/30 g) confectioners' (icing) sugar
1 tablespoon Grand Marnier or 2 teaspoons vanilla extract
1 cup (8 fl oz/250 ml) heavy (double) cream

Have ready a pan of ice cubes, mixed with a little water.
∾ In a heatproof bowl, combine the egg yolks, sugar, and Grand Marnier or vanilla extract. Whisk until frothy. Place the bowl over (but not touching) barely simmering water in a saucepan. Using a whisk or an electric mixer, beat until light colored and thickened, 5–6 minutes. Do not beat too long, and do not allow the yolks to get too hot or they will curdle. Nest the bowl in the pan of ice and continue beating until cold. The mixture will become quite thick. Set aside.
∾ In another bowl, whip the cream until thick, soft folds form. Stir the cream into the cooled egg yolk mixture just until blended and smooth. Serve immediately or cover and refrigerate for up to several hours, stirring again just before serving.
∾ Any leftover sauce can be covered and refrigerated for up to 24 hours and then stirred well before serving.

TECHNIQUES

The following pages focus on practical cooking techniques used in this book that may not be familiar to some readers.

BONING AND SKINNING CHICKEN BREASTS

These days so many people buy chicken breasts already skinned and boned at the market that they might not stop to realize the economy that comes with buying whole breasts and taking a few minutes to do the skinning and boning themselves. You can save the bones and any other trimmings to make a simple stock, simmering them with some onion, celery, carrot, parsley, and a bay leaf. For healthier results, be sure to pull or cut off any yellow fat adhering to the surface or edges of the breast or to any trimmings you might use.

1. Removing the breastbone.
Hold a whole chicken breast skin side down and, using a sharp knife, slit the thin membrane covering the breastbone along its center. Grasp the breast firmly at each end and flex it upward to pop out the breastbone. Pull out the bone, using the knife, if necessary, to help cut it free.

2. Cutting the whole breast in half.
Place the breast skin side down on a cutting board. Cut along the center of the breast to separate the two breast halves.

3. Skinning a breast half.
Place the breast half, skin side up, on a cutting board. Steady the breast meat with the side of a sturdy knife blade or with your hand; with the other hand, firmly grasp the skin and strip it away from the meat.

4. Boning a breast half.
Starting along the rib side, insert the knife between the bones and meat. Pressing the knife edge gently against the bones, gradually cut the bones away from the meat. Neatly trim the edges of the breast.

5. Flattening a breast half.
If a recipe calls for flattening a breast half to help it cook more evenly, place it between two sheets of plastic wrap. Using a rolling pin, flatten it to a uniform thickness.

CUTTING CITRUS ZEST

Zest, the thin, brightly colored, outermost layer of a citrus fruit's peel, contains most of the peel's aromatic essential oils—which provide a lively source of flavor for savory and sweet dishes alike. Depending upon how the zest will be combined with other ingredients, how intense a citrus flavor is desired, and what decorative effects are called for, the zest may be removed in one of several different ways, shown below. Whichever way you use, take care to remove the colored zest only; the white, spongy pith beneath it is bitter and, if included, can mar the flavor of the dish.

Grating zest.
For very fine particles of citrus zest, lightly rub the fruit against the small rasps of a hand-held grater, taking care not to grate away any of the bitter white pith beneath the zest.

Shredding zest.
Using a simple tool known as a zester, draw its sharp-edged holes across the fruit's skin to remove the zest in thin shreds. Alternatively, use a fine-holed shredder, which has small indented slots to cut shreds.

Cutting wide strips.
Holding the edge of a paring knife or vegetable peeler almost parallel to the fruit's skin, carefully cut off the zest in strips, taking care not to remove any white pith with it.

DRAINING AND SAUCING PASTA

The cooking time for any pasta will vary with its shape, size, and degree of dryness. You can use the package instructions as a guide, but start to test the pasta at the earliest time it might be done by pulling out a piece, blowing on it to cool it slightly, and then biting into it. In Italy, perfectly cooked pasta is described as al dente—*literally, "to the tooth"—tender but firm to the bite. Don't drain the cooked pasta so thoroughly that its surface becomes dry. Italian cooks leave some water on the pasta, making it easier to mix with the sauce before serving.*

1. Cooking and draining.
Cook the pasta in an ample quantity of boiling salted water until *al dente*—tender but firm to the bite. Drain immediately.

2. Adding pasta to the sauce.
The moment excess water has drained from the pasta, add the pasta—with water still clinging to its surface—to the hot prepared sauce.

3. Mixing pasta and sauce together.
With wooden spoons, gently mix the sauce into the pasta to coat evenly. If necessary, warm over medium-high heat for a few seconds. Serve at once.

KNEADING DOUGH

Today, more and more people are making bread with the help of food processors and automatic bread machines. But those who make use of such modern conveniences are missing out on the simple, satisfying pleasure of kneading dough by hand. Kneading develops the texture of bread, knitting its gluten into a tight, elastic network that traps the gas emitted by yeast; and there is no better way to tell when a dough has been properly kneaded than by the human touch. That's not to say you can't take some shortcuts: try the new strains of quick-rise yeast, widely available in stores today, which can significantly reduce the rising time of bread dough.

1. Folding over the dough.
Mix the dough as directed in the recipe and turn it out onto a well-floured work surface. Using the heel of your hand, press the dough down and away from you. Then fold the dough over onto itself. Rotate the dough slightly.

2. Continuing to knead.
Once more, press down with the heel of your hand, fold the dough over, and rotate it. Continue kneading in this manner, working in more flour if necessary to reduce stickiness, until soft, smooth, and elastic, about 10 minutes.

PEELING AND SEEDING TOMATOES

Tomatoes are one of the great pleasures of the table—especially at the height of summer, when you should seek out the best sun-ripened tomatoes you can find. At other times of year, plum tomatoes, sometimes called Roma or egg tomatoes, are likely to have the best flavor and texture. Often when tomatoes are made into sauces or combined with other ingredients, recipes call for removing their skins and seeds, neither of which contributes much to the prized flavor or texture of the vegetable-fruit.

1. Scoring the skin.
Bring a saucepan three-fourths full of water to a boil. Using a small, sharp knife, cut out the core from the stem end of the tomato. Then cut a shallow X in the skin at the tomato's base.

2. Loosening the skin.
Submerge each tomato in the boiling water for 20–30 seconds. Using a slotted spoon, remove each tomato and submerge in a bowl of cold water.

3. Peeling the tomato.
Starting at the X, peel the skin from the tomato, using your fingertips and, if necessary, the knife blade.

4. Seeding the tomato.
Cut the tomato in half crosswise. Holding each half over a bowl, squeeze gently to force out the seed sacs.

PREPARING FRESH SHRIMP

Raw shrimp (prawns) are usually sold with the heads already removed but with their shells still on. Most recipes call for peeling shrimp before cooking. And their thin, veinlike intestinal tracts are often removed—principally for the sake of appearance but also to remove a hint of bitterness. After deveining, larger shrimp may be butterflied to help them cook more quickly and evenly. To freshen shrimp before cooking, soak them in salted water for 10–15 minutes, then rinse well in fresh water.

1. Peeling.
Using your thumbs, split open the shrimp's thin shell along the concave side, between the two rows of legs. Peel away the shell. If the recipe calls for it, leave the last shell segment with tail fin intact and attached to the meat.

2. Deveining.
Using a small, sharp knife, carefully make a shallow slit along the peeled shrimp's back, just deep enough to expose the long, usually dark, veinlike intestinal tract. With the tip of the knife or your fingers, lift up and pull out the vein.

3. Butterflying.
To butterfly the shrimp, continue slitting down into the meat just far enough so that, with your fingertips, you can open it out and flatten it easily into two equal-sized lobes. Take care not to cut completely through the shrimp.

ROASTING BELL PEPPERS

Bell peppers (capsicums)—especially the ripened red, yellow, and orange varieties—have a natural sweetness and juicy texture that are heightened by roasting. While many different methods exist for roasting peppers, the one shown here streamlines the process by halving, stemming, and seeding them first, leaving only the peeling of the blackened skins after the peppers have cooled.

SECTIONING CITRUS FRUIT

When citrus fruit is used as a garnish or featured in a dessert or salad, recipes frequently call for it to be sectioned, or segmented—that is, cut free from its pith and membranes, the better to enjoy the fruit's flavor, texture, and color. The only tool needed to perform this task is a good, sharp knife. Bear in mind that the process yields the most attractive results when you start with citrus fruits that have few if any seeds; use the tip of a small, sharp knife to remove any visible seeds after sectioning.

1. Halving, stemming, and seeding.
Preheat a broiler (griller) or an oven to 500°F (260°C). Using a small, sharp knife, cut each pepper in half lengthwise. Cut out the stem, seeds, and white ribs from each half.

1. Trimming the fruit.
To enable the citrus fruit—here, a grapefruit—to be steadied on the work surface, use a sharp, thin-bladed knife to cut a thick slice off its bottom and top, exposing the fruit beneath the peel.

2. Roasting the peppers.
Lay the pepper halves, cut sides down, on a baking sheet. Place under the broiler or in the oven. Broil (grill) or roast until the skins blister and blacken.

2. Cutting off the peel.
Steadying the fruit upright on the work surface, thickly slice off the peel in strips, cutting off the white pith and membrane with it to reveal the fruit sections.

3. Peeling the peppers.
Remove from the oven and cover with aluminum foil. Let steam until cool enough to handle, 10–15 minutes. Then, using your fingers or a knife, peel off the skins.

3. Cutting out the sections.
Hold the peeled fruit in one hand over a bowl to catch the juices. Using the same knife, carefully cut on each side of the membrane to free each section, letting the sections drop into the bowl.

TRIMMING AND CLEANING LEEKS

Leeks add a wonderfully mild, sweet, oniony flavor to many French dishes. Grown in sandy soil, they frequently have grit trapped between their green leaves and the layers of their white bulb ends. As a result, they require careful cleaning before use in any recipe. The toughest part of the green leaves must be trimmed off as well; and some recipes call for only the white or the white and pale green parts of the vegetable, requiring even further trimming.

1. Trimming the leeks.
Using a sharp knife, trim off the root end of each leek. Then, cut off the tough, dark green portions of the leaves, leaving about 1 inch (2.5 cm) of the tender green portion.

2. Slitting the leeks.
To expose the leeks' layers for more thorough cleaning, cut each leek in half lengthwise, starting at the green end and working down the stalk about three-fourths of the way toward the root end.

3. Washing the leeks.
In a basin filled with cold water, or under a stream of running water, swish the leeks to clean them thoroughly, gently separating the layers with your fingers to wash away any grit or sand trapped inside.

TRIMMING ARTICHOKES

If you grow up eating artichokes, as most Italians do, these thistlelike vegetables seem commonplace. But those of us who first encounter them in adulthood may be a bit intimidated by the idea of preparing them. As with any vegetable, the secret to getting them ready for cooking is to cut away the parts you wouldn't eat anyway: the tough outer leaves and prickly top, the tough stem portion, and, in the case of mature artichokes, the fibrous choke. Be sure to keep some lemon juice close at hand to coat the cut surfaces of each artichoke, which otherwise would quickly turn brown.

1. Removing outer leaves.
Working with 1 artichoke at a time and starting at the wide bottom, remove the tough outer leaves. Pull each leaf straight down and snap it off. Remove 3 or 4 layers until you reach pale green leaves.

2. Cutting off the stem.
Using a sharp knife, cut off the stem of the artichoke even with the bottom.

3. Trimming the top.
Cut off the top half or more of the artichoke to eliminate the tough portion. For fully grown artichokes, spread open the center and, using a small spoon or melon baller, scoop out the prickly choke from the center and discard.

TRUSSING A CHICKEN AND TESTING FOR DONENESS

Tying, or trussing, whole poultry before roasting gives it a more compact, uniform shape, ensuring that it cooks more evenly. The result is a bird that not only has moister meat and looks more attractive when presented at table, but is also easier to carve. Many different methods exist for trussing; the one shown here is among the simplest, requiring just a single piece of kitchen string at least long enough to wrap twice lengthwise around the bird. At the earliest possible time that the bird might be finished, start checking for doneness with an instant-read thermometer.

1. Securing drumsticks.
Place the bird breast side up and slide the center of the string under its tail. Cross the ends above the tail and loop each around a drumstick; then cross them again (shown here) and pull them tight to draw together the tail and the ends of the drumsticks.

2. Completing trussing.
Turn the bird over and tuck the wing tips across the neck flap. Pull one string along the side, loop it around the nearest wing, pull it tight across the neck flap and loop it around the other wing. Tightly tie together the string ends; cut off any excess string

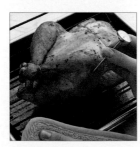

3. Testing for doneness.
After roasting, insert an instant-read thermometer into the thickest part of the thigh, taking care not to touch the bone and to insert from above so juices will not run out. A temperature of 180°F (82°C) indicates doneness.

USING A FOOD MILL

A food mill is a mechanical sieve that produces an even-textured purée. Although cranked by hand, in some cases it can do a job faster than the time it would take to purée in a food processor and then sieve that purée. Cooked vegetables or fruits are pushed against the holes in the bottom of the mill by a paddle fitted with a tension spring; the solids are forced through the holes, which hold back any seeds, skins, and fibers. Imported models usually come with both medium and fine disks, offering a choice of coarser or finer purées.

1. Ladling in the ingredients.
Set the food mill securely atop a large bowl. Ladle in the food to be puréed—here, a cooked soup—making sure to include any liquids along with the solids.

2. Turning the mill.
Steadying the mill with one hand, turn its handle clockwise to force the ingredients through the disk. From time to time, turn the handle counterclockwise to dislodge fibrous material from the disk's surface.

3. Finishing the purée.
Continue ladling ingredients and turning the mill until the purée is complete. Remove the mill and stir the purée to give it an even consistency, returning it to a pan if necessary for gentle reheating.

KITCHEN EQUIPMENT

A selection of cookware and tools used in the preparation of the recipes in this collection.

BAKEWARE & COOKWARE

Sturdy pots and pans for stove top and oven.

Baking dishes—select heavy-duty glazed porcelain, stoneware, earthenware, glass, or tinned copper for oven baking.

Baking pan
Heavy, durable, shallow metal sheet pans for a wide variety of uses, from roasting peppers to toasting nuts to baking breads.

Baking or roasting pan
Heavy, durable metal pan large enough to hold roasts. Sturdy metal V-shaped rack facilitates lifting and turning, promotes even cooking, and prevents sticking.

Baking sheet
All-purpose shallow-rimmed metal baking sheet for such tasks as roasting bell peppers (capsicums) or eggplants (aubergines), toasting nuts or bread crumbs, or baking cookies and wafers.

Broiling pan
Heavy, durable metal pan for cooking foods under a broiler (griller). Raised insert allows fat to drain away.

Casserole or dutch oven
Large-capacity enameled cast-iron cooking vessel with tight-fitting lid holds pot roasts, braises, and stews. For use on the stove top or in the oven.

Deep-dish pie dish
For fruit pies without bottom crusts, chose a dish about 2 inches (5 cm) deep made of earthenware, which absorbs and transfers heat more efficiently than metal or glass, thus preventing uneven baking and scorching of fillings.

Double boiler
A large saucepan topped with a heatproof bowl is excellent for gently warming or melting heat-sensitive foods.

Frying pan
Choose good-quality heavy aluminum, stainless steel, cast iron, or enameled steel for rapid frying or browning. Shallow, flared sides promote evaporation of moisture.

Gratin dish
Shallow baking dish that promotes the formation of a golden crust atop gratins.

Omelet pan
French-style pan with gently sloping sides that make cooking and rolling classic omelets easier. Select a heavy metal pan that absorbs heat well and transfers it quickly. The 10-inch (25-cm) size may also be used for sautéing.

Pasta pot
Large stainless-steel pot includes pierced insert for easy draining.

Round cake pan
Standard-sized cake pan, 8 or 9 inches (20 or 23 cm) in diameter and 2 inches (5 cm) deep, in aluminum, stainless steel, or tinned steel.

Saucepan
A versatile pan, available in several sizes, used for cooking vegetables and making simple soups, sauces, and small quantities of broth. Select saucepans made of heavy anodized aluminum, cast aluminum, stainless steel, or enameled steel for the best performance.

Sauté pan
For quick searing or browning or for gentle sautéing, stewing, or braising, select a well-made heavy metal pan large enough to hold food in a single layer without crowding. Straight sides help retain and contain splattering.

Soufflé dish
Classic, deep, straight-sided 1½-quart (1.5-1) circular baking dish for the preparation of soufflés.

Springform pan
Deep, circular pan with spring-clip sides that loosen for easy removal of hard-to-unmold cakes.

Stew pot
Deep pot with ovenproof handle, for cooking stews on the stove top or in the oven. Heavy enameled cast iron is a good choice, as it holds heat well.

Stockpot
Deep, medium- to large-capacity pot with close-fitting lid, for making stock or soup or for boiling or braising foods. Select a good-quality heavy pot that absorbs and transfers heat well. Enameled steel cleans up easily and does not react with the acidity of any wine, citrus juice, or tomatoes added during cooking.

Stove-top grill
Sturdy grilling surface of cast aluminum for stove-top grilling of vegetables or other foods.

Tart pan
Shallow baking pan with fluted sides and removable bottom, for attractive shaping and easy umolding of tarts.

PREP TOOLS

To help speed along food preparation.

Colander
For draining pasta, beans, and other foods.

Cutting board
Choose a hardwood or good-quality acrylic cutting board for preparing vegetables and meats. Clean thoroughly after every use.

Electric blender
Powerful motor with various speeds for chopping, puréeing, or liquefying small quantities of ingredients. Especially suited to puréeing soft foods, mixing liquids, and blending smooth sauces. Newer improved models are excellent for puréeing.

Food mill
Hand-cranked mill purées soups, vegetables, and fruits by forcing ingredients through its conical grinding disk, which also sieves out fibers, skins, and seeds.

Food processor
For chopping, shredding, grating, puréeing, or slicing large quantities of ingredients with great efficiency and speed. Also used for making pastry dough.

Heavy-duty stand mixer
Mixer with powerful motor, large capacity, and multiple speeds for mixing batters or doughs. Special attachments include a dough hook for kneading bread dough and a balloon whisk for whipping.

Kitchen string
For trussing poultry and tying up a bouquet garni. Select linen string that will withstand intense heat with minimal charring.

Mixing bowls
Sturdy bowls in a range of sizes for mixing, holding, and serving all kinds of ingredients.

Mortar and pestle
For crushing whole spices, such as aniseeds to flavor biscotti.

Parchment (baking) paper
Stick-resistant ovenproof paper for lining baking sheets for delicate meringues and for enclosing oven-baked fish.

Pepper mill
For freshly grinding peppercorns.

Ricer
Sturdy, hinged stainless-steel apparatus forces boiled potatoes through small holes, producing smooth, fine-textured mashed potatoes and purées.

UTENSILS

Handheld tools for general and specific tasks.

Asparagus peeler
Small, tonglike stainless-steel device that grasps and strips away the tough, thin layer of peel from thick asparagus stalks.

Basting brush
For all-purpose brushing of thin, even coatings of oil, lemon juice, and other liquid ingredients.

Box grater/shredder
Sturdy stainless-steel tool for grating or shredding ingredients.

Carving knife
Long serrated blade for cutting bread and roasted meat.

Cherry pitter
Small, sturdy device that grips a cherry and pushes out its pit in one squeeze. Can also be used to pit olives.

Dry measuring cups
In graduated sizes, for measuring dry ingredients. Straight rims allow ingredients to be leveled for accuracy. Choose stainless steel for precision.

Fine-holed shredder
Handheld utensil perforated with sharp slots for cutting thin shreds of citrus zest or other ingredients.

Ginger grater
Rough surface of porcelain grater easily grates whole fresh ginger.

Handheld grater
Fine rasp surface for grating citrus zest or whole nutmeg.

Handheld shredder
Sturdy, stainless-steel utensil perforated with sharp slots for cutting thin shreds by hand.

Instant-read thermometer
Insert into the thickest part of roasted meat or poultry at the earliest moment it might be done for a quick and accurate measure of internal temperature.

Kitchen knives
Large chef's knife for chopping; thin-bladed, flexible knife for slicing meat and poultry; paring knife for peeling vegetables, cutting up small ingredients, and testing meat and poultry for doneness; long serrated blade for cutting bread and roasted meat; two-pronged fork for steadying food during carving.

Liquid measuring cup
For accurate measuring of liquid ingredients, choose heavy-duty heat-resistant glass, marked on one side in cups and ounces and on the other side in milliliters.

Measuring spoons
For measuring small quantities of ingredients such as chopped herbs, salt, or baking powder. Select good-quality, calibrated metal spoons with deep bowls.

Meat pounder
Heavy stainless-steel disk with sturdy handle, to flatten meat or poultry for quick sautéeing.

Melon baller
Small, sharp-edged, hemispherical scoop cuts melon or other soft fruits or vegetables into perfectly shaped balls. Can also be used for removing seeds from cucumbers.

Mushroom brush
Small brush with short, soft bristles for cleaning the delicate surface of mushrooms.

Olive pitter
Small, sturdy device that grips an olive and pushes out its pit in one squeeze.

Parmesan cheese grater
Half-cylindrical utensil with coarse rasp surface for quickly grating blocks of Parmesan cheese.

Parmesan knife
Traditional Italian knife for cutting chunks of Parmesan or other hard cheeses.

Pastry blender
Sturdy curved wires for cutting butter or shortening into flour when making pastry by hand.

Ravioli cutter
Rolling cutter with decorative serrated edge for cutting ravioli dough.

Round cutter
Stainless-steel biscuit or cookie cutter for cutting sheets of rolled pastry dough or fresh pasta dough into round ravioli.

Skimmer
Wide disk with fine mesh for efficient removal of froth from simmered recipes and for removing small pieces of food from skimming liquid.

Whisks
For beating eggs or blending liquids. Choose stainless steel. Use the wider balloon whisk for whisking the maximum amount of air into egg whites.

Zester
Small, sharp holes at the end of a stainless-steel blade cut citrus zest into fine shreds.

OTHER UTENSILS

You may want to keep these utensils handy:

Ladle for serving soups and stews

Mesh sieves for draining and straining

Metal tongs for picking up or turning ingredients

Potato masher for mashing potatoes by hand

Rolling pin for rolling out dough and for flattening chicken breasts

Rubber spatula for gentle blending and folding of batters

Slotted spoon for transferring cooked meats or vegetables without their liquid

Wooden pasta serving forks

Wooden spoons for all-purpose mixing and stirring

COOKING PRIMER

The following terms for the cooking methods used in this book are seen so often in recipes that many people now take them for granted. I find that a basic grasp of the principles behind them can dramatically improve your everyday cooking.

Baking

Cooking uniform pieces of meat, poultry, seafood, or vegetables with a small amount of fat or liquid (or a combination of foods mixed with a sauce) in an open pan or dish in the hot, dry air of an oven. Basting helps to keep the food moist and to develop an attractive surface. Also refers to the cooking of breads, cakes, pastries, and puddings in an oven's dry heat.

Braising

Slow, moist-heat cooking of tougher, small cuts or pieces of meat, poultry, seafood, or vegetables. The food is generally first browned in a minimum of fat and then added to a tightly covered pot or other vessel with a small amount of liquid. It is then cooked at low heat in an oven or on top of a stove.

Broiling (Grilling)

Generally refers to the cooking of relatively tender, thin cuts or pieces of meat, poultry, seafood, or vegetables, using an overhead dry heat source and little or no fat. Food to be cooked is usually placed on a rack in a broiling pan, which in turn should be placed on a shelf adjusted so that the top of the food is generally 3–4 inches (7.5–10 cm) from the heat source. Careful attention must be paid to avoid undercooking, overcooking, or burning the food.

Frying

Refers to the fast browning and cooking of food in varying but fairly shallow amounts of fat, most often at high heat—a method commonly used for steaks, chops, fillets, chicken pieces, sausages, bacon, sliced vegetables, and eggs. Best done in a large, heavy-bottomed frying pan with 2-inch (5-cm) sloping or curved sides that allow moisture to escape easily. Frying pans of cast iron, extra-thick aluminum, or heavy stainless steel with an extra-thick aluminum or copper bottom all hold and conduct heat well. Pans with a nonstick surface are good for foods that are apt to stick and to be difficult to turn, such as fish.

Poaching

Gentle simmering of fish, chicken, some meats, fruit, or eggs, usually in a flavorful liquid, just until cooked through and tender. The size and shape of the food to be poached determines the size and shape of the pan: a sauté pan or deep frying pan for chicken breasts, fish fillets, or fruit halves; a large, deep pot for whole chickens; a long, narrow fish poacher for whole fish. Use a minimum amount of liquid—just enough to submerge the food.

Pot roasting

A form of braising, pot roasting is the slow, even cooking of large, tougher cuts of meat or whole poultry in moist heat, enclosed in a deep, tightly covered pot on top of a stove or in an oven. The meat or poultry may be browned first, and only a very small amount of liquid or fat is included. Recommended are enameled cast-iron pots with covers that have rings on the underside for rapid and even self-basting.

Roasting

Usually refers to the slow or moderate cooking of whole cuts of meat or whole poultry in an open pan in the dry heat of an oven. Little or no fat or liquid is added. Basting helps to keep the food moist and to develop an attractive surface. A roasting pan should have 2- to 3-inch (5- to 7.5-cm) sides and be large enough for air to circulate well around the food being roasted.

Sautéing

The light searing or browning and quick cooking of tender, small or thin pieces of meat, poultry, seafood, or vegetables, done with minimal fat and with little loss of natural juices. Recommended is a heavy, wide sauté pan with straight sides, 10 or 11 inches (25 or 28 cm) in diameter with sides 2½–3 inches (6–7.5 cm) high. Thick aluminum, or stainless steel with a laminated copper or aluminum bottom, conducts and holds heat well. A nonstick surface may be desirable for some foods. A heavy frying pan can be used in place of a sauté pan, but the sauté pan's straight sides help concentrate the heat and reduce splattering.

Simmering

Refers to the cooking of liquid or ingredients in liquid over low to medium heat. Bubbles should rise to the surface but not break.

Stewing

Refers to the slow cooking of small, uniform pieces of meat, poultry, seafood, or vegetables in a moderate amount of liquid in a covered pot, casserole, or other lidded vessel. Meat or poultry pieces may be browned, or not, before liquid is added. Stewing can be done on top of a stove or in an oven.

INGREDIENTS

An illustrated primer of distinctive Italian, French, and American ingredients, all sold in specialty-food stores and well-stocked markets.

Avocados

Sometimes mistakenly referred to as a vegetable, the avocado is actually a fruit. It comes in two varieties: the Haas, which has a dark-green, dimpled skin; and the Fuerte, which has a paler, smoother skin. Haas avocados tend to have a richer flavor and texture and are best used in salads or eaten out of hand.

Belgian endive

Also known as chicory or witloof, this leaf vegetable has refreshing, slightly bitter, spear-shaped leaves, white to pale yellow-green—or sometimes red—in color, tightly packed in cylindrical heads 4–6 inches (10–15 cm) long. Grown in northern France and Belgium, Belgian endive was developed relatively recently, in the late 19th century, cultivated from the roots of wild chicory.

Calvados

Distilled from cider and aged for at least one year in oak casks, this dry, fragrant apple brandy is named for the area of Normandy in which it has been produced for centuries. Sipped on its own as a digestive after dinner, calvados is also used to flavor both savory and sweet dishes of the region and is frequently combined with apples.

Cannellini beans

These small to medium-sized, white, thin-skinned oval beans are among the most popular in Italy, appearing in soups, salads, appetizers, stews, and vegetable side dishes. If cannellini cannot be found, Great Northern or white (navy) beans may be substituted. Canned cooked cannellini beans may also be used in some recipes; they should be drained and well rinsed before use.

Chicory

Grown around Paris and in western France, this curly-leafed salad green—also occasionally cooked as a side dish—is prized for its refreshing bitterness, present most mildly in the pale green to white leaves found at the center of its loose, open head. Also known as curly endive.

Couscous

A North African staple, these small, granular particles of semolina pasta became a French favorite after Algeria was colonized by France in the 1820s. Couscous has a fluffy consistency resembling rice pilaf when cooked, making it an ideal accompaniment to stews, braises, or other foods with sauces. Traditional couscous takes as long as 1½ hours to steam. Instant couscous, available in well-stocked food stores, has been precooked and then redried, and is ready to serve in a matter of minutes.

Crab

Crabmeat is a delicacy enjoyed the world over, and the United States is no exception. Along the Atlantic and Gulf coasts, blue crabs are the most prevalent; in southern Florida, stone crabs are served; and the along the Pacific Coast, the Dungeness is the crab of choice. Crabs, like lobsters, must be kept alive until cooking. You may buy crabmeat already prepared but you'll get the best flavor if you extract the meat yourself.

Cranberries

Native to North America, cranberries are an integral part of American cooking, especially for holiday meals. The best time to buy them is in autumn and early winter when they are harvested. They are too tart to eat raw, but they make wonderful additions to both savory and sweet preparations. Fresh cranberries should be plump, firm, and scarlet red. Usually sold packaged in sealed plastic bags, they can go straight into the freezer, where they will keep for up to 10 months. Widely available bags of prefrozen cranberries are also excellent in quality.

Crème fraîche

Fresh pasteurized cream is lightly soured and thickened by the addition of lactic bacteria culture to produce this popular product, used throughout France as a topping or an enrichment for a wide range of savory and sweet dishes. It may be found in the refrigerated case of well-stocked food markets. To make your own crème fraîche at home, stir 1 teaspoon cultured buttermilk into 1 cup (8 fl oz/250 ml) heavy (double) cream. Cover tightly and leave at warm room temperature until thickened, about 12 hours. Refrigerate until ready to serve. Store for up to 1 week.

Curry powder

Most curry is associated with India, but varieties of curried dishes can be found throughout Southeast Asia, Thailand, the Caribbean, and Africa. Curry powder does not refer to one pepper or plant but is actually a generic term for blends of spices. Most common blends contain coriander, cumin, ground chile, fenugreek, and turmeric. Some may also include cardamom, cinnamon, cloves, allspice, fennel seeds, and ginger.

Dijon mustard

Among the many varieties of mustard made in France, that produced in and around the leading mustard-producing city of Dijon is distinguished by a pale yellow color and fairly hot, sharp flavor resulting from its blend of brown mustard seeds—or, if marked *blanc,* lighter seeds—and white wine or wine vinegar. Similar non-French blends may be labeled Dijon style.

Escarole

Popular in France both raw in salads and cooked, this variety of chicory has broad, curly, bright green leaves with a refreshingly bitter flavor. Also known as Batavian endive.

Flageolet beans

Small and pale green, these popular dried beans, harvested before they reach maturity, come from Brittany in northern France. They are now being grown in the United States as well. Their earthy flavor complements lamb dishes particularly well.

French bread

A wide variety of different breads are produced in France. But the daily bread most often is the baguette, a long, slender loaf with a tender, dense white crumb and a well-developed, crisp crust. When "crusty French bread" is suggested as an ingredient or accompaniment to a recipe in this book, widely available French-style baguettes serve the purpose well.

French cheeses

With hundreds of cheeses produced throughout France, and many dozens exported as well, lovers of French cheese have a wide variety from which to choose. Among these, some of the most popular are goat's milk cheeses, known by the collective French term *chèvre,* which are generally fresh and creamy, with a distinctive tang; they are usually sold shaped into small rounds, and are sometimes coated with pepper, ash, or mixtures of herbs, which add mild flavor. Excellent fresh goat cheeses are also now produced in the United States. Also finding favor, particularly as a melted topping for French onion soup and for vegetable gratins, is Gruyère, a variety of Swiss cheese with a firm, smooth texture, small holes, and a strong, tangy flavor. Rich, creamy, ripened Brie cheese is always a French favorite. It is usually sold in wedges cut from whole wheels, with a white, powdery rind.

Green lentils

This popular variety of the small, disk-shaped dried legume may be used in soups and salads or as a side dish. Although lentils originated in Asia, they are grown throughout France today, with the green Puy lentil (from Le Puy in the Auvergne) widely favored and exported. When preparing any lentils, make sure to pick through them carefully before cooking to remove such impurities as stones, fibers, or misshapen beans.

Italian bread

Everyday Italian meals are most often accompanied by crusty country bread made from unbleached wheat flour and noted for its firm, coarse-textured crumb. Look for round, oval, and long loaves in good bakeries and Italian delicatessens, variously labeled Italian, country-style, rustic, or peasant bread.

Leeks

Leeks, which originated in the Middle East, were introduced to France under the Roman Empire. Grown year-round in the northern and western parts of the country, they flavor soups, stews, and braises, as well as being enjoyed cooked on their own as appetizers or side dishes. Grown in sandy soil, leeks require thorough cleaning before use (see page 291).

Madeira wine

Ranging from dry to sweet, this amber dessert wine comes from the Portuguese island of Madeira. The labels of most Madeiras include an indication of the type of grapes from which they were made, with Bual and Malmsey being sweetest and fullest in body; Verdelho having a nuttier, more mellow quality; and Sercial being the driest. Madeira wine is popularly drunk as an aperitif in France and is used in sauces and other preparations.

Marsala

A specialty of the region of Marsala, in Sicily, this aromatic amber wine, which is available in both dry and sweet versions, finds widespread use as a flavoring in the Italian kitchen. It is most often used as the base of a sauce for chicken or veal, for adding color and flavor to carrots, and for enhancing a wide variety of cakes and other desserts.

Mesclun

A specialty of southern France, with a name derived from the Niçois word for "mixture," this assortment of tiny greens is frequently served as a salad on its own or as a garnish or base for other ingredients. Although the mixture will vary, mesclun typically includes chicory (curly endive), lamb's lettuce, and dandelion leaves, combined with such other greens as oak leaf lettuce, chervil, arugula (rocket), and purslane. Well-stocked food stores and greengrocers sometimes carry mesclun, which is often prewashed and bagged for sale.

Olives

Ripe black olives may be cured in various combinations of salt, seasonings, brines, oils, and vinegars. European olives generally offer the most superior flavor and texture. Some of the most delicious are Gaeta, Spanish olives, Greek Kalamata, or French Niçoise olives. If the olives are too salty for your taste, drain and rinse well with cold running water, or soak them in cold water to cover for 30 minutes or more. To pit olives, use an olive pitter (see page 294), which grips the olive while pushing out its pit. Or use a small, sharp knife to carefully slit the olive lengthwise down to the pit, then pry away the flesh.

Niçoise olives

Picked when ripe and then pickled in brine, these small, brown to black olives are a specialty of the Provençal city of Nice.

Olive oil

One of the greatest sources of character in Italian cooking, olive oil contributes its fruity flavor to a wide range of savory dishes. Extra-virgin olive oil, the most flavorful of all, is extracted from the fruit on the first pressing, without the use of heat or chemicals; it is used most often in dressings and as a seasoning. Each brand sold displays its own distinctive taste and color; higher-priced labels usually offer the best quality. Pure olive oil, which is less aromatic and flavorful, is used most often in cooking. Store all olive oils in airtight containers away from heat and light.

Paprika powder

Derived from the dried paprika pepper, paprika powder is available in sweet, mild, and hot forms. The best kind of paprika is from Hungary, but if you prefer a less spicy version, you can substitute Spanish paprika. Paprika powder works very nicely as a garnish as well as a flavoring. A dusting gives color to such foods as potato salad, macaroni salad, and deviled eggs.

Parmesan cheese

Sharp, salty and richly flavorful, this hard-crusted cow's milk cheese is aged for up to two years. When grated or shredded, it enriches stuffings and sauces, and is used as a garnish for pastas and other savory dishes. The name of the cheese refers to the city of Parma, in central Italy, but the cheese actually was first developed in an area midway between Parma and the town of Reggio. For the best flavor and texture, buy Parmesan imported from Italy in block form—to grate, shred, or shave fresh as needed. Parmesan cheese bearing the official Italian mark "Parmigiano-Reggiano" is considered the best quality of all.

Polenta

The term polenta refers both to Italian yellow or white cornmeal and to the cooked mush made from it and served as a first course or side dish. In Italy, the best polenta is made from cornmeal freshly ground within the two- to three-week harvest period. I find that long-cooking polenta imported from Italy, with its fine, even grind, has a better flavor and cooks to a smoother and more even consistency than American cornmeal or quick-cooking varieties.

Rice:
Arborio

A specialty of Italy's Piedmont and Lombardy regions, Arborio rice has short, round grains that cook to a pleasantly chewy texture while developing their own creamy sauce—the distinctive characteristics of risotto. Similar varieties include Vialone Nano and Carnaroli, which some cooks consider the best. Other types of medium-grain white rice can be substituted if Arborio is unavailable.

Basmati

A highly aromatic, long-grained variety, basmati rice is grown primarily in India, Iran, and the United States. It is prized for its sweet, nutlike flavor and perfume. White and brown basmati rice may be found, both of which are wonderful to use when making pilaf.

Jasmine

Grown in Thailand, jasmine rice is a long-grained variety with a sweet, floral scent similar to that of basmati.

Shallots

Grown in France for well more than a thousand years, these small cousins of the onion have brown skins, purple-tinged white flesh and a flavor resembling a cross between sweet onion and garlic. A traditional flavoring in the foods of Bordeaux in southwestern France, they appear in sauces, dressings, marinades, and salads. Store them in a cool, dry place, as you would onions and garlic.

Tarragon

Delicate and sweetly flavored, with a faint hint of licorice, this herb—used both fresh and dried—flavors many French sauces, salads, pickles, and egg dishes. Tarragon-flavored white wine vinegar is a popular ingredient in salad dressings.

Vermouth

Vermouth takes its name from *Wermut,* the German word for wormwood, an ingredient in many traditional recipes for this commercial, delicately aromatic dry or sweet wine enhanced with herbs and barks. Two of the world's three leading centers for vermouth production are found in France—Marseilles and Chambéry. The wine frequently flavors French sauces and stuffings, and is particularly complementary to seafood and chicken.

Walnuts

California supplies nearly two-thirds of the world's walnut supply, making possible the use of these delicious nuts in everything from salads to turkey stuffings, to cakes and cookies. The most common variety is the English walnut, which has a light brown shell that cracks easily. Black walnuts, native to North America, have dark shells that are difficult to break. When buying walnuts, look for whole nuts that are free of holes, cracks, and mold. To toast walnuts, which develops their full flavor, aroma, and texture, spread the shelled nuts in a single layer on a baking sheet and toast in a preheated 325°F (165°C) oven until they just begin to change color and are fragrant, 5 to 10 minutes. Remove from the oven and let cool to room temperature.

INDEX

CREDITS

Front Cover: Roast chicken with apple and sage (page 125) is served with green beans with shallots (page 203) and mashed potatoes with rosemary and lemon (page 214).

Back cover photos, from left to right: Farfalle with Tuna and Black Olives (page 176), Minestrone (page 55), Rack of Lamb with Flageolet Beans (page 151), Mixed Berry Shortcake (page 262).

ADDITIONAL PHOTOGRAPHY
Philip Salaverry: Recipes on pages 118, 231, and 232; Suggested Menus, Section Openers on pages 18, 36, 62, 86, 176, 188, 194, 226, 234, 246, 256, 272

Noel Barnhurst: Cover, Chapter Openers on pages 16–17, 84–85, 192–93, 244–45

ADDITIONAL PROOFREADING
Ken DellaPenta, Arin Hailey

ADDITIONAL COPYEDITING
Anne Weinberger

ADDITIONAL TEXT
Barbara Ignatius

SPECIAL THANKS
John and Jane Weil for the generous use of their home, Dean Alvarez, Sarah Gifford, Mario Amador, Emily Jahn, Chris Hemeseth, Kathryn Meehan